the Nasdaq® trader's toolkit

M. ROGAN LaBIER

John Wiley & Sons, Inc.

New York • Chichester • Weinheim • Brisbane • Singapore • Toronto

Published by John Wiley & Sons, Inc.
Published simultaneously in Canada.

No part of this publication may be reproduced, stored in a retrieval system or transmitted in any form or by any means, electronic, mechanical, photocopying, recording, scanning or otherwise, except as permitted under Sections 107 or 108 of the 1976 United States Copyright Act, without either the prior written permission of the Publisher, or authorization through payment of the appropriate per-copy fee to the Copyright Clearance Center, 222 Rosewood Drive, Danvers, MA 01923, (978) 750-8400, fax (978) 750-4744. Requests to the Publisher for permission should be addressed to the Permissions Department, John Wiley & Sons, Inc., 605 Third Avenue, New York, NY 10158-0012, (212) 850-6011, fax (212) 850-6008, E-Mail: PERMREQ@WILEY.COM.

This publication is designed to provide accurate and authoritative information in regard to the subject matter covered. It is sold with the understanding that the publisher is not engaged in rendering professional services. If professional advice or other expert assistance is required, the services of a competent professional person should be sought.

Although the author believes the information, data, and contents presented are accurate, he neither guarantees their accuracy nor completeness nor assumes any liability. It should not be assumed that the methods or techniques presented in this book will be profitable or that they will not result in losses. Trading involves the risk of loss as well as profit. Past performance is not a guarantee of future results.

Nasdaq is a registered service trademark of the National Association of Securities Dealers, Inc.

Designations used by companies to distinguish their products are often claimed as trademarks. In all instances where John Wiley & Sons, Inc. is aware of a claim, the product names appear in initial capital or all capital letters. Readers, however, should contact the appropriate companies for more complete information regarding trademarks and registration.

Library of Congress Cataloging-in-Publication Data

LaBier, M. Rogan.
  The Nasdaq trader's toolkit / M. Rogan LaBier.
     p.   cm.—(Wiley online trading for a living)
  Includes index.
    ISBN 0-471-40403-9 (cloth : alk. paper)
    1. Electronic trading of securities.   I. Title.   II. Series.
  HG4515.95 .L33   2001
  332.64'273—dc21   00-043912

Printed in the United States of America

10 9 8 7 6 5 4 3 2 1

acknowledgments

Thanks to all the many professional traders whose experiences led to the writing of this book. Without their input and constant fight to keep ahead of the constant change that is today's electronic market, I doubt this trader would've written a thing. Special thanks to my friends at Nasdaq, the various electronic brokerages, and all the ECNs that have kept me posted on all the newest and latest changes to the execution routes and software platforms. Without your input, this book would never have been written. I owe special thanks to a friend who some years ago tore a dollar bill in half as a bet on who could make their first $5,000 in the market. The thought that this Swedish marine was gunning in earnest to beat me at this game focused my first efforts. That I won the dollar is not significant; that I discovered a new world of amazing possibility is.

contents

chapter 1

introduction

I'd like to start by saying I like "get-rich" books. Often they're fun and simply written, and they make me feel that hope and possibility is right here within my grip. Sometimes the books contain great ideas, sometimes not; sometimes they contain partial truths or outdated formulas. I think they tell us loads about our times and reaffirm a part of our basic human nature. Reading get-rich books from the turn of the century—nineteenth to twentieth, that is—is a lot of fun. For one thing, not much has changed regarding human nature, for all our technological prowess. The urge to trade, to speculate, and, yes, to gamble has been around since before recorded history. Anyone who gets a kick out of the great tech stock rally of the 1990s will get an even bigger kick out of the great tulip rally of seventeenth-century Holland. If one were to line up every get-rich book about the stock market, I suspect the line would be very long indeed.

This is *not* a get-rich book. In my time as proprietary trader, market maker, and head trader at one of the largest direct-access electronic brokerages, I've talked to thousands of people who, like me, have also read all the get-rich stuff and all the "stock-picking" books around. Like me, they are interested and even amused by the writings, but, in their attempts to better their financial lives, they have never encountered anything that deals with the realities of trading your own account in the digital age. There are unlimited books on stock picking, trading strategies, and sophisticated sales pitches, and pompous books by major institutional money managers who manage multibillions. While many of the books are very helpful, none seems to deal with the realities of how to buy and sell stock in the fast-moving electronic market. To that end, I decided to put on paper what I know about transacting in the electronic markets. Consider the following: If you own 1,000 shares of EBAY (eBay), RHAT (RedHat), or CIEN (Ciena), or any of the really volatile stocks—stocks that can drop two points in as many minutes—and you go to sell that stock, using the wrong route can wind up taking several minutes. Several minutes can mean several dollars. And on 1,000 shares, this can mean the difference between a healthy profit and a harsh loss. If this sounds familiar, read on.

So how do you buy and sell stock? You can hire a full-service brokerage to do it for you, and you can even enter your orders online (Charles Schwab, Datek, E*Trade, DLJ Direct, and many others offer excellent full service online) and suffer exorbitant commissions or less than stellar execution—one or the other, sometimes both at once. And if you are investing for the long term, this may be fine. But if you actively trade for a living, eventually you know you just have to do it yourself.

Full-service discount brokerages often take the other side of your trades, and nondiscount brokerages rape you with high commissions *and* take the other side. Eventually, if you trade for a living, you get burned enough to want to cut the broker's and trader's cost out of the equation. And due to new laws and technological advances, *you can.* While formerly reserved for market professionals at extreme, prohibitive cost, direct access to the stock, options (and soon the world's currency) markets is now available to individuals. Some electronic brokerages now offer the individual *direct* access to the securities markets for a small fee. It is a brave new world. If you have a computer and a phone line, you yourself can trade directly with the specialist on the floor of the New York Stock Exchanges (NYSE), and actually appear, along with all professional participants, on the "virtual floor" of the Nasdaq from anywhere in the world. You can have the control, you can do the execution, and you can keep all the proceeds that formerly went to the broker and trader.

But trading your own account directly entails certain responsibilities. Anyone who has ever traded through a direct-access–oriented electronic brokerage knows you don't just buy or sell. The securities markets *are markets*; there has to be a buyer if you're going to sell, and as a trader you have to locate that buyer and sell to him. We all know about the electronic communications networks (ECNs), and some brokerages claim their network is "the best"—but why? In what way? Every route of execution works differently in different situations. Given certain circumstances, all are truly amazing; in other circumstances, they fail dismally. The best of the electronic brokerages offer full access to a multitude of routes, so you can point and click to designate one or another, but which route is best to use in which situation? Anyone who does not take this question seriously has obviously never traded his or her own account.

And no discussion about which route is the fastest, surest way to transact would be possible without a thorough discussion of the road map of buying and selling: the Nasdaq Level II Quotes Montage. What is Level II and, more important, how do you interpret it? How do you tell what the market makers are doing? And what games and tricks do market makers play? Even though doing so will not endear me to my market-making friends, in this book I'm going to outline just what it is that market makers do, how they do it, and how to spot it. And it's okay that they'll be upset, because I'm the least of their problems. The world is changing. An electronic revolution in the truest sense is sweeping the world's equity markets, and many pillars of strength in the financial communities are reinventing themselves to avoid obsolescence.

This is, therefore, the first book about the new tools of the trade. What are those tools; how do you use them? With a little knowledge and today's technologies, you can buy and sell stock faster and more transparently than market makers themselves.

It's possible to turn a small trading account into an account worth millions. Many people worldwide have done just this. But it is more important to note that many more people have lost everything on the anvil called Speculation. Unscrupulous get-rich-quick schemes can be found in all industries and are especially prevalent in the fields of gambling and stock speculation. These may consist of simple or complex "systems" that can be purchased from a so-called expert, or they may be sold as very expensive courses guaranteed to turn anyone into a successful trader. The least scrupulous systems usually recommend a particular brokerage (which will give you a huge credit line) and "scalping" as a business plan to people new to trading. (Scalping is the practice of holding position for often no more than mere seconds, in order to capture a small gain. Practiced scalpers often do this hundreds of times a day.) People brand new to trading, by the way, are the *last* people who should use huge lines of credit or scalp. Many traders make great livings scalping, but for reasons to be discussed shortly, it is one of the hardest ways to make a buck long term. Additionally, it is a craft—and one not easily learned. Scalping with great success requires experience and knowledge. Knowledge and experience must be acquired, through hard work, practice, and study. I hope this book will shorten part of the learning curve.

Are great traders born, or do traders become great? It's the age-old question of education or evolution. I believe that they become great and that those few traders who actually turn their accounts into massive empires worth more than the gross domestic product of many small countries also have a certain gift, a knack for the game. And they are persistent. And they educate themselves, through all means available, including the jungle of hard knocks: the stock market.

This book may help you turn your account into the massive sort of empire described. But it is my hope that you don't read it with that in mind. I'll leave that to the get-rich books. Trading is a ruthless, competitive game, where the losses are real and instantaneous. Day trading, in particular, is a hard, hard game. The purpose of this book is not to turn you into a supertrader, to give you some secret that will make you rich overnight. Rather, this book's single purpose is to assist you to become a successful trader, defined in the following way: one who understands the game, understands the risks involved, and has the necessary skills and tools to minimize risk and implement a trading plan. The goal: Profit and loss will be limited by the quality of your trading thesis, not your ability to execute.

That's all. If you are one of the gifted, that's your business. If you are one of the gifted and have the persistence to work hard and accept the heartbreak that will come with inevitable loss from time to time, and the foresight to continually educate yourself in an ever-evolving game, my hat's off to you. This book may be the start of something wonderful.

day trading defined

Simply put, day trading is the practice of profiting from intraday moves in the equity market and closing all positions by end of day. Day trading can be highly profitable. Scalping (a kind of day trading) also can be profitable—at least for a time. I think, however, that to limit yourself only to scalping is to take tremendous risk for minimal gain; it's missing the big picture. Many stocks move four, five, or more points in a single day. It would be silly to ignore all the real potential out there and take more risk for tinier profits. (Chapter 9 explains my view in depth.) Many active day traders don't scalp. Preferring to capture larger intraday moves they'll hold a stock from seconds to hours, and capture a large part of the move.

In any case, watching the market intraday allows you to buy during rallies and sell short (see Chapter 11) on sell-offs, thereby profiting from volatility. The securities markets become more volatile everyday. On an awful day, like those of the March 2000 sell-off, prepared traders reaped massive, life-changing profits.

Day traders close all positions by the end of the day. Why close all positions by end of day? Doing this insulates the trader from adverse happenings overnight. Say you own 1,000 shares of a biotech company whose new technological widget is widely expected to win approval from the Food and Drug Administration (FDA). Then the news comes out after market hours, and it is bad: The FDA doesn't approve. By market open the next day, the price of your 1,000 shares has been cut in half. Similar situations happen all the time. Holding no positions overnight contains losses. You may lose potential profit as well, but you must decide if you are better safe than sorry. But note: I am not giving a carte blanche recommendation for closing all positions by end of day; in fact, many of the best profits I have seen came from holding overnight. I'm just explaining the reasoning behind the day traders' approach. As a trader, you may find that you sleep better if you are flat at market close . . . or not. But this book is not just about day trading, short-term speculation, or position trading (several day to several month price targets) or investing for the long term. It is about how to actually buy and sell your positions in the fastest, most agile way possible and how to determine which approach to execution best serves your needs at a particular time. Countless profitable trades have become losses due to a lack of information about the execution systems that everyone uses.

is it possible to profit by scalping?

Yes. Absolutely. But keep in mind it is very difficult, and there are bigger fish out there. In an average day, a scalper may buy a $10 stock and sell it for 10⅛. An eighth doesn't sound like a lot, but keep in mind that on 1,000 shares, that's $125. And when you realize the average scalper makes dozens of such trades a day, it adds up fast. Of course, so do the commissions.

The best scalpers sometimes trade 300 or more times a day. They are like sharks swimming in shallow water, waiting for a moment of weakness. And those moments occur all the time. But this is not to say that scaping is easy! And, truth be told, with scalping as a plan you will miss out on all the major moves, like Yahoo! going from $27 a share to a split-adjusted $340. But the Yahoo! move would have been in your long-term investment account, right? At least it should have been. Successful traders speculate only with a small percentage of their total account. Day trading is a highly risky endeavor and should be done only with purely speculative capital—that is, money you can afford to lose.

But scalping, in my personal opinion, is a largely uneconomic activity. New order-handling rules regulating the Nasdaq make scalping profitably much, much more difficult. And scalping involves much higher risk, because you need to buy or short more shares to beat commission costs. It is truly sad, in my opinion, that scalping holds such an allure, and that often the traders most eager to scalp—and trade the most volatile, hardest-to-trade stocks—often are the newest to trading. Avoid get-rich-quick thinking! Scalping in today's market (as opposed to before August 1998, when Nasdaq order-handling rules were different) really requires skill; you have to fully understand the order execution systems and have split-second decision-making powers. You *develop* this kind of knowledge with experience. It doesn't come from a five-day course. And as far as I know, this is the first book that deals with how execution systems actually work.

I'll say it again here and later in the book: As a rule, scalping for an eighth in today's markets is uneconomic for those brand new to trading. It may enrich your broker and seminar instructor, but until you have a firm understanding of the basics of trading, with scalping as an m.o., you probably will be the one getting scalped.

swing trading

Swing traders tend to take a more conservative approach. They watch a comparatively small number of highly volatile or strongly trending stocks and employ strict risk management controls to hold a position open from hours to several days. Getting to know some few stocks well can be an excellent way of avoiding some of the risk taken by scalpers, who often know nothing about the stocks they trade. Many of the stocks swing traders work with move several or more points intraday or over several days. At the time of this writing, I can name almost a dozen stocks that move 5 to 20 points intraday every day. Swing traders tend to take buy or sell positions with time frames already in mind. And in the same way that the best day traders close all positions every day, swing traders close positions once their particular thesis/time frame is proven wrong. Some swing traders approach trading with a momentum-driven philosophy, buying stocks during periods of unusual buying pressure and holding overnight for potential gap-ups (opening in the morning at a higher price than where it closed) to sell before the market opens; others buy stock splits with the intention of holding for several days to capture speculative price run-ups. Coupled with strict money management, these sorts of knowledge-driven, risk-averse plans can often be easily and safely accomplished.

position trading

Successful traders often take positions for a number of weeks to months based on their observance of short- or intermediate-term trends. "The trend is your friend" is what they'll tell you. Short- to intermediate-term trends are not sexy or exciting because they don't provide the instant gratification of day trades. But they get results. And you can make educated decisions based on reason, and plan, and remove as much risk as possible. Take a look at the oil services industry during spring and summer 1998. A trend like this is gold for the taking.

trading vs. investing

Trading is *not* investing. Trading involves taking a specific position for a specific reason. Traders must consider opportunity cost, price, slippage, risk, and a multitude of other factors in real time. Trading and speculation are similar: For various reasons, you think X is going to happen, and so you do Y to take advantage of it. If X happens, you get out with a profit. If it doesn't, you get out with a loss. You are actively involved and watching events as they occur.

Investing, on the other hand, involves much longer time frames and complex strategies. You may own a stock for its earnings, for its growth, or for any number of reasons. The main thing is, you *own* it long term—3, 5, 10 years. Think of retirement. Investing is what you should do with the majority of your account and certainly with your individual retirement account (IRA). Some firms allow individuals to actively trade their IRAs. I can't understand this. IRA money has *got* to be there for retirement! Don't do anything risky with it, especially if you are approaching retirement age. Consult a professional financial advisor for strategic financial planning before risking anything in a self-directed trading account. Don't speculate until you truly have money you can afford to lose.

If you are reading this book, you've probably already made the decision to actively trade your own account. Maybe you've even started to and are considering switching from a full service brokerage to one that offers direct access to the markets. If so, the following section will be of interest.

full-service vs. direct-access brokerage

The choice of whether to use a full-service or a direct-access brokerage is a fairly simple one, based on the number of trades you are doing. If you are doing two or fewer trades a week, you will do fine with one of the better online discount brokerages, for the following reasons:

- *Discounted commissions* (and probably less-than-wonderful execution). You are clearly not subject to the intraday vagaries of the market, so you probably won't need absolute control of your executions. Remember: Direct-access trading will require your full attention. You will need to become an expert trader to enjoy the benefits of direct access, but if you are only doing a few trades a week, you are not trading enough to make the effort worthwhile. You will probably benefit from the low commissions found at the discount houses. The money you will lose due to slippage is probably less than the monthly cost of a top-of-the-line, real-time, front-end order execution platform.

- *Full, easily-accessed information.* Most of the better full-service online brokerages offer news, financial reports, and well-designed account information, all set up for easy access for someone whose life doesn't revolve around the markets. The news may not be real time, but you probably can afford the 15- to 20-minute delay, since your trading plan probably doesn't include scalping based on news hot off the press.

- *24-hour access.* You can peruse your account at leisure from the luxury of your home over the Internet.

- *You will still be able to work at your job.* Unless you're going to devote yourself to a new career, there's no reason to get a full direct-access trading platform. It's overkill.

If you actively trade your account intraday and are committed to trading full time, you probably want to consider a direct-access electronic brokerage, for the following reasons:

- *Control.* There is no control like the ability to trade anytime direct. Real-time information coupled with the best, fastest execution systems in existence has no substitute. Of course, there is a price to pay: You will be truly responsible for your decisions. Sometimes taking responsibility is not a good thing, if you aren't ready (with knowledge) and fully committed. Trading direct requires full commitment. Remember: The traders at the market-making firms whom you are trying to beat are trained, licensed, practiced, and sharp. There aren't many professional suckers working for the majors; the high stakes of the game weed them out.

- *Lower costs overall.* Electronic brokerages will charge a hefty data feed fee and higher ticket charges than a discount online brokerage. However, you will not be subject to the slippage that occurs when using a full-service discount brokerage. Remember: Nothing in life is free. If the brokerage is charging you a discounted commission, the additional money used to pay the broker and trader a living wage is coming from somewhere.

- *Be the middleman—and own his profit.* If the stock is bid 10 by 10¼, and you buy it at your discount broker, the broker may take the other side: Buy it at 10 and sell it to you at 10¼. On 1000 shares, that's $250 the broker will keep for his trouble. And when you go to sell the stock, the broker may do it again. So those two $9 commissions really cost you $500. When you add it all up, if you are aggressively trading your own account several times a day, you're missing out on a lot of money.

- *Work from anywhere.* The better direct-access brokerages offer remote trading platforms. In other words, you can load the software onto your laptop computer and trade from anywhere as long as you have a good Internet connection. I had a client who called to say hi while trading the New York Stock Exchange directly during a visit to the Great Pyramids at Giza, Egypt. But trading really isn't a vacation. It's a hard, often boring job. The fact that some people travel while doing it shouldn't make you lose sight of the rigors. And I didn't say whether my friend in Egypt made any money, did I? If it's a vacation you want, take one! Don't imagine trading your own account will be a stress-free Shangri-La; quite the opposite. With responsibility comes pressure. Putting your butt on the line every day is no joke. The fact that you can do it from home might actually ruin your home as a sanctuary.

Before you start to trade directly, you'll need to get the facts. You'll need a firm grasp of Level II interpretation (understanding just what the Level II quotes mean) and an understanding of all the order-execution routes. The rest of this volume provides the map and all the routes are marked.

chapter 2

the toolbox

This analogy is goofy but appropriate: While you might use a steak knife to screw in a screw, and it will work, eventually, there are better ways to do the job. You might also cut a steak with a screwdriver, and it will work, eventually, but there are better ways to do the job. The proper tool for the job is nowhere more important than here, the cyber jungle of the trader. New tools for buying and selling stock that used to only be available to institutions are now available to retail traders, and they have turned the market on its ear. They are the real-time Level II quotes, and the various execution routes by which you can execute against these quotes—or represent your own quotes—directly in the Nasdaq quotes montage (see Chapter 3), competing directly against major institutions and other traders alike. If you have command of these tools, including Level II, SuperSOES, and ECNs, which are now legal and affordable to individual users, you can buy at the bid, sell at the ask, and actually participate in the Nasdaq market at dealer prices, the same way a market maker does, without the legal responsibilities of being a market maker. And the SuperDot, the execution vehicle long in use by institutions and brokerages for trading the New York Stock Exchange direct, is now available for personal use as well.

These tools truly enable the individual to buy at the bid, sell at the ask, and move in and out of positions with greater speed and agility than the market makers themselves. (See Chapter 10 for a description of what it is that market makers do, how they do it, and the unique legal responsibilities of making a market.)

No wonder market makers don't want you to have access.

The following chapters discuss all the new means available to individuals to purchase and sell both listed and over-the-counter (OTC) securities, methods that recently were available only to institutions.

As well as in-depth discussion of the Level II montage, the "order book" of the Nasdaq, and SuperMontage—the new proposal-stage next generation Level II, by the end of this chapter, you'll have a thorough understanding of what Level II is, how it works, how to interpret it, and why you might want to have access to it if you're trading over-the-counter stocks. Coupled with a thorough understanding of the methods with which you can buy and sell securities, this information will enable you to buy at the bid, sell at the offer, ascertain in real time the strength and direction of a stock *before* it moves, and enter and exit positions with greater speed and agility than the market makers themselves.

understanding Level II

If you have ever traded your own account, undoubtedly you have run into situations where it seemed impossible to sell or buy stock, no matter what you did. The hard truth is that in different situations, which can be readily identified once you have an understanding of Level II, some order-entry "routes" have distinct advantages over others.

You must understand Level II and how it works as a prerequisite for understanding how and why the various tools (SelectNet, Super-SOES, SuperDot, and ECNs) work. With understanding, Level II can be like a map, showing you the fastest route to your destination. You then can select the route, and you're on your way.

Regarding the fastest route: Some routes will create a near-instantaneous fill, whereas others, *in the same circumstances*, will result in "nothing done." Understanding just how these tools work and when to use each one is an absolute necessity to trading effectively. If you have been trading your own account, then you know that there is no single sure-fire way of instantaneously entering or exiting a position that works equally well for all situations. This book will provide you with an understanding of how all the tools work and when to use them. Fortunately, there are not so very many routes, and all can be mastered quickly and easily. The advantages and disadvantages are as easy to know as the knife vs. the screwdriver.

Now the hard, boring stuff.

Level I

There are three "levels" of quotes in the Nasdaq market. Level I is what brokers generally have access to. It is also referred to as the "inside market," and it is what is given when you ask your broker for a quote. You may ask for a quote in Microsoft (MSFT) and your broker will respond something like this "Microsoft is currently bidding $93^{13}/_{16}$ by $^{7}/_{8}$" or "Microsoft is bid $93^{13}/_{16}$, offered $93^{7}/_{8}$." Simply put, that means that a market participant is willing to pay $\$93^{13}/_{16}$ to buy a certain number of shares and that a market participant (maybe the same one) is willing to sell a certain number of shares at $\$93^{7}/_{8}$. So if you want to sell MSFT, you can currently sell it at $\$93^{13}/_{16}$ per share; if you'd like to buy it, you can, at $\$93^{7}/_{8}$ per share. This is also the sort of quote you get from Yahoo! or any full-service traditional or online brokerage.

	Bid	*Ask*
MSFT	$93^{13}/_{16}$	$93^{7}/_{8}$

But Level I is only the very tip of the iceberg. It tells you what the best bid and offer (offer = ask) are; in other words, it says what is the most you can sell your shares for or the cheapest you can buy shares. But there is much much more information to know. Suppose you could tell that in the next few moments, the price probably will go up? Or suppose you could tell it probably will go down? You don't need a crystal ball. But you do need practice, knowledge, and, most important, Level II.

Level II

Figure 2.1 is a Level II snapshot of Microsoft and all the market participants. Nasdaq market makers have something called Level III. As shown in Chapter 3, although the Nasdaq Level III screens are organized differently, it is important to note that as far as information

figure 2.1   Nasdaq Level II quotes montage (MSFT)

TOOLS OF THE TRADE									_ □ ☒

MSFT	Last	93 7/8					15:57		—15:57—
High	94 1/16	Low	91 51/64	Tot Vol		17991500			93 7/8 100
BID ↓	93 13/16	ASK	93 7/8	Close		92 1/4			93 7/8 1000

93 7/8 300
93 7/8 100
93 7/8 1100
93 7/8 4000

NAME	BID	DIR	SIZE	#BEST	NAME	ASK	DIR	SIZE	#BEST ▲
ISLD	93 13/16	+0	83	576	INCA	93 7/8	+0	37	378
INCA	93 13/16	+0	42	576	MWSE	93 7/8	-1/16	11	22
NITE	93 13/16	+0	22	180	SBSH	93 7/8	+0	10	51
FBCO	93 13/16	-1/16	10	19	REDI	93 15/16	-1/16	10	146
MSCO	93 13/16	+1/4	10	63	ISLD	93 15/16	+0	73	562
BEST	93 13/16	+1/8	10	32	MONT	93 15/16	-9/16	10	14
SLKC	93 13/16	+3/16	10	69	MSCO	93 15/16	+0	10	51
SBSH	93 13/16	+0	10	69	WARR	93 15/16	+1/16	10	9
EVRN	93 13/16	+0	9	2	GFIN	93 15/16	+1/16	10	31
ARCA	93 13/16	+1 13/16	2	40	AGIS	94	+0	10	37
GSCO	93 3/4	+1/8	10	39	PRUS	94	-1/2	10	25
PWJC	93 3/4	+1/4	10	24	HRZG	94	-1/2	10	25
DKNY	93 3/4	+0	1	6	MHMY	94	-1 1/8	10	1
JPMS	93 11/16	+0	1	6	GSCO	94	+1/8	10	37
REDI	93 5/8	+0	40	163	NFSC	94	+0	5	20
MLCO	93 5/8	+1/4	10	21	NITE	94	+0	3	127
PRUS	93 5/8	+1/4	10	23	LEHM	94	+0	1	11
BRUT	93 5/8	+3/8	2	22	SELZ	94	-1/16	1	3
LEHM	93 5/8	+0	1	31	MADF	94	+0	1	50
BTRD	93 9/16	+0	10	30	BRUT	94 1/16	+0	1	49
MHMY	93 9/16	-5/8	1	6	MLCO	94 1/8	-1/16	10	27
AGIS	93 9/16	+0	4	1	BTRD	94 1/8	+1/4	30	18
GFIN	93 9/16	+0	2	0	EVRN	94 1/8	+0	10	3
WARR	93 9/16	+0	1	0	SHWD	94 1/8	+0	1	1

93 13/16 10
93 7/8 1000
93 7/8 1200
93 7/8 300
93 7/8 200
93 7/8 3600
93 7/8 1000
93 7/8 3600
93 7/8 1000
93 7/8 1000
93 7/8 1100

goes, the information on a Level III Nasdaq workstation screen is fundamentally identical to that on a Level II screen. In other words, if you have Level II, you have all the same information that the market makers do.

Now you can see why the Nasdaq market makers are so miffed: Their playing field has been leveled, and now any Tom or Jane can compete with them on near-equal terms.

Life was hard enough for market makers before, but at least all the professional participants had the unwritten practice of maintaining nice fat spreads. But now, in come Tom and Jane Trader. And

Jane's not so greedy. She's willing to make only an eighth, only a six-teenth, and on only a few shares. But due to the increased liquidity of Tom's and Jane's accounts, the market makers can no longer make their big fat spreads. And it's hurt them.

For a while, traders at major firms raised their hands to the sky and bellowed "Where'd all the money go?" There were layoffs, firms closed their doors permanently, and compensation packages at major firms were substantially reduced. Now market makers have resigned themselves to not making those big, fat spreads. They have to split it with Tom and Jane.

But Darwin's law rules the cyber jungle: That's just the way it is. The market maker system must adapt or be evolved out of existence. For now, at least, individuals have powerful tools at their disposal, tools never before available to the "nonprofessional" individual. The following chapters are devoted to those knives and screwdrivers, those arrows and blades of successful trading. Keep in mind there is a quiet war raging; market makers are fighting for their very lives. And since we know they won't go quietly into the night, we must educate ourselves and train ourselves to play the game at its highest level. It is a zero-sum game; somebody wins, somebody loses. "Scalping" is ex-actly what it sounds like. Level II is the virtual battlefield where great campaigns are waged. You must carefully examine Level II if you hope to see the market for what it is, to not be fooled by the melee, and to profit from the madness of crowds.

chapter 3

Level II: definitions

Please examine the Level II screen shot of Microsoft (MSFT) in Figure 3.1 and review the following definitions. The Level II screen is officially referred to as the Nasdaq Level II Quotes Montage.

Level II (L2) shows the current bids and offers of all market participants in a chosen stock. It updates dynamically, as the market participants change their price and desired transaction size. In a very busy stock, L2 will be in a constant state of frenzied flux. In an illiquid stock that few people care about, L2 often remains static and unchanged for much of the day. Many of the smaller, less active stocks have only several active market participants. Heavily traded stocks, such as Microsoft (MSFT), have many participants, often several dozen. The screen shot in Figure 3.1 was taken at 15:57 (3:57) P.M. EST on a typical day. As you can see from the volume indicator (item #6), almost 18 million shares were traded on that day!

During premarket hours, particularly just before the market opens, prices often seem bizarre, with bid prices often higher than offers; this is because some participants have not yet changed their price and size from where they were the day before. In addition, market participants will jockey around, raising and lowering their prices before the market opening to try to determine who's more desperate to buy or sell. Keep in mind that any premarket displays by market

figure 3.1   Level II quotes montage

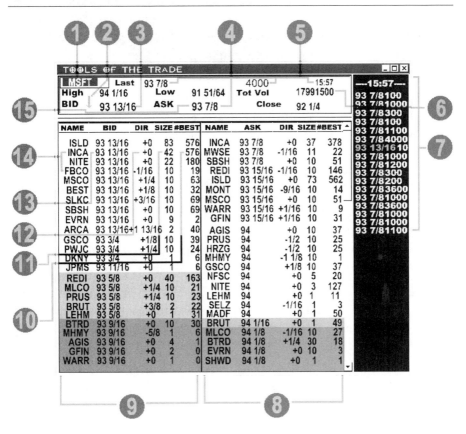

makers are just that: premarket. No one is under any obligation to honor displayed intentions until the market is open. Think of the market makers' premarket machinations as banks on opposite sides of a street. At 6:30 A.M., the president of one bank comes in and sees that the guy across the street has posted a new, higher rate of interest. So the president at this bank raises her rate too, and a bidding war ensues, until one or the other is unwilling to do business at that price level. The doors of the banks are closed, mind you, and the banks still are not open for business. Who knows what will be the best rates once they actually start transacting with customers?

Generally, Level II is organized in the way it is displayed. Each color in the figure represents a different price level. There is no special significance to the colors themselves; you can choose a color scheme that is pleasant to your eye. The colors simply give you a quick visual indication of the depth of market participants at each price level. The 15 numbered circles on the figure correspond to the following.

1. *Symbol.* The symbol of the stock.

2. *Tick Arrow.* This arrow points down on a "down tick," when the last trade is at a price the same or lower than the previous trade, or points up on an "up tick," when the last trade occurs at a price equal to or higher than the previous one. This is important information, especially when trying to sell short.

3. *Bid.* This is "the best bid," the highest price at which a market participant is willing to buy stock. Also known as the "inside bid," it is the bid price your broker typically quotes you.

4. *Ask/Offer.* The "best offer," the lowest price at which any market participant is currently willing to sell. Also known as the "inside offer," it is the offer price your broker typically quotes you.

5. *Last Sale.* This information tells you that MSFT last traded 4,000 shares at $93\frac{7}{8}$, and that the trade occurred at 15:57, or 3:57 P.M. EST.

6. *Volume.* This is the number of shares traded so far today.

7. *Ticker.* This provides simple sales data: time of sale, price of sale, and size of sale. The complete "Time of Sales" reports, which will be described in detail shortly, contain much more information regarding a stock's activity. But as a quick reference, many traders find the ticker invaluable.

8. *Offer Side.* This "side" of the quotes montage contains the postings (not unlike those postings found in a newspaper) of all market participants wishing to sell. Notice the very best price—the lowest price at which anyone is currently willing to sell—is at the very top of the montage. Remember, each color represents a price level.

9. *Bid Side.* This "side" of the quotes montage contains all the postings of all market participants currently willing to buy stock. The highest price anyone is currently willing to pay for stock appears at the very top of the montage.

    The left side of the Level II montage represents the bid (buyer) side of the participant's quote. Everyone on the left desires to buy at the prices, sizes noted. The right side is the offer (selling) side, displaying everyone's intentions to sell. So, if you wish to buy stock and you have direct access to the market, you can do it in two ways: You can either "take" the inside (best) offer and buy the stock right away, or you can join the market participants bidding for the stock and perhaps buy the stock cheaper, when someone decides to "hit" your bid. You would then keep the spread for yourself!

    Important terminology: You "hit" bids, and you "take" offers. If you call a trader and tell him to "hit the offer," he will not understand whether you want to buy or sell. Use of incorrect terminology will wind up in confusion at best and, at worst, maybe even a sell when you really wanted a buy. Of course none of this will have any significance at a full-service brokerage; the brokers there don't even know the difference—they are salesmen, not traders. When you want to buy through a full-service brokerage you'll get the best offer. But of course, their traders may take the other side. If possible, they will buy the stock at the bid and keep the difference!

10. *Number Best.* Also called "hammer," this is an optional informational item found in the better direct-access trading platforms. It tells you the number of times in the current trading session that a market participant has remained at the best bid/offer *after everyone else has left.* This feature is nearly indispensable for the following reason: It clues you in immediately to whom the buyer/seller may be. If the montage shows one guy bidding for only 100 shares, at a price only $1/16$ above everyone else, and that everyone else is bidding for similar size, you might not think much. But if you found out that the guy at the best bid has been there 132 times today (even

though he's only bid 100 shares), and nobody else has been there more than 10 times, you might conclude that he is a buyer of size. And if this was coupled with a huge increase in volume on the day, well— To repeat, let's say the stock has traded 1,000,000 shares today, and every market participant (as in the preceding example) is showing only 100 shares. Who is doing all the trading? Number best/hammer can clue you in. I find the "number best/hammer" feature a very valuable piece of information.

11. *Size.* This is the number of shares the market participant is willing to transact at the displayed price. You may configure your L2 screen to show size in multiples of 10, where 10 means 100 shares, as is the screen in Figure 3.1, or you may configure it to show "actual" size—100 shares, 500 shares, and the like.

12. *Direction/Change.* This is also a very valuable feature, since it shows you whether the market participant has recently raised or lowered the bid or offer. Suppose you are looking at a stock, and all of a sudden you notice that in the last minute or two, nearly all the market participants on the bid side have raised their price. Now, for whatever reason, they're all willing to pay more for the stock than they were five minutes ago. Then you notice that on the offer side, nearly all participants have raised their offers too, indicating they're not willing to sell so cheap anymore. Direction/ change is a valuable indicator of short-term trader sentiment. Some trading platforms offer you a + or – indicator; others offer + or – and the amount by which participants have changed their quote. Figure 3.1, for example, is of the latter variety, showing not only + or – but also by how much participants changed their price.

13. *Price.* This is the price that market participants are holding out to the world that they will transact at. They can change it at any time, provided they are fulfilling their liabilities and duties as either market makers or ECNs.

14. *Market Participant.* This is the firm that is bidding or offering the stock. It is identified by a four-letter acronym. Ex-

amples: GSCO (Goldman, Sachs), SBSH (Salomon Smith Barney), and MASH (Meyer, Schweitzer). There are also the ECNs such as ISLD (the Island), ARCA (the Archipelago), and INCA (InstiNet). Detailed information on the ECNs is provided later in this volume. The participants highlighted here are INCA (InstiNet) and FBCO (Credit Suisse First Boston). INCA is an ECN and FBCO is a market maker. For reasons soon to be discussed, you must *memorize* the symbols for the ECNs, so as to readily distinguish them from market makers. This won't be hard—there are only a dozen or so. Memorizing the market makers, however, would be hard; there are thousands.

All market makers must maintain a firm, two-sided quote. That means they must always stand ready to both buy and sell at their displayed prices/sizes during market hours. Note that the market makers' bid price and offer price may be very far apart—that is their spread. Since market makers may change their price and size whenever they like, their individual spread (difference between the bid and the offer) will vary throughout the day. Note also that the quote is two sided. That is, market makers may appear *only* at one place at a time on each side of the market. *Note:* ECNs are not market makers and are therefore not required to maintain two-sided quotes.

15. *Inside Market.* This is what traditional brokers quote you. Note that unless brokers have access to Level II (and most don't), then they will see *only* the best bid and offer—not any of the actual montage! Most traditional brokers don't even know what Level II is—though this is changing fast.

time of sales

"Time of Sales" reports are also known as "Time and Sales" reports, "Print Reports," "Sales Data" reports, and "Sales Reports." What you call them is simply your preference. I like "Time of Sales" because I think that's the most accurate description.

Time of sales reports are not part of the Level II montage, yet sales data is absolutely necessary to understanding and monitoring your interpretation of Level II data and executions. Time of sales will allow you to see whether the print (one official record of your transaction) received was in line with all the transactions at the time of execution and give you additional information, such as whether that last print half a point above the market was really a print at that price, or whether it is simply a record of a transaction that occurred earlier. Time of sales differs from a simple stock ticker in that it includes a time-stamped record of all the bid/offer changes of the market participants as well as records of every transaction executed.

So if, in an extremely liquid stock, you have ever placed a stop loss or even a market order with your broker or online yourself, and received a print that looks out of line considering other trades at the time, by referring to the time of sales report, you have the means to determine whether the execution price was fair and equitable. It is of special value when considering prints on the NYSE. For example, if the price is the only print at that price, and every other print was three-quarters of a point higher, there may be very good reasons for this. But then again, something may have gone awry. In any case, you'll need to contact your broker if you feel an error has been made.

If you request it, your broker is required to represent you in an investigation of the print. This will involve filing a complaint with the regulatory organization governing the exchange where the trade took place. StockWatch keeps thorough time-coded records of every transaction and bid/offer in every stock. If there is a questionable print, StockWatch and the regulatory organizations will support you in investigation of the trade. Just make your broker aware of the trade, and he or she will advise and assist you in investigation of the print. Remember: You are a client, and it is in the brokers' best interests to keep you happy. Your broker will be glad to assist in any investigation of a seemingly unreasonable print. If he or she is not, then report him or her and change brokers.

Keep in mind that a print with which you are not happy is not necessarily a bad trade. A quick investigation of time of sales will clue you in as to possible causes for the print. For example, a client once called me and said he had just bought 300 shares of an NASD NM (National Market) security at market. As he placed his market order, the prints were going off at $14\frac{1}{4}$. About 20 seconds later, he received his print: $14\frac{3}{4}$! Then he saw prints at $14\frac{1}{4}$ again! He called me screaming bloody murder.

So I looked at time of sales. Seconds before he entered his order, the offer changed to $14\frac{3}{4}$. And 5,200 shares printed at $14\frac{3}{4}$. It was the high of the day. It was very close, so I offered to investigate. I was told by the Nasdaq that several seconds before he placed the trade, the one market maker offered out at $14\frac{3}{8}$ moved his quote. Next in line were market makers, at $14\frac{3}{4}$. They were happy to sell there, and filled the order between them. But then the spread being wide, more market makers jumped on the offer; in mere seconds, the offer was $14\frac{1}{4}$ again. So I had to give my client the bad news: All in all, it was a bona-fide trade. If my client had entered a limit order, then this would not have happened. But as a market order, it executed immediately. And he was legitimately peeved. But the print was "good."

The following figures are examples of time of sales reports (see Figures 3.2 and 3.3), for both listed stocks and an over-the-counter (OTC) stock (see Figure 3.4). Please note these important identifiers; they'll come in handy when examining a report.

- *Exch.* This refers to the exchange where the trade took place. NYS is New York Stock Exchange, and the rest are the regional listed exchanges. In certain situations, listed stocks can trade on the Nasdaq, provided the firms trading them have met certain qualifying criteria. You will see the identifier NAS in the exchange field for Nasdaq trades.

- *Trade.* This reflects that an actual trade took place at the time shown.

- *Irg. Trade.* This identifies an irregular trade, having most likely been reported out of sequence or having occurred on another exchange. For example, InstiNet trades are reported as irregular trades.

- *Bid/Ask.* At times no trades take place, but the specialists on the exchange changed their price/size. Every change in price/size is time coded and noted.

- *Best Bid/Best Ask.* When a price is quoted that creates a new inside market, you will see the identifier "Best . . ." identifying that a new price/size has been entered, changing the inside market.

- *Closing/Opening.* On the listed exchanges, during opening and closing procedures, specialists will match the largest number of trades possible. The arrived-at price will serve as the "opening price" and the "closing price" for "market on close" or "market on open" orders.

- *Sld/Sold.* This refers to the fact that the trade being reported actually occurred at least 20 minutes ago.

- *Form T/.T.* This refers to the fact that the trade occurred aftermarket, between 4:02 P.M. and 4:39 P.M.

- *Intra.* This designates a trade taking place intraday.

figure 3.2   AOL time of sales report

Date	Time	Price	Volume	Exch	Type	Bid	BSize	BEx	Ask	ASize	AEx	Cond
9/3/99	16:00	97 1/16	1000	NYS	Trade							
9/3/99	16:00	96 3/8	300	NYS	lrg Trade							Intra
9/3/99	16:00	96 3/8	2000	NYS	lrg Trade							Intra
9/3/99	16:00	96 3/8	200	NYS	lrg Trade							Intra
9/3/99	16:00	96 3/8	200	NYS	lrg Trade							Intra
9/3/99	16:00				Bid	96 1/2	100	PHS	97 3/16	100	NAS	
9/3/99	16:00				Ask	96 1/2	100	PHS	97 1/2	100	PHS	
9/3/99	16:00				Bid	96 7/8	100	NAS	97 1/2	100	PHS	
9/3/99	16:00				Ask	96 7/8	100	NAS	97 3/16	100	NAS	
9/3/99	16:00				Best Bid	97 1/16	1000	CIN	97 3/16	100	NAS	
9/3/99	16:00				Best Ask	97 1/16	1000	CIN	97 3/16	100	NAS	
9/3/99	16:00				Bid	96 15/16	1000	NYS	97 3/16	100	NAS	
9/3/99	16:00				Ask	96 15/16	1000	NYS	97 3/16	75000	NYS	Closing
9/3/99	16:00	96 3/8	3000	NYS	lrg Trade							Intra
9/3/99	16:00				Bid	97 1/16	1000	NYS	97 3/16	75000	NYS	
9/3/99	16:00				Ask	97 1/16	1000	NYS	97 3/16	75000	NYS	Closing
9/3/99	16:00				Bid	96 7/8	100	CSE	97 3/16	75000	NYS	
9/3/99	16:00				Ask	96 7/8	100	CSE	97 3/8	100	CSE	
9/3/99	16:00				Bid	96 15/16	200	CIN	97 3/8	100	CSE	
9/3/99	16:00				Ask	96 15/16	200	CIN	97 1/4	600	CIN	
9/3/99	16:00				Best Bid	96 15/16	700	BSE	97 1/4	600	CIN	
9/3/99	16:00				Best Ask	96 15/16	700	BSE	97 3/16	100	NAS	
9/3/99	16:00	96 1/2	4400	NYS	lrg Trade							Intra
9/3/99	16:00	96 1/2	2000	NYS	lrg Trade							Intra
9/3/99	16:00	96 1/2	1000	NYS	lrg Trade							Intra
9/3/99	16:00	96 1/2	200	NYS	lrg Trade							Intra
9/3/99	16:00	96 1/2	200	NYS	lrg Trade							Intra
9/3/99	16:00	96 1/2	1000	NYS	lrg Trade							Intra
9/3/99	16:00	96 1/2	200	NYS	lrg Trade							Intra
9/3/99	16:00	96 1/2	100	NYS	lrg Trade							Intra
9/3/99	16:00	96 1/2	1200	NYS	lrg Trade							Intra

Please note that the modifiers just listed will appear only if the specific conditions described by the "modifier" have been fulfilled. Normal transaction prints require no modifier.

Figure 3.2 shows a time of sales report for America Online (AOL). The elements found in time of sales for listed stocks are very similar to the elements found in a Nasdaq time of sales report. This report shows the closing minute of the market. Why did I choose the close? Several items of interest appear only at the time of close, including the "closing price" of the stock and the modifiers describing when the trade actually took place.

Figure 3.3 presents the Nasdaq time of sales report for Microsoft (MSFT).

Figure 3.4 presents an OTC bulletin board stock. The larger issues in the bulletin board market display their quotes in the Nasdaq

figure 3.3 MSFT time of sales report

Date	Time	Price	Volume	Exch	Type	Bid	BSize	BEx	Ask	ASize	AEx	Cond
						MICROSOFT CORP						
9/9/99	15:59				Best Ask	94 1/16	20000	NAS	94 1/8	7000	NAS	up
9/9/99	15:59	94 1/8	2800		Trade							
9/9/99	15:59				Best Bid	94 1/16	25000	NAS	94 1/8	7000	NAS	
9/9/99	15:59				Best Ask	94 1/16	25000	NAS	94 1/8	7000	NAS	up
9/9/99	15:59	94 1/16	1000		Trade							
9/9/99	15:59	94 1/8	2200		Trade							
9/9/99	15:59				Best Bid	94 1/16	27000	NAS	94 1/8	7000	NAS	
9/9/99	15:59				Best Ask	94 1/16	27000	NAS	94 1/8	7000	NAS	up
9/9/99	15:59	94 1/16	500		Trade							
9/9/99	15:59				Best Bid	94 1/16	29000	NAS	94 1/8	7000	NAS	
9/9/99	15:59				Best Ask	94 1/16	29000	NAS	94 1/8	7000	NAS	up
9/9/99	16:00	94 1/8	100		Trade							
9/9/99	15:59				Best Bid	94 1/16	30000	NAS	94 1/8	7000	NAS	
9/9/99	15:59				Best Ask	94 1/16	30000	NAS	94 1/8	7000	NAS	up
9/9/99	16:00	94 1/8	800		Trade							
9/9/99	16:00	94 1/8	500		Trade							
9/9/99	16:00	94 1/8	2000		Trade							
9/9/99	16:00	94 7/64	100		Trade							
9/9/99	16:00	94 1/8	3000		Trade							
9/9/99	16:00	94 1/8	1000		Trade							
9/9/99	16:00	94 1/8	1000		Trade							
9/9/99	16:00	94 1/8	2500		Trade							
9/9/99	16:00	94 7/64	1000		Trade							
9/9/99	16:00	94 1/8	300		Trade							
9/9/99	16:00	94	300		Trade							
9/9/99	16:00	94 1/8	400		Trade							
9/9/99	16:00	94 1/8	2000		Trade							
9/9/99	16:00	94 1/8	2000		lrg Trade							FormT
9/9/99	16:00	94 1/8	1000		lrg Trade							FormT
9/9/99	16:00	94 1/8	5000		lrg Trade							FormT
9/9/99	16:00	94 1/8	100		lrg Trade							FormT
9/9/99	16:00	94 1/8	700		lrg Trade							FormT
9/9/99	16:00	94 1/8	1000		lrg Trade							FormT

figure 3.4   an over-the-counter bulletin board stock

XDSL		9.187	↓	+.031	1000	Kk	10:31	----10:31----
High	9.375	Low		9.187	Acc. Vol.	66100		9.187 1000
Bid	9.156	Ask		9.250	Close	9.156		

Name	Bid	Size	#Best	Name	Ask	Size	#Best
NITE	9.156	0	0	SHWD	9.250	0	2
USCT	9.125	0	3	ERNS	9.250	0	2
PCOS	9.125	0	4	MHMY	9.312	0	1
HILL	9.062	0	1	ALEX	9.375	0	0
MHMY	9.062	0	1	NITE	9.406	0	0
FRAN	9.000	0	0	POND	9.437	0	0
WIEN	9.000	0	1	KBRO	9.500	0	0
MASH	9.000	0	4	FRAN	9.500	0	0
FAHN	8.968	0	0	WIEN	9.500	0	1
HRZG	8.937	0	0	USCT	9.531	0	1
ERNS	8.937	0	1	HILL	9.562	0	1
ALEX	8.875	0	0	MASH	9.562	0	2

OTC bulletin board system, but it is important to note that these stocks are not Nasdaq stocks. Bulletin board stocks have different order-handling rules due to their exchange status. Therefore, they are not eligible for electronic trading. You will not be able to trade a bulletin board stock over your computer. The easiest way to identify a bulletin board stock is by the Size bid offered, which is always zero. The reason for this is that the quotes are "subject," and not firm. Firm quotes mean that market makers are liable to transact at their quoted bid/offer; "subject" means that their quote will have to be confirmed with the market makers. So, generally, you will need to call a trader at your brokerage to transact these issues for you, since you cannot trade them over the computer.

If you know and understand this information, you will have a good basic understanding of what Level II is and how to review through sales data what actually occurred. After you study a few Level II quotes, all the information will come to you without even thinking about it.

Simple, right? It only takes a few minutes to learn what Level II is. But your interpretive skill of Level II may take some time to develop. Don't be worried or befuddled; it's not brain surgery, but it is more complex than it appears and requires a lot of careful real-time observation to perfect. It is absolutely necessary to perfect your understanding of Level II if you are or are planning on trading actively.

chapter 4

Level II: interpretation

Now that you know what all the stuff on a Level II screen is, let's look at what the Level II doesn't say—the fun part: what it means. The trickier parts of this subject will be dealt with further in Chapter 10, which deals specifically with just what market makers do. But now, the basics: the conventional Level II interpretations and how they apply to getting your order filled.

To gain any real understanding of what is going on in a given stock, you must watch it and know the participants. I like to compare the participants in the market to those in horse races. Just because a horse is favored to win a race (and everyone knows it; the odds are published) doesn't mean that the horse will win. Nevertheless, you must know the participants in order to form your own interpretation of a given situation and to remove from the equation as much serendipity as possible.

the axe

It may be surprising to the uninitiated that in many stocks, one or two of the market makers trade a disproportionate amount of those stocks' volume. Names like Goldman Sachs (GSCO), and Salomon Smith Barney (SBSH) come to mind when one thinks of 800-pound gorillas. Market participants watch each other and follow each other's cues. A great game of follow the leader is afoot everyday in most stocks, and knowing who the axe—the major player—is will help you determine the short-term direction of the stock. Knowing that GSCO, for example, is on the bid, has been on the bid all day, and is the axe in this stock, may influence the timing of your sell decision. Laws of supply and demand suggest that if demand outstrips supply, the price is going up; if supply outstrips demand, the price is going down. Conventional wisdom says "Don't trade against the axe." If the axe is a seller, you don't want to be a buyer, and vice versa. But this conventional thinking is not enough. In today's market, the axes are fully aware of their reputation. They use the public's perception to their advantage, trying to disguise their real intentions. This topic is dealt with more in Chapter 10.

It isn't enough simply to know the huge firms that trade the majority of a stock's liquidity because the axe in a particular stock may change from day to day or hour to hour. Institutions and mutual funds may use GSCO or SBSH as brokers to buy or liquidate large positions. And when an institution wants out, it wants out for a reason, and will sell a million shares as quickly as possible without driving the market down due to excess supply. The extent to which market makers are able to buy or sell huge amounts of stock without noticeably affecting the stock's price is a measure of their skill.

Today a company may hire Salomon Smith Barney to sell 100,000 shares; tomorrow it may hire Herzog (HRZG) to buy 50,000; and so on. You will not know how many shares the axe is ordered to buy or sell, but there is a way to surmise if the market participant is a buyer or seller of size. This is important information because you may want to reconsider buying a stock if, for example, the axe has been selling huge amounts of stock today and is on the offer. Such information is available only on Level II quotes, not on Level I; in other words, brokers, with their Level I quotes, won't be able to give you this information. (Remember, brokers are salespeople, not traders.)

Most Level II quote screens come with a configurable option of #Best. Figure 4.1 provides further description and shows where on the screen #Best appears. #Best refers to the number of times in the current session that that particular market participant has been on either the best bid or the best offer *after everyone else has left.*

figure 4.1   #Best: identifying the axe

TOOLS OF THE TRADE									
ODETA		11 1/4	↓	+1/16		200	Ot	14:10	
High	11 7/16		Low	10 7/8		Acc. Vol.	15300		
Bid ↓	11 1/4		Ask	11 3/8		Close	11 3/16		

Name	Bid	Chg.	Size	#Best	Name	Ask	Chg.	Size	#Best
CWCO	11 1/4	+0	1	7	MASH	11 3/8	-1/8	23	4
INCA	11 1/8	+1/8	10	5	REDI	11 7/16	+0	5	1
SHWD	11 1/8	+0	1	1	RILY	11 1/2	+0	10	0
ALLN	11	+1/8	10	0	HRZG	11 1/2	+0	1	0
CRUT	11	+1/2	4	0	SLKC	11 1/2	+1/4	1	0
BTRD	10 7/8	+0	10	0	ALLN	11 13/16	+0	38	0
HRZG	10 7/8	+0	1	0	NITE	11 7/8	-1	10	1
RILY	10 3/4	+0	10	0	CRUT	12	+0	1	0
ISLD	10 3/4	+1/8	2	0	CWCO	12	+1/4	1	0
NITE	10 5/8	+0	1	0	SHWD	12 1/2	+0	1	0
SLKC	10 5/8	+0	1	0	BLUE	13 1/4	+0	1	0
AVLN	10 1/2	+0	1	0	AVLN	17 1/2	+0	1	0
BLUE	10 1/4	+0	1	0	INCA	0	+0	0	0
MASH	10	+0	3	0	ISLD	0	+0	0	0
REDI	0	+0	0	1	BTRD	0	+0	0	0

Being on the best bid or offer means that this participant has been willing to transact more stock at a particular price than anyone else has, or has been willing to sell more stock than anyone else has. In other words, in this current session, this participant is the axe. This fact can be incredibly important not only when deciding whether to take a position, but it may also affect *how* you enter or exit the position. This will be covered in depth later.

So, an examination of #Best is extremely helpful in determining if there is buyer/seller of size on a particular day. And if, for example, you have determined that a certain market maker is buying a huge amount of stock on the day, and he is currently on the best bid, you might think twice about selling now. The laws of supply and demand suggest that as long as the market maker is buying, the price may continue rising.

this is the axe

Please refer to Figure 4.1 again. Note how the buyers/sellers of size on the day are easily identified here using #Best/Hammer. This is an exaggerated situation of the kind you are looking for; you will rarely find one that is so clear. Market makers are fully aware of what those numbers indicate, and will go to great lengths to disguise their intentions (manipulate these numbers). So then, if market makers might hop on and off the bid/offer to change those numbers, then what use is #Best/Hammer? In my opinion, it is of very great utility. But as in any situation where duplicity is involved, you must interpret what you see, not just accept it as fact. When you read Chapter 10, you will have a clear understanding of just what it is market makers do, and you will be in a better position to interpret these kinds of numbers.

So then why, you may be wondering, are the market makers in Figure 4.1 displaying their intentions so clearly? The answer is simple. The security shown in the figure is not an actively traded one. Most of the trades in it are by institutional and retail *investors* who are interested in the stock long term. And because there is very little relative liquidity and volatility in this stock, intraday speculators are not attracted to it. Market participants may feel a little more free to show their hand because there are no day traders waiting to pick them off and cut into their profits. Is it viable to day-trade stock like this? Probably not. You can better spend your time elsewhere. An illiquid stock with low to no beta (beta is a measure of a stock's volatility) is simply not an environment friendly to active intraday speculation. Why did I use this stock as an example? For two reasons: first, to show clearly how #Best/Hammer works; and second, to show that size bids and fat spreads don't necessarily mean a stock is suitable for day trading; #Best and a little interpretation have been invaluable in countless situations, even in stocks with scores of participants, where numerous market makers show large numbers.

Once there was a buyer of size in a stock, and I had gotten long the stock in anticipation of a run-up. At this point, the price of the stock was up about one point from where I had bought it—a healthy profit on my 1,000 shares.

But then I noticed the axe, whom I had identified using #Best and carefully observing trading, had dropped his bid, and actually appeared on the offer, showing larger size offered as well. At the same time, I noticed InstiNet appear on the best bid. A number of trades went off at the bid, and I was considering liquidating my long position. (If the axe was done buying, and his buying was the reason for the price run-up, then the moment he disappeared would be the moment I'd sell). But then I noticed several more sellers appear, including some ISLD and ARCA offers (day trader driven liquidity) at prices in between the spread. They were either liquidating their long positions or selling short in front of the axe, whom they thought was a seller. And InstiNet (remember INCA on the bid?) was soaking up all the shares that were being sold. I surmised that the InstiNet bid might really be the axe in disguise, so I waited, deciding to risk a little profit. Several moments later, InstiNet left the best bid, and the axe appeared on the best bid and disappeared off of the offer. The price of the stock paused for a moment, then rocketed up. Many prints hit the tape, as I assumed the axe was taking the offers. You see, the axe, a size buyer on the day, wasn't really finished buying. He just wanted to let the stock "breathe" for a few moments. By offering out shares (perhaps he had a client who wanted to sell too?), he hoped to induce others to sell, so he could buy the stock cheaper. When no real sellers emerged, he decided to just buy the stock and finish his order. From the looks of things, he just started taking the offers. Several large prints hit the tape, and moments later I got out three-quarters of a point higher because I had pegged him accurately as a buyer of size who wasn't finished.

This type of action requires careful study of the stock *and* the market maker, and is not foolproof. Careful observation and practice help, but remember: #Best in and of itself is not sufficient. See Chapter 10 for a better understanding of interpreting market maker behavior.

typical situations

Now that you know what Level II and all the items found on it are, let's examine what to look for when determining how to enter and exit positions. This section will give you an idea of what you should be looking for when entering an order; it is oriented toward facilitating your ability to execute with the greatest speed. It will also help you understand which stocks will move and in what direction. The things you look for when deciding to enter or exit positions are the same things you look for when identifying movers, but the emphasis is different.

Conventional Level II interpretation centers on a supply-and-demand price model; if there is lots of demand relative to supply, the price should move up. And likewise, if there is lots of supply relative to demand, price should fall. And though conventional interpretation is a very good starting point, in my opinion it should never be used in a vacuum to determine strength and direction. Consider Figure 4.2, and note the number of buyers relative to sellers. In theory, the price will move up faster than it will move down, given equal buying and selling, due to the number of shares bid for compared to those offered. However, in this case, the stock was *down* several moments later. There were many reasons for this, including the fact that the markets were strongly down on that day and Yahoo (YHOO) had just reversed a very nice run. The point is that Level II is not the end all and be all. It must be interpreted, and many times conventional interpretation falls short.

figure 4.2   Yahoo (YHOO): appearances may be misleading

YAHOO INC								_ □ ×
YHOO	173 3/16 ↓ -11/16 100 Ot 13:32							----13:32----
High 177	Low 172 3/16	Acc. Vol. 5834800						173 1/4 400
Bid 173 3/16	Ask 173 1/4	Close 173 7/8						173 1/4 600

Name	Bid	Size	#Best	Name	Ask	Size	#Best	
ISLAND	173 3/16	400	1	MONT	173 1/4	300	9	173 1/4 400
ISLD	173 3/16	400	592	ISLAND	173 5/16	294	0	173 1/4 600
INCA	173 3/16	300	589	ISLD	173 5/16	200	613	173 1/4 100
BTRD	173 3/16	200	112	ISLAND	173 7/16	300	0	173 1/4 100
ARCHIP	173 3/16	200	1	ISLAND	173 15/32	100	0	173 1/4 200
ARCA	173 3/16	200	47	INCA	173 1/2	2500	505	173 3/16 100
AGIS	173 3/16	100	36	ISLAND	173 1/2	800	0	173 3/16 300
REDI	173 3/16	100	77	BTRD	173 1/2	500	113	173 1/4 100
MWSE	173 1/8	1000	7	REDI	173 1/2	500	90	173 1/4 300
ISLAND	173 1/8	6	1	SBSH	173 1/2	300	2	173 1/4 300
ISLAND	173 1/64	100	1	SWCO	173 1/2	100	5	173 1/4 100
								173 3/16 100

This section will give you a feel of what to look for and, more important, why you need to look for certain things when interpreting Level II. And when combined with the later chapters on the actual execution routes and market maker games, you'll have a good understanding of how to execute with confidence.

Although conventional interpretation provides a good understanding of what to look for in determining stocks on the move, it is not enough. Who is on the bid/offer: Is it the axe, the axe in disguise (as an ECN), a market maker fulfilling his duty of providing liquidity in the stock, or perhaps an ECN or market maker showing a complete natural customer order? All of these factors and more are crucial to your plan of execution. For example, some routes will work very well against ECNs; others will not work at all against ECNs. So an understanding of just who bid/offered is very important to your choice of route. Additionally, who it is on the other side of the market will affect your decision. Are there already many orders working for the stock you are trying to trade? For example, if you are trying to sell 100 shares of a stock that currently has only 100 shares bid, and there are already 10 orders entered by other traders (with an aggregate size of more than 2,000 shares), your order has little hope of being filled. Then you can make alternate plans and save time, which would otherwise have been wasted.

So first, the conventional interpretation. Take a look at the Level II screen in Figure 4.3.

Take note of several things: first, the huge buying pressure on the bid side. As you can see, many ARCHIPs are seen bidding for the stock. (I discuss ARCHIPs and ARCA ECN in detail later.) *Note:* I have used ARCA ECN here simply for ease of explanation due to common knowledge of ARCA. Several ECNs, notably REDI and NTRD, behave similar to ARCA; however, I'm using ARCA at this time because many day traders are familiar with it through their RealTick software platforms. ARCA, REDI, NTRD, and others have fantastic functionalities, and do have differences. But these will be looked at in Chapter 6: ECNs.

Notice the enormous number of buyers in this stock relative to sellers. Note also the direction indicator; almost everyone has raised his bids and offers recently. This indicates the current sentiment, that the price is going up. Market participants are willing to pay more for the stock than they were five minutes ago and also are unwilling to sell it as cheaply as they recently were.

figure 4.3 **ETEL**

	Name	Bid	Chg.	Time	#Best		Name	Ask	Chg.	Time	#Best
p	ARCHIP	5 3/4	+0	9:47	1	P	ARCHIP	5 1/2	+0	9:47	0
P	ARCHIP	5 3/4	+0	9:47	1	O	HRZG	5 3/4	+0	9:47	0
P	ARCHIP	5 3/4	+0	9:47	1	O	USCT	5 3/4	+0	9:47	2
P	ARCHIP	5 3/4	+0	9:47	1	O	SLKC	5 13/1(	+1/8	9:47	0
O	ARCHIP	5 3/4	+0	9:47	1	O	INCA	5 7/8	-3/8	9:47	0
P	ARCHIP	5 3/4	+0	9:47	1	O	MASH	5 7/8	-1/8	9:47	3
P	ARCHIP	5 3/4	+0	9:47	1	O	BRUT	5 7/8	+1/8	9:47	0
O	ISLD	5 23/3:	+0	9:47	14	O	ISLD	5 7/8	+0	9:47	7
O	NITE	5 23/3:	+0	9:47	1	O	FAHN	5 7/8	+7/3	9:47	4
O	REDI	5 11/1(	+3/1	9:47	2	O	GRUN	5 7/8	+0	9:47	1
O	ARCA	5 5/8	+0	9:47	9	O	ARCA	5 15/1(	-7/1	9:47	2
O	ARCHIP	5 5/8	+0	9:47	1	O	ARCHIP	5 15/1(	+0	9:47	0
O	ARCHIP	5 5/8	+0	9:47	0	O	REDI	5 15/1(	+0	9:47	0
O	ARCHIP	5 5/8	+0	9:47	0	O	BACH	6	+1/8	9:47	0
O	ARCHIP	5 5/8	+0	9:47	0	O	WIEN	6	+0	9:36	0
O	SHWD	5 5/8	+0	9:47	1	O	HILL	6	+0	9:43	0

Note all the buying pressure and the fact that this stock is still bid $5^{23}/_{32}$, offered $5^3/_4$. All the ARCHIPs you see reflect individual orders in the ARCA ECN.

These two things tell you that if laws of supply and demand hold up, at least in the very near term, this stock is going up. If you were to decide to sell now, you would have a good chance offering out and being taken. The Level II screen in Figure 4.4 was taken several moments later. You can see that this stock has indeed bid up a little bit. Had you purchased it when you first looked at the screen, or held off a few moments in selling, you might have been able to offer it out at $6\,^1/_8$, for a profit of around one-quarter a share, or $250 on 1,000 shares.

An excess of supply or demand for a given security certainly warrants attention. It is one of many indicators that you can use to evaluate your trade. When there is an inordinate amount of buying pressure, and when the directional indicators are almost uniformly positive (individuals are both willing to pay more to buy the stock and less willing to sell for cheap), you'll want to take notice.

figure 4.4   ETEL, minutes later—still strong

E-NET INC										_ □ ☒
ETEL			5 31/32	↑	+2 31/32	500		Os	9:53	
High		6 1/8	Low		4	Acc. Vol.		2030200		
Bid		5 31/32	Ask		6	Close		3		

	Name	Bid	Chg.	Time	#Best		Name	Ask	Chg.	Time	#Best ▲
P	ARCHIP	6 1/8	+0	9:53	1	P	ARCHIP	5 15/16	+0	9:53	1
P	ARCHIP	6 1/8	+0	9:53	1	O	USCT	6	+0	9:53	2
P	ARCHIP	6 1/8	+0	9:53	1	O	MASH	6	-5/1	9:52	4
P	ARCHIP	6 1/8	+0	9:53	1	O	ISLD	6	+0	9:53	14
P	ARCHIP	6 1/16	+0	9:53	1	O	INCA	6	-1/4	9:52	2
P	ARCHIP	6	+0	9:53	1	O	NITE	6	-1/1	9:52	14
P	ARCHIP	6	+0	9:53	0	O	ARCA	6 1/8	+0	9:53	5
P	ARCHIP	6	+0	9:53	0	O	ARCHIP	6 1/8	+0	9:52	0
P	ARCHIP	6	+0	9:53	0	O	SLKC	6 1/8	+1/8	9:51	0
P	ARCHIP	6	+0	9:53	0	O	ARCHIP	6 1/8	+0	9:52	0
P	ARCHIP	6	+0	9:53	1	O	FAHN	6 1/8	+0	9:52	6
O	NITE	5 31/32	+0	9:52	2	O	REDI	6 1/4	+0	9:51	0
O	MASH	5 7/8	+0	9:52	3	O	HRZG	6 1/4	+0	9:52	1
O	USCT	5 7/8	+1/2	9:53	3	O	ARCHIP	6 1/4	+0	9:51	0
O	ISLD	5 13/16	-1/1	9:53	16	O	PENN	6 1/4	+1/4	9:51	0
O	SLKC	5 3/4	+1/8	9:51	1	O	GRUN	6 1/4	+0	9:52	3
O	HILL	5 3/4	+1/4	9:52	0	O	BACH	6 3/8	+1/8	9:52	1
O	HRZG	5 3/4	+0	9:52	3	O	ARCHIP	6 3/8	+0	9:52	0
O	MHMY	5 11/16	-1/4	9:52	0	O	MHMY	6 1/2	+0	9:52	1
O	PENN	5 5/8	+1/4	9:51	0	O	WDCO	6 1/2	+1/2	9:47	0
O	GRUN	5 5/8	+0	9:52	0	O	SHWD	6 1/2	+0	9:51	2
O	INCA	5 3/8	+0	9:52	1	O	HILL	6 1/2	+0	9:52	0
O	ARCHIP	5 3/8	+0	9:46	0	O	FLVL	7	+0	9:47	0 ▼

Memorize the way a stock looks when it is under considerable buy-ing or selling pressure. You'll need the ability to appraise situations like this in an instant. But there are several important points to consider here. First, the stock is on its way up and is showing no sign of weakness.

Figure 4.5 depicts a stock that, using conventional interpretation, looks like it is going down.

Note that in this stock there are very few buyers relative to sellers. There is very little ARCA or ISLD activity, and "direction indicator" is not configured here. However, there is an awful lot of volume on the sell side, and very little on the bid. Notice how many of the partic-

figure 4.5 Yahoo (YHOO)

YAHOO INC								
YHOO	172 11/16	−1 3/16	300	Ot	13:37		172 11/16	700
High 177	**Low** 172 3/16	**Acc. Vol.** 5947300					172 11/16	200
Bid ↓ 172 5/8	**Ask** 172 11/16	**Close** 173 7/8					172 11/16	200

								172 5/8	500
Name	**Bid**	**Size**	**#Best**	**Name**	**Ask**	**Size**	**#Best**	172 5/8	100
MLCO	172 5/8	100	51	INCA	172 11/16	3500	516	172 5/8	100
MSCO	172 9/16	1000	25	REDI	172 11/16	1000	95	----13:37----	
NITE	172 1/2	700	66	ARCA	172 11/16	500	95	172 5/8	600
INCA	172 1/2	500	592	ARCHIP	172 11/16	500	1	172 11/16	300
MWSE	172 1/2	100	8	ISLAND	172 11/16	200	1	172 11/16	100
SWCO	172 1/2	100	5	ISLD	172 11/16	200	626	172 11/16	500
MASH	172 1/2	100	31	MLCO	172 11/16	100	20	172 11/16	100
ISLAND	172 7/16	1000	0	MONT	172 11/16	100	13	172 5/8	100
ISLD	172 7/16	1000	599	ISLAND	172 13/16	910	1	172 5/8	100
USCT	172 7/16	100	10	AGIS	172 13/16	100	51	172 5/8	100
ISLAND	172 3/8	200	0	BRUT	173	100	27	172 11/16	300

ipants on the bid are showing the smallest size possible—only 100 shares each. And several thousand are offered. Again, if rules of supply and demand hold true, unless something changes, this stock may be headed down, at least in the short term.

By watching Level II update dynamically, you will be able to gauge the strength and direction of the stock, at least in the very short term.

This is not meant to guide you in picking stocks—but when you see such situations, you can make educated guesses about a stock's short-term movement. And this short-term movement will certainly influence your timing and choice of route.

By gauging strength and direction (momentum) and taking quick action, you can make quick profits. But it is much much more risky than it looks.

The risk here is that the party ends the moment you buy—and that you wind up buying at a higher price than you may have wanted to *because* of the stock's strength. Also, you may be forced to sell at a lower price a few minutes later due to the supply that has come into the market (all the people who just bought, you included, now rush to sell when you realize the error). The first example (the one with all the ARCAs) seems a cut-and-dried profit on first examination—until you consider execution.

Take another look at Figure 4.3, which shows strong upward pressure. Just how would you buy this stock? Many bids are in the ARCA book for stock at $5^3/_4$; if you were to try and buy stock from USCT of HRZG at $5^3/_4$, simple addition tells you that unless there's a miracle, you'll *never* get it at that price. No chance! To try to take those 100 shares at $5^3/_4$ would guarantee you nothing but frustration. And this frustration can cause you to chase the stock higher. You must constantly evaluate your risk/reward at each price level; as the run continues, the chance for reversal grows as well. It is all too easy to buy too late, at too high a price, and then sell into weakness as the tiny move reverses. In other words, the price momentum is a consideration, not *the* consideration.

This is a dramatic example of upward pressure, and it will be well to recognize the telltale signs—both for picking a stock on the move and for choosing your entry/exit strategy. In both Figures 4.3 and 4.4, it would be simple to sell; you could offer the stock out at the ask and rest assured you'd be taken. However, if you wish to *buy* in a situation like this, things are a little more complicated. In real-life trading, you will have to make fast decisions that take risk and other factors into account.

Were you to decide to buy here, you might have to go higher right away. If you were able to purchase, right now, at $5^7/_8$, you might prevent the sort of aggravation generated by "chasing" a stock up or down. Sometimes it is better to make a decision and stick to it, recognizing the vagaries of the market. Keep in mind that there is no single route to guarantee a purchase price in a dynamically changing market. You just have to adapt to changing circumstances. However, if you buy at a higher price, you're taking on much more risk. One thing not often discussed, but nevertheless important to be aware of, is the presence of limit orders around round numbers. For example, there may well be many "hidden" orders to sell at or near $6. They are "hidden" because the price has not traded there yet; trading there will trigger the orders. You'll have to take this into account when considering a buy at $5\frac{7}{8}$, and also if you are selling. If you are considering holding off selling, or offering out at 6, and a seller emerges just shy of 6, you may have to reevaluate your plans and consider this new information.

Later I discuss just what routes work in given situations. For now, your mind-set is important. You'll need to judge just what's happening on Level II, and estimate what your chances are of getting filled using that particular route.

Now, if you happened to be short this stock, and it suddenly takes off with runaway buying pressure, you'll need to focus and still see the situation for what it is. You'll have to consider who is bid, who is offered, how many shares bid/offered, are they market makers or ECNs, which way is the stock headed . . .

So in addition to simple supply and demand, you must take into account the *condition* of the market in that security. If many sellers suddenly appear just when you are getting ready to sell your stock, be prepared for a fight. The market is indeed a market; if you are a seller, you bear the responsibility of locating a buyer. Offering out in the hopes that someone may take your stock may or may not be the best approach.

These examples are not the easy sort of no-brainers that you'll find in most execution tutorials. They are more like the everyday battlefields where you will fight in order to profit by day trading. It would be wonderful if there were always enough stock to go around for everyone. But with the increasing volatility of the markets, combined with the entry of more and more inexperienced players—who will buy the stock too dear and be forced to take a loss—executing will only get harder as time goes on. This isn't a game for the weak of heart, and the sad thing is that it is often the very most inexperienced players who are attracted to trade these most-difficult-to-trade stocks, like moths drawn to the plasma beam.

I hope this section will give you a clear understanding of what you're up against when it comes to getting in or out of positions.

Recognizing a problem is the first step toward solving it. Learn to recognize situations like the ones just described. Later we'll examine just how the routes work and which ones work in which situations. Train yourself to have confidence and knowledge in the worst of situations; that way you'll be prepared for everyday situations—and for the occasional ones where everything goes wrong. Always be prepared.

Figure 4.6 shows another stock that's going up. Note all the buying pressure in the ARCA book and all the prints going off at the offer price. And, you'll notice there are 1,800 shares bid for at 6 but only 600 offered.

At this time, if you were to try to buy at 6, how likely is your order to be filled? Not likely, unless one of the offers is hiding size. Hiding size will be dealt with more in Chapter 10, but basically it refers to a market participant who shows a particular size (say 100 shares) but really transacts much more at that price (say 5,000). This is currently legal. You need to recognize that a market participant may really be working an order well in excess of what is showing. The reason for this is an obvious one: In volatile stocks, where the price fluctuates greatly, if the market maker were to show 5,000 shares offered, he

figure 4.6   ETEL: it's offered at 6, but could you buy it there?

E-NET INC

ETEL	6	↑ +3		500	Os	14:23	6 200
High	7 5/16	Low	4	Acc. Vol.	17891000		10000
Bid	5 31/32	Ask	6	Close	3		6 500

Name	Bid	Chg.	Size	#Best	Name	Ask	Chg.	Size	#Best	
ARCHIP	6	+0	9	1	ISLD	6	+0	5	502	6 100
ARCHIP	6	+0	5	1	NITE	6	-1/4	1	156	6 700
ARCHIP	6	+0	4	1	FAHN	6 1/32	+0	1	53	6 1000
ISLD	5 31/32	+0	280	410	REDI	6 3/32	+3/3	5	29	6 500
ARCA	5 31/32	+0	30	143	ARCHIP	6 1/8	+0	10	0	6 500
ARCHIP	5 31/32	+0	10	1	ARCA	6 1/8	+0	10	94	6 100
ARCHIP	5 31/32	+0	10	1	GRUN	6 1/8	+0	5	21	900
ARCHIP	5 31/32	+0	10	0	BACH	6 1/8	+1/8	5	22	
NITE	5 31/32	+0	1	192	USCT	6 1/8	+0	2	72	6 100
SHWD	5 15/16	+0	5	17	SHWD	6 1/8	+0	1	49	6 2000
ARCHIP	5 29/32	+0	10	1	MASH	6 1/4	+0	60	83	6 500
ARCHIP	5 29/32	+0	10	1	MHMY	6 1/4	-3/8	5	19	6 300
ARCHIP	5 29/32	+0	10	1	HRZG	6 1/4	+0	5	42	6 200
HRZG	5 29/32	+1/3	10	94	SLKC	6 5/16	+13/	5	22	6 500
ARCHIP	5 7/8	+0	10	1	HILL	6 5/16	+0	1	0	6 1000
ARCHIP	5 7/8	+0	10	1	ARCHIP	6 7/16	+0	12	0	6 500
ARCHIP	5 7/8	+0	10	0	ARCHIP	6 1/2	+0	30	0	6 300
MASH	5 7/8	+0	10	118	ARCHIP	6 1/2	+0	20	0	6 600
SLKC	5 7/8	+13/	5	16	BTRD	6 1/2	+0	5	0	6 300
USCT	5 7/8	+1/1	2	48	PENN	6 1/2	-1/4	1	1	6 200
ARCHIP	5 7/8	+0	1	1	ARCHIP	6 9/16	+0	25	0	6 300
ARCHIP	5 27/32	+0	10	0	BRUT	6 25/32	+0	50	2	6 500
ARCHIP	5 27/32	+0	10	0						6 100

500

6 100
6 1500
6 500

might induce selling. To represent his client fairly, he will show only as much stock as he feels he can, given current market conditions. The only way to determine that he's hiding size is to watch the stock and the market participants. Prior to the screen shot shown in Figure 4.6, many participants offered at 6. All of these offers were taken, as you can see reflected on the ticker. Now all that's left are ISLD and NITE, with a combined total of 600 shares. Clearly, given this situation, this stock is poised like a compressed spring. How far it will move is anybody's guess, but at the moment, it certainly looks like there's more demand than supply.

And minutes later as shown in Figure 4.7, the stock is indeed higher, and many limit orders hover at $6^{1}/_{2}$ offered. There is still a lot of buying pressure, but the picture has changed dramatically.

figure 4.7   ETEL, minutes later

E-NET INC										
ETEL		6 15/32	↑	+3 15/32	200		Os	14:40	6 1/2	500
High	7 5/16	Low		4		Acc. Vol.	18639600		6 15/32	500
Bid	6 15/32	Ask		6 1/2		Close	3		6 7/16	200
									6 15/32	500
									6 1/2	3000

Name	Bid	Chg.	Size	#Best	Name	Ask	Chg.	Size	#Best		
USCT	6 15/32	+1/3	2	53	HRZG	6 1/2	+0	97	44	6 1/2	1000
NITE	6 15/32	+0	1	211	ISLD	6 1/2	+0	75	550	6 1/2	500
ISLD	6 7/16	+0	17	442	FAHN	6 1/2	+0	45	59	6 1/2	500
ARCA	6 7/16	+0	16	156	MASH	6 1/2	+0	42	88	6 1/2	300
ARCHIP	6 7/16	+0	14	0	ARCA	6 1/2	+0	40	100	6 1/2	200
SHWD	6 7/16	+0	10	17	ARCHIP	6 1/2	+0	30	0	6 1/2	200
ARCHIP	6 7/16	+0	225S	1	INCA	6 1/2	+0	22	56	6 1/2	300
INCA	6 13/32	+0	2	54	NITE	6 1/2	+0	16	166	6 1/2	1500
BACH	6 3/8	+0	20	1	ARCHIP	6 1/2	+0	10	0	6 1/2	200
REDI	6 3/8	+1/4	2	31	BTRD	6 1/2	+0	5	0	6 7/16	500
MHMY	6 3/8	+0	1	9	GRUN	6 1/2	-1/8	5	23	6 7/16	400
MASH	6 1/4	+0	45	121	BACH	6 1/2	-1/1	5	22	6 7/16	400
PENN	6 1/4	+3/4	10	0	SLKC	6 1/2	+1/1	5	23	6 1/2	200
HRZG	6 1/4	-1/8	10	37	HILL	6 1/2	-1/2	5	0	6 1/2	200
ATTN	6 3/16	+2 11/	10	5	SHWD	6 1/2	+0	4	52	—14:40—	
SLKC	6 3/16	+1/1	5	17	PENN	6 1/2	+0	1	1	6 1/2	100
FAHN	6 1/8	+0	1	8	MHMY	6 17/32	+1/3	1	21	6 1/2	400
BRUT	6 1/16	-3/1	80	2	ARCHIP	6 9/16	+0	10	0	6 1/2	500
HILL	6	+0	5	3	USCT	6 5/8	+0	10	73	6 7/16	100
ARCHIP	5 3/4	+0	22	0	BRUT	6 25/32	+0	50	2	6 15/32	500
GRUN	5 11/16	+0	5	10	ARCHIP	6 31/32	+0	5	0	6 15/32	700
FLVL	5 1/8	+0	1	1	REDI	7	+0	20	31	6 1/2	300
										6 15/32	800
										6 7/16	800

If you really needed to sell now, would you stand your shares in line with the other 40,700 (!) offered? In this sort of scenario, try to stay ahead of the crowd. If things were to turn ugly—and they could easily in such a situation—it's just better to stay ahead of the crowd. When you see a storm brewing, take measures against it. Here many sellers currently offered at $6\frac{1}{2}$ might reevaluate, and sell at $6\frac{15}{32}$, then $6\frac{7}{16}$, then $6\frac{13}{32}$, and so on. Panic could easily set in, and send the stock tanking.

So, if you really need to be done right now, you won't offer out along with 40,700 other shares! You might consider selling at $6\frac{15}{32}$, however, and just being done with it. After all, $\frac{1}{32}$ on 1,000 shares equals around $30. And your peace of mind might be worth it.

At least there is a lot of ECN liquidity in this stock. Execution against an ECN often takes place at electronic speed, by virtue of the lack of human intervention in the transaction. If you do decide to be done, chances are you can be—and quickly too.

Weakness looks like the example in Figure 4.7. But there are some weak stocks without all the ARCHIPs and Archipelago ECN activity. The converse of a strong up-pressured stock, a down-pressured stock will have lots of liquidity offered out and fewer shares bid for. Ideally, when you look at the direction indicators, you'll see that many of the participants have recently lowered their bids and offers. (The direction indicator will tell you this.) In Figure 4.8, you'll note almost 5,000 shares offered out and only 1,000 bid for. And at the next respective price levels, you'll note 7,500 shares offered and only 1,100 shares bid for. And under those bids, there is little interest at all; many participants are bidding 100 shares only. If this thing starts to sell, or if someone hits all the bids, this stock could tank.

Figure 4.9 shows another stock with significant downward pressure. Note the similar conditions.

Direction change indicators show uniform minuses. If the change in direction is zero, a plus sign will show; however, the market participant has not changed his price recently. Also note how many shares are offered relative to the number of shares bid (300 bid, 5,900 offered). If some selling starts, this stock may move down quickly. If the sizes shown are real (i.e., if players aren't hiding size), a market sale of only 1,600 shares at this point would drop the price a full point.

figure 4.8   CDNW under selling pressure

CDNW		21 7/8	↑ +7/8	100	Ot t 10:56
High	22 1/4	Low	21 1/8	Acc. Vol.	895000
Bid ↑	21 3/4	Ask	21 7/8	Close	21

Name	Bid	Size	#Best	Name	Ask	Size	#Best
INCA	21 3/4	10	38	ISLD	21 7/8	19	30
PWJC	21 5/8	10	11	SHWD	21 7/8	15	1
MONT	21 5/8	1	1	REDI	21 7/8	9	10
BTRD	21 9/16	4	0	OGRU	21 7/8	5	4
NITE	21 9/16	1	3	PRUS	21 7/8	1	5
OGRU	21 1/2	5	0	HRZG	22	23	4
MASH	21 1/2	5	0	NFSC	22	10	0
NEED	21 1/2	1	0	MLCO	22	10	1
VOLP	21 1/2	1	0	PWJC	22	10	0
SLKC	21 1/2	1	0	NITE	22	10	16
JOSE	21 1/2	1	0	PERT	22	5	5
PRUS	21 7/16	1	0	MASH	22	4	5
ADAM	21 3/8	1	0	MONT	22	1	4
CASS	21 3/8	1	0	BEST	22	1	2
USCT	21 1/4	2	0	DEAN	22	1	0
MHMY	21 1/4	1	0	BTRD	22 1/16	1	2
BEST	21 1/4	1	0	SLKC	22 1/8	1	1
MLCO	21 3/16	10	0	BRUT	22 1/8	1	3
DBKS	21 1/8	1	1	INCA	22 1/4	49	19
PERT	21 1/16	5	0	ARCHIP	22 1/4	10	0
REDI	21	10	0	ARCA	22 1/4	10	6
HRZG	21	10	3	MXXX	22 1/4	10	0
RSSF	21	1	0	USCT	22 1/4	2	0
LEGG	21	1	0	GRUN	22 1/4	1	0
ISLD	21	1	29	DBKS	22 3/8	2	2
GRUN	20 15/16	1	0	FBLC	22 1/2	10	0
MWSE	20 7/8	1	0	FBRC	22 1/2	1	0
FBRC	20 1/2	1	0	ALLN	22 1/2	1	0
SHWD	20 1/2	1	0	NEED	22 1/2	1	0

figure 4.9   Yahoo under selling pressure

NAME	BID	CHG	SIZE	#BEST	NAME	BID	CHG	SIZE	#BEST
INCA	155 15/16	+0	3	275	ISLD	158	+0	14	541
REDI	155 3/4	-11/16	1	62	PERT	156	+0	11	88
ISLD	155 5/8	-3/16	5	572	MWSE	156	+0	10	11
SLKC	155 9/16	-1/16	1	53	INCA	156	-3/16	7	217
FBCO	155 7/16	-3/4	1	3	MASH	156	+0	6	30
MWSE	155 1/16	-1/8	1	17	NITE	156	-1/16	5	34
MASH	155	+0	2	7	BRUT	156	+0	4	22
NITE	154 7/8	+0	5	24	HRZG	156	-3/4	2	9

TOOLS OF THE TRADE

YHOO

slow movers

To use an old mariner's term, the next stock could be said to be stuck "in irons." In the long-ago days of sail, a ship, particularly a warship, could get itself into a position of being "in irons" (stuck motionless, dead in the water) by the wind. A hove-to vessel unfortunate enough to be in irons could take several hours to turn and get going again, allowing the enemy ample time to circle. In the end, being stuck in irons meant annihilation for the vessel and crew. Though less dramatic in trading, you don't want to trade stocks that are stuck in irons, as the stock in Figure 4.10 is. This stock is stuck and going nowhere, at least in the next few minutes. Note the enormous number of buyers bidding and the equally huge number of sellers selling. How much buying or selling would be necessary to get this stock moving? A whole lot. And the prints show many transactions at the offer and many at the bid. This stock is undecided as to which way to go. Right now this stock is just a no-mover.

But the good news in this sort of situation is that you can buy or sell practically all you want. Getting in or out of a position in this stock will not be difficult due to the sheer amount of size available. But keep

figure 4.10   Dell "in irons"

DELL COMPUTER CORP									
DELL		49 11/16	↓ +1/4		1000	Qt	14:12		49 11/1
High	49 15/16	Low	48 15/16		Acc. Vol.	17890200			49 11/1
Bid ↓	49 11/16	Ask	49 3/4		Close	49 7/16			----14:1

Name	Bid	Chg.	Size	#Best	Name	Ask	Chg.	Size	#Best
ISLD	49 11/1	+0	119	157	ISLD	49 3/4	+0	42	148
INCA	49 11/1	+0	58	119	MASH	49 3/4	-1	31	49
MWSE	49 11/1	+0	14	15	INCA	49 3/4	+0	25	131
BTRD	49 11/1	+0	12	51	NITE	49 3/4	+0	24	53
DLJP	49 11/1	+11/1	10	15	DEAN	49 3/4	-1/8	10	10
BEST	49 11/1	+11/1	10	7	HMQT	49 3/4	-1/8	10	5
SLKC	49 11/1	+1/16	10	34	PWJC	49 3/4	+0	7	15
PRUS	49 11/1	+0	10	20	HRZG	49 3/4	+0	6	30
MLCO	49 11/1	+0	5	24	SHWD	49 3/4	+0	5	29
REDI	49 11/1	+0	5	55	BRUT	49 3/4	+0	4	26
SWST	49 11/1	+0	1	9	SWST	49 3/4	-1/8	1	9
SBSH	49 11/1	+0	1	25	JEFF	49 3/4	-1/16	1	1
JPMS	49 11/1	+1/2	1	7	RAMS	49 3/4	+0	1	15
GSCO	49 5/8	+1/8	10	4	PIPR	49 3/4	-1/16	1	17
MSCO	49 5/8	-1/16	10	31	BRAD	49 3/4	+0	1	3
ARCHIP	49 5/8	+0	9	1	MADF	49 13/1	+0	14	50
ARCA	49 5/8	-1/16	9	59	NFSC	49 13/1	-7/16	10	26
NFSC	49 5/8	+0	7	7	DLJP	49 13/1	+0	10	12

in mind that situations can and do change. Were we to look at this stock again in an hour or two, it could be in play.

The L2 screen in Figure 4.11 is an example of where you sometimes need to read between the lines. There is no massive demand on the bid side and no particularly weak show on the offer. However, there is significant interest, if you note the ticker. Look how many trades are printing, and all at the offer price! Within the last few seconds, an awful lot of trades have gone off. If you watch this stock and know the participants, you might be getting ideas. Nobody's conceded this is a mover yet, but this kind of buying, if continued, can only drive a price up.

Figure 4.12 shows the same stock three minutes later. Some sellers are starting to come in, but the stock is $1\frac{1}{2}$ points higher! While there still is no sizable interest on the buy or sell side, clearly this

figure 4.11   a screen where you must "read between the lines"

NAME	BID	CHG	SIZE	#BEST	NAME	ASK	CHG	SIZE	#BEST
ISLD	111 11/16	+0	1	296	REDI	111 15/16	+0	1	15
RSSF	111 5/8	+0	10	6	ISLD	112	-1 3/8	2	292
MWSE	111 1/4	-1/16	1	11	MWSE	112	+0	1	6
USCT	111 3/8	+ 3 15/1	1	14	SLKC	112 3/8	+1/2	1	8
MASH	111 1/16	+0	1	33	BRUT	112 7/16	+7/16	2	27
NITE	111	+0	3	42	NITE	112 1/2	-1/8	10	16
SLKC	111	+1/2	1	29	HRZG	112 1/2	+1/2	4	2
BMUR	111	+0	1	0	USCT	112 3/4	+0	11	7
BRUT	111	+0	1	24	BMUR	112 3/4	+0	1	4
PERT	110 3/4	+ 3 3/4	3	1	NFSC	112 13/16	+0	1	7
HRZG	110 1/8	+0	1	17	MSCO	113	-1/8	2	0
MSCO	110	-1/8	2	0	LEHM	113	+2	1	0
NFSC	109	+0	1	2	PERI	113 7/16	+0	1	7
SHWD	108 11/16	+0	1	6	SELZ	113 7/8	+0	1	0
SBSH	108	+0	1	0	SBSH	114	+2	1	2
LEHM	108	+2	1	0	MASH	114	+2	1	26
REDI	107 1/4	+0	10	26	INCA	114 1/2	+2 7/8	10	55

stock is moving. If you know the behavior of a stock and the participants involved, you can move into this sort of trade. But be very careful; here the sizes of all the prints are very small and the volatility is
great. And everyone seems to be bidding or offering only 100 shares!
Imagine if a slew of sell orders hit the market at the same time. Lack of
liquidity breeds volatility, and volatility is a double-edged sword. But
if you know and watch a stock, you will be able to see these sorts of
scalps all the time. On the other hand, if you don't know how these
stocks behave, you could easily be misled into making a bad decision.
Newbies should keep away from stocks that are extra volatile. Though
potential reward is great, the risk is simply too big.

summary

Use Level II to determine not only the strength and direction of a
stock in the very near term, but also to determine what route you

---

figure 4.12　same screen, minutes later

```
TOOLS OF THE TRADE                                          _ □ ×
```

RBAK	Last	113 3/8				12:44		113 1/2	200
High	113 5/8	**Low**	106 13/16	**Tot Vol**	742200			113 1/2	100
BID ↓	113 3/8	**ASK**	113 1/2	**Close**	111			113 1/2	100

NAME	BID	CHG	SIZE	#BEST	NAME	ASK	CHG	SIZE	#BEST		
										113 1/2	100
										113 1/4	100
MASH	113 3/8	+5/16	5	34	NFSC	113 1/2	+0	3	9	113 1/2	200
ARCA	113 3/8	+3/8	1	23	MWSE	113 1/2	-1/2	3	7	113 3/8	300
ALKC	113 3/8	+0	1	32	ARCA	113 1/2	+0	1	11	113 3/8	200
ISLD	113 1/4	+0	6	310	ISLD	113 3/4	-1/8	4	301	113 1/2	200
NITE	113 1/4	+0	1	43	MASH	113 3/4	+0	1	27	113 1/4	200
BRUT	113	-3/8	3	26	SELZ	113 7/8	+0	1	0	113 1/2	200
MWSE	113	+0	2	11	BRUT	114	+0	4	29	113 1/2	200
BMUR	113	+0	1	0	SBSH	114	+2	1	2	112 7/8	2800
RSSF	112 1/2	+0	10	6	INCA	114 1/2	+1	10	57	113 1/2	500
MSCO	112	+2	2	0	PIPR	114 3/4	+0	1	0	113 1/2	100
USCT	111 3/16	+0	1	14	USCT	114 3/4	+2	1	7	113 1/2	200
PERT	110 3/4	+0	3	1	NITE	114 3/4	-1	1	16	113 1/2	100
HRZG	110 1/8	+0	1	17	SHWD	114 7/8	+0	1	4	113 1/2	200
LEHM	110	+2	1	0	PERT	114 15/16	-1/2	1	7	113 5/8	100
NFSC	109	+0	1	2	HRZG	115	-1 3/16	5	3	113 5/8	100
SHWD	108 11/16	+0	1	6	MSCO	115	+0	2	0	113 3/8	100
SBSH	108	+0	1	0	LEHM	115	+2	1	0		

---

should use to execute. Several important concerns in analyzing Level II are:

- What is the strength and direction of the stock?
- Is there a size buyer or seller causing the move?
- Who is on the bid and offer? Is it the axe, is it liquidity driven mostly by day-trader activity; are a large number of market makers trading size?
- How many shares are generally bid/offered by non-ECN participants? Is it generally the very minimum allowed (100 shares), or are the participants offering a significant amount of shares? (In DELL, at time of this writing, for example, market makers often show several thousand shares.)
- How liquid is the stock? Is volume increasing or decreasing?
- Are the participants on the bid/offer ECNs, or market makers?

All of this information is directly applicable in your choice of execution vehicle. Think of Level II as a map—it will tell you what route to use. Each and every one of these considerations will affect your choice of execution route. After you learn how all the routes work, you will have a context and framework from which to decide with confidence, on an ongoing basis, how to execute and know you'll get filled. Next we'll take an in-depth look at the execution routes, and you'll see how it all ties together. Then we'll take a look at what market makers do to enhance your ability to read between the lines of Level II.

decimalization

Of course, all the Level II displays you've seen so far are in fractions, because, at the time of this writing, stocks and options are still quoted in fractions. But this will soon change! By the end of second quarter 2001, if all goes well, all U.S. stocks and options will be quoted in decimals. The change to decimals has been planned for some time and has been pushed back several times. But now the actual process of converting to decimal pricing has finally begun.

The final "Decimals Implementation Plan for the Equities and Options Markets" was released by the Securities and Exchange Committee on Decimals on July 24, 2000. It provided the plan for the complete roll-out of the conversion from fractional pricing convention to decimal pricing in the U.S. equity and option markets. The exchanges have until April 9, 2001, to fully complete implementation.

The change from fractional pricing to decimal pricing is a major, major step in the modernization of the U.S. financial markets and should have dramatic impact on liquidity and volatility. It represents the end of a historic era, begun during the times of the great Spanish Armada. It is a real and figurative break from the past and an acceptance of change to come.

the plan
Phase 1 of the plan began on August 28, 2000, with limited stocks on the NYSE. Each phase-in period of the plan will be followed by detailed reporting and monitoring. The plan may be changed subject to these findings. The first phase will be followed by expansion of the listed stocks traded in decimals, as well as further monitoring and re-

porting. After examining the results of the phase-in, a determination may be made to roll out decimal pricing in all listed stocks and/or all options, including options on Nasdaq stocks. This decision should be made between November 2000 and April 2001.

If all goes well, initial roll out of decimal pricing for Nasdaq securities could commence on or before March 12, 2001, beginning with a limited number of issues and a follow-up period, and then, finally, after careful review, full implementation.

minimum price variation
For equities, the new minimum price variation (the minimum difference in quoted prices) will be 1 cent, or $.01. So you'll be able to bid or offer in increments of a penny. However, trade prints will go off at prices with up to four decimals. This happens because an order may be filled at different prices, and the total aggregated average price per share may come out to be a decimal value of up to four digits. Interestingly, clearinghouses will keep track up to six decimal places, but the exchanges will round them off to four for reporting purposes. For options, minimum price variation will be as follows: for option issues quoted under $3 the MPV will be $.05; for option issues quoted $3 and greater, the MPV will be $.10.

interesting note
Currently, data is sent from the exchanges in the same way as it has been for many years—in *decimal* form. Your software platform converts the decimals to fractions. However, the Nasdaq will soon quit accepting orders in fractions and will start to quote stocks in decimal form on all its market maker workstations.

Currently most software platforms do not allow for orders to be entered in decimal form. Therefore, most orders are sent to the Nasdaq as fractions and converted back to fractions for viewing in Level II. However, this will change. In the coming months, software platforms will begin to offer decimal pricing for orders as an option and will start displaying Level II in decimals. As April 2001 approaches, order entry in fractions will be completely phased out and decimal pricing will become the default.

ECNs like Island have always internally priced their orders in decimals. However, software end users would not be aware of this because all platforms converted the decimals into fractions for display in Level II. ISLD was the first ECN to begin quoting exclusively in decimals, in June 2000.

why were prices quoted in eighths anyway?
There's a historical tradition. To trace the origins, we must go back to the sixteenth century. Spain was at the zenith of its power, and Spanish money was the worldwide fungible instrument of choice. Spain minted large, soft, gold coins called dubloons. People who wanted smaller amounts of money (change) created it themselves by cutting the coins into eight pieces, called pieces of eight. The dubloon was standard currency for the Spanish Armada and all of Spain's trading partners. Centuries later the dubloon and Spain's glory are all but forgotten, but the practice of trading in eighths remains. Pricing convention on the NYSE was in eighths until 1997. The Nasdaq led the way in 1997 when it introduced a further reduction into the pricing convention, that of pricing in sixteenths. Other exchanges soon to followed. And soon ECNs began pricing in thirty-seconds, sixty-fourths, and even 256ths. Realizing that the fractional system was outdated, unnecessary, and possibly hurting the efficiency of the markets, the Nasdaq decided to lead the way into decimal-based pricing convention.

effects
Reducing the pricing convention to sixteenths in 1997 led to greater volume on the exchange immediately. It is thought that buyers and sellers, now finding more agreeable prices, were more willing to transact. This placed a huge burden on the exchange hardware, as volume hit record levels. Industry analysis promulgates that the transition to decimal pricing convention may further facilitate transactions and therefore lead to greater volume of executed trades as well as fairer pricing. This may, of course, add substantially to the load of the already overburdened Nasdaq hardware.

One result of the diminished spreads in 1997 was reduced profitability of the trading houses, brokers, and market makers whose fees and/or profits were derived from capturing the spread. As spread diminished, and as online traders became more and more active—further reducing spreads—the profitability of these firms diminished. To some degree this loss of profit has been made up for by lowered transaction costs, which have been facilitated by automated electronic streamlining of the transaction/clearing process. However, it is widely believed that the already small spread will wither away as decimalization is implemented. So, in short, there will be more volume and better prices, and the market makers will be squeezed again.

SuperMontage: Nasdaq's proposed completely new updated Level Ii

The Nasdaq has proposed significant changes to the Level II quotes montage. If approved by the SEC, a new quotes window, called the Nasdaq Order Display Facility (NODF), or SuperMontage, will replace the current Level II quotes montage. SuperMontage is proposed to roll out only after decimalization is fully implemented in the Nasdaq.

At first glance, the system is a bit complicated—but it's easy after you learn the basics. Because SuperSOES and SuperMontage are designed to be integrated and complement one another's performance, *it is best to understand SOES, SelectNet, and the ECNs as well as SuperSOES before reading this.*

Designed to complement and enhance the new execution system SuperSOES, the new quotes montage is the long-awaited upgrade of Nasdaq's current legacy Level II system. This is a description of the proposed system. Figure 4.13 presents the proposed new screen. You'll notice that it is divided into three sections. The windows are as follows:

1. Top. The top consists of three parts, subwindows representing the three best price levels bid/offered. The subwindows are aggregated for price/size; that is, in each window the entire aggregated size per price level available is shown, without attribution to any specific market participant. In addition to displaying more information than Level II, this facility adds enhanced performance, as will be discussed.

2. Middle. Inside market/Level I quotes—same as you're used to.

3. Lower-Level II. Presents the first three price levels *only*. By using a simple query function that will display a static, frozen-in-time picture of total interest, you will be able to see all

figure 4.13   what the proposed SuperMontage will look like

Bid	Total	Ask	Total
$20.00	9,000	$20.05	4,400
$19.95	15,000	$20.10	5,000
$19.90	25,000	$20.15	15,000

Inside: $20.00 Q $20.05 Q 5,700 - 3,400 PCL: $19.75
Last: $20.05 Q +0.30 11:52 Vol:10,500,000 Hi:$20.25 Low:$19.75

MLCO	$20.00	1,000	ISLD#	$20.05	1,000
SIZE	$20.00	5,700	SIZE	$20.05	3,400
SBSH@	$20.00	1,500	INCA#	$20.10	800
INCA#	$20.00	800	SBSH@	$20.10	500
SBSH	$19.95	500	GSCO@	$20.10	3,400
ISLD#	$19.95	1,500	MLCO	$20.15	500
BRUT#	$19.95	100	BTRD#	$20.15	2,500
HRZG@	$19.95	1,000	HRZG	$20.15	100
MLCO@	$19.90	1,000	SBSH	$20.20	1,000

interest at all price levels, depending on the functionality of your software. You'll notice a market participant id "SIZE" in the montage. This is an aggregate representation of *nonattributed* (i.e., anonymous) orders at the best price level. "SIZE" will appear once on either side of the market, showing the aggregated, nonattributed best price available.

This new montage has significant advantages over the old system—but these advancements come at a price. You'll have to decide for yourself whether you find it an improvement or not. Certainly, from the standpoint of maintaining a fair and orderly market, the new system represents a major leap forward.

what it does

The new SuperMontage will allow for a single point of entry for orders, eliminating the current dual liability for market makers (liability for SOES executions as well as for orders sent to them via SelectNet). By creating SuperSOES, the dual liability has been all but eliminated. Because of this single gateway for orders and quotes, things should speed up quite a bit. Additionally, in theory, market participants will be coaxed into showing larger size, since in this new environment they'll have total control of their liability.

changes to Level II

SuperMontage may be integrated directly with market participants' order books. In SuperMontage, market participants are able to input quotes representing multiple orders; gone is the current stipulation that market participants may only show their best bid and offer in the Nasdaq quotes montage. Market makers would still be required to keep at least a two-sided quote in the security, but they may elect to represent multiple client and proprietary orders in SuperMontage. Indeed, should the participant choose to integrate his or her internal order book with SuperMontage, many orders may appear at once at different price levels representing different orders. It will be the market participants' choice. When a market participant ID shows alongside a quote in the new Level II window, this is said to be an "attributable order"—one that may be attributed to that specific market participant. And theoretically, there could be many attributable orders by the same market participant at different quoted prices/sizes, according to the new rules. However, there also will be nonattributable (anonymous) quotes. These nonattributable quotes will be designated (in aggregate of all nonattributable quotes at that price level) the market participant id "SIZE" for display in the Level II. I believe this should increase the reliability of stop and GTC orders and the like. With the new system, market participants will be able to place orders that stay live in the Nasdaq system. In the current NWII system, there is no way to place individual orders as such; a trader (at the firm that accepts the order) currently has the responsibility of monitoring the stock and executing the order properly when the time comes. This current system is, in my opinion, hopelessly obsolete. It is hoped that the new system will provide some improvement in execution of nonmarketable orders.

In SuperMontage, you will see both attributed and anonymous quotes. This has raised criticism from many of the ECNs, because the offering of anonymous quotes may be seen as competing with ECNs, who make a business of offering participants the ability to display quotes to the market anonymously. The Nasdaq has cited numerous legal arguments in its favor as well as citing common sense: the Nasdaq exists to be a marketplace; this is its function. Offering these kinds of orders facilitates liquidity in the Nasdaq and may tend to diminish market fragmentation, encouraging a more centralized transaction environment and better serving the investor. Quotes are arguably less likely to be traded through if displayed in SuperMontage (which is what the ECNs do, anyway). The Nasdaq has not asked for any restrictions to be placed on the ECNs with regard to the argument that the very existence of ECNs potentially causes market fragmentation. Unauthorized quotes, though obviously distasteful to the ECNs, should encourage liquidity in the Nasdaq. To the ECNs, however, this proposed system must be like salt in the wound.

changes to Level I
There are none.

new top window
This window displays the aggregated interest at each of the top three price levels without respect to attribution. This facility will allow traders to know the immediate depth of market at a glance and will be especially useful for SuperSOES use, since with SuperSOES, one will not need to direct orders to specific market participants. It serves other purposes as well. For example, it will allow for sweep orders to be executed.

how it will operate
There are some new rules here; please pay particular attention to these, as they will directly affect your executions.

Market makers are subject to auto-execution. When you place an order in SuperSOES, the market maker in queue will receive the report of an execution. However, ECNs have a choice in their level of participation. They can either sign up to receive auto-execution (which may be injurious to them) or they can remain accessible for "order delivery" through SelectNet. SuperSOES knows whether the ECN is an auto-ex participant or not. It presents the auto-ex participant with an immediate execution or delivers a SelectNet order to the nonparticipant. End users of SuperSOES probably won't be aware of this distinction, but it is well to be aware of it. Auto-execution is just that: immediate. However, the new SelectNet doesn't create an auto-execution. If the order is routed by SuperSOES to the ECN via SelectNet, execution should be near immediate—but remember, since SelectNet is an order-delivery vehicle, it will not create auto-executions against market participants. It will deliver the order, and then it is up to the ECN to process the order and create an execution. An ECN may set itself to accept any SelectNet order immediately. However, the order is being sent through the Nasdaq to the ECN, and you must allow time for the ECN to process the order and send a report back to Nasdaq. If for any reason the ECN doesn't respond within five seconds, the order will be canceled and sent elsewhere, if sent through SuperSOES.

Nasdaq divides the ECNs into two additional categories for purposes of execution: ECNs that charge a fee for nonsubscribers (expressed in cents per share and generally passed on to the trader) and those that don't. Those ECNs that do not charge any fees will take priority in the execution protocol over those that do charge a fee. The reasoning is this: If an ECN charges the user a fee per share, then the real cost of the stock is not the quoted price but the quoted price plus or minus (depending on whether you're buying or selling) the fee. Obviously, the ECNs that charge fees per share feel persecuted for this, because they wind up being last in the routing protocol.

So the Nasdaq has instituted one more policy: You may still place directed orders to the ECNs via SelectNet. (See the SuperSOES section for further explanation.)

You may place nondirected limit or market orders in SuperSOES, which will execute against any market participants (via SelectNet as well) according to the order execution algorithm to be described. However, you can still place directed orders, subject to the description in the SuperSOES section.

Additionally, if an order is placed such that it would trade through all available shares at the three price levels and still leave a portion unexecuted (e.g., a stock is bid 100 shares at each price level, and you place a nondirected market sell for 500 shares), the system will pause for five seconds before moving to the next level and providing execution. Orders behind you will remain in queue, waiting to be executed in the order in which they were received. This was done to combat some of the volatility in the market. The five-second delay is thought to give market participants time to add or remove quotes.

order execution algorithm
Nondirected orders placed in SuperSOES will be executed in the following five steps against:

1. Market makers and ECNs that do not charge a fee
2. ECNs that do charge a fee
3. Market makers reserve size (if any)
4. Reserve size of ECNs that do not charge fee
5. Reserve size of ECNs that do charge a fee (if any)

Directed orders placed in SuperSOES will go through SelectNet to the market participant designated; they will be nonliability for market makers but liability orders for ECNs.

So, if, for example, you were to place a bid on an ECN that charges a fee, say InstiNet, and, further, you were to display a bid of 1,000 shares with 4,000 shares in reserve, and someone were to place a nondirected order of ample size into the system, you would receive an execution of 1,000 shares (your display size) *after* all shares from both market makers and ECNs that don't charge were exhausted. You would then execute the rest of your order (the reserve) only after market makers' *and* the ECNs that don't charge have exhausted their reserve size.

A cumbersome explanation indeed! But it is important to know all this stuff, so you know exactly what to expect when you go to buy or sell.

It will become important to know which (if any) ECNs elect to participate in auto-execution and more important to know which ECNs don't. Also, you will need to remember which ECNs charge a fee.

You'll always be able to place a directed SelectNet order to an

ECN (preference), just as you do today. Or better yet, you can execute directly in the ECN if you have direct access to it. Going directly to the ECN would save you the time of having Nasdaq send the ECN a Select-Net order.

aftermarket

Both before and aftermarket, keep in mind that the vast majority of market makers are not participating. However, the ECNs that bid and offer in the aftermarket certainly do participate. Their bids and offers are good as shown, and may be executed against just as during market hours—with some not insignificant differences.

pools of liquidity

You can bid and offer on the ECNs subject to their individual policies. Months ago Datek Securities sent a message to all of its clients stating that it was the "first brokerage to offer after-hours trading to its clients." Maybe that is so for the full-service brokerages, but direct-access traders have had access to after-hours markets for more than two years now. Yes, liquidity is limited, and yes, not all ECNs (InstiNet in particular) post their bids/offers to the Nasdaq data feed after hours, but this is changing. Datek's announcement stirred great interest in after-hours trading, and in the not so distant future, trading after hours may be ubiquitous. Volume increases continuously, like a slow tide. Will it overtake the beach?

Trading after hours is problematic, at this time, because none of the ECNs connect directly with one another at that time. So separate "pools" of liquidity exist: the liquidity in ISLD, the liquidity in MKXT, the liquidity in ARCA, but no pipeline between! (SelectNet has extended its hours, but after it is closed, how do you execute against the various ECNs? Right now the only way to do it is to use a brokerage house that has direct connections to the ECNs.) So, your choice of broker will impact your ability to trade afterhours.

But this situation is sure to change; several months ago nine ECNs wrote a letter of intent to link up somehow. When they do, however they do it, it will be great. Because currently price discovery in the aftermarket is less than ideal. Several proposals have crossed the desks of all the ECNs, but so far, nothing has caught the fancy of the group.

Figure 4.14 is a screen shot typical for the after-hours market. Note the active ISLD, ARCA, and MWSE bids and offers.

Note the live orders on ARCA and ISLD. All of these live orders may be executed against if you have access to the ECN. Today the whole issue of afterhours online trading is overemphasized. There is so little liquidity after hours that you cannot trade in all stocks. However, some stocks do trade quite actively in the aftermarket, and stocks that announce significant information after hours may show

figure 4.14   aftermarket

RED HAT INC									
RHAT	R	108	↓	+23 1/16	200		Ot	16:01	
High	109 7/8	Low		83 3/8	Acc. Vol.		8215800		
Bid ↑	108	Ask		108	Close		84 15/16		

Name Bid	Chg.	Size	#Best	Name Ask	Chg.	Size	#Best
MWSE 107 1/16	-7/16	1	34	ISLD 108 1/4	+0	2	1253
ISLD 107	+0	11	1640	ARCA 108 5/16	+1/16	1	111
ARCA 0	+0	0	122	MWSE 108 15/1	+0	1	45
DKNY 107 15/1	+0	2	56	NITE 108	+0	1	209
SHWD 107 15/1	+0	2	56	RAMS 108 1/16	+0	2	77
SLKC 107 15/1	+0	1	101	USCT 108 1/8	+0	1	11
MONT 107 7/8	+0	1	31	GSCO 108 3/8	+0	2	5
INCA 107 3/4	+0	10	163	INCA 108 3/8	+0	2	169
MASH 107 11/1	+0	10	64	MASH 108 1/2	+0	10	35
HRZG 107 5/8	+0	1	33	PFSI 108 1/2	+0	1	1
MLCO 107 1/2	+0	2	41	NFSC 108 9/16	+0	1	61
SUSQ 107 1/2	+0	1	15	PERT 108 3/4	+0	1	14
NITE 107 1/4	+0	1	239	EVRN 108 13/1	+0	1	19
AGIS 106 15/1	+0	2	10	HMQT 108 15/1	+0	1	7
BEST 106	+0	1	15	SHWD 108 15/1	+0	1	28
GSCO 105 5/8	+0	2	29	HRZG 109	+0	4	30

significant price moves. But remember, often the next day, during market hours, these stocks reverse their after-hours moves.

It's only a matter of time until the after-hours markets become much more active across the board. Remember, when the Chicago Board of Options opened, there was no liquidity either. Now it is one of the most vibrant, active exchanges. You can count on few things in life; that after-hours trading will become ubiquitous is one of them.

chapter 5

Level III

Level III provides similar information to Level II. It is organized differently, however. Figure 5.1 provides an example of a Level III screen. Please note that the workstation may change with the advent of SuperMontage, if and when it is approved and implemented. See Chapter 4 for further information on SuperMontage.

Just like typical Level II screens, the bid is on the left and the offer is on the right. The only real difference between the Level II and Level III quotes montage is that Level III shows both sides of the market participants' market. So in Figure 5.1, the best bid is FAHN at $27\frac{1}{16}$, and the best offer is NEED at $27\frac{1}{8}$. You will note that FAHN's offer is at $27\frac{1}{2}$, and that NEED is bid at 27. Why is the screen arranged this way? Well, keep in mind this was designed in the 1980s, and change doesn't come quickly.

The real difference is that box on the left which allows the market maker to move his bid, offer, or both at the same time. You see the up or down buttons, as well as the increment of the move, which is currently $\frac{1}{8}$, the default. Note that there are no routes to select; typically, market makers have access only to SelectNet and SOES. And they are prohibited from using SOES for their own account.

Many people believe that Level III screens provide much more information than Level II screens, as well as special, secret information,

figure 5.1 Nasdaq Level III quotes montage

COMB ▼	Sec: ABCD	A TEST SECURITY		US ▼
Last: 27 1/16	Q -7/16	11:53 Vol 19200	PCL: 27 1/2	OP

Hi: 28 1/16   Lo: 27 1/16   NM5 S1

Ins: 27 1/16   Q 27 1/8   Q 10 - 10   MKT- LMT-   NSDQ

Your: 27 1/16   27 1/2   10 - 15   D3-1

⊙ Both ○ Bid ○ Ask   ○ RPT ⊙ ORD ○ QTE ○ TKO   Send
Up | 1/8 ▼ | dn   ⊙ SeNT ○ Nasdaq   Clear

FAHN	27 1/16	27 1/2	10-10		NEED	27	27 1/8	10-10
RSSF	27 1/16	27 1/2	5-5		SHWD	27	27 1/8	10-10
TOOL	27 1/16	27 1/2	10-15		MASH	27	27 1/8	5-5
NEED	27	27 1/8	10-10		REED	27	27 3/16	5-10
NITE	27	27 1/2	10-10		REDI	27	27 3/16	10-5
OPCO	27	27 3/8	10-10		NFSC	27	27 1/4	5-5
NAWE	27	27 3/8	10-10		MLCO	26 7/8	27 1/4	10-10
SHWD	27	27 1/8	10-10		PWJC	26 7/8	27 1/4	5-5
MASH	27	27 1/8	5-5		EVRN	26 15/16	27 1/4	10-10
RILY	27	27 1/4	5-5		DKNY	26 7/8	27 1/4	5-10
TSCO	27	27 1/4	5-5		RILY	27	27 1/4	5-5
HJMY	27	27 3/8	5-5		TSCO	27	27 1/4	5-5
REED	27	27 3/16	5-10		PIPR	26 15/16	27 5/16	5-5
REDI	27	27 3/16	10-5		JEFF	26 15/16	27 5/16	5-5
NFSC	27	27 1/4	5-5		HJMY	27	27 3/8	5-5
JEFF	26 15/16	27 5/16	5-5		NAWE	27	27 3/8	10-10
PIPR	26 15/16	27 5/16	5-5		OPCO	27	27 3/8	10-10
EVRN	26 15/16	27 1/4	10-10		NITE	27	27 1/2	10-10
PWJC	26 7/8	27 1/4	5-5		RSSF	27 1/16	27 1/2	5-5
DKNY	26 7/8	27 1/4	5-10		TOOL	27 1/16	27 1/2	10-15
MLCO	26 7/8	27 1/4	10-10		FAHN	27 1/16	27 1/2	10-10

1Adv	2Index	3Decl	4Dial	5TenAct	6MktSum	7ekTS	8NsdNws

such as the "location" of stop and limit orders held by other market makers. Nothing could be further from the truth. At this time, *there is no central order book for the Nasdaq.* Unlike the listed exchanges, where one specialist controls each stock, and the specialist keeps all stop and limit orders in a central order book that no one is allowed to see, *there is nowhere to "keep" stop and limit orders* in the current Nasdaq. Individual traders on the Nasdaq maintain their own book of orders and are responsible for executing them when they become marketable. At this time, brokerage houses are not even required to accept stop orders. Many do, however, especially those with traders who are willing to take on the responsibility.

In other words, people trading their own accounts are responsible for the execution their own orders. In a sense, all stop orders must be "mental stops" for those trading their own accounts directly. Those desiring the services of a "full-service" brokerage must consider this fact before taking on the responsibility of trading their own accounts. However, many software packages offered by brokers do allow for the placement of stop orders—this is a software functionality. Check with your broker to see whether the platform they're offering supports these kinds of orders.

But there is hope on the horizon. Currently, the Nasdaq is developing SuperMontage, and with any luck, it will be online soon.

In some ways, the Level III workstation has less information than can be found in top-end retail software platforms now available to individuals. Level III is easy to understand once you get used to it, but several market makers have told me that they prefer the style of organization found in retail Level II platforms.

The only fundamental difference found on Level III is that registered market makers can raise or lower their price and size directly on the screen by the point-and-click method. Day traders, as they are not market makers, must enter bids and offers through their broker, then cancel and enter a new order to change price or size. While individuals may use the point-and-click method, their order goes to an ECN—a registered market participant—and then to the Nasdaq system. Using an Internet-based order execution system, this method can be nearly as fast as market makers can change their price/volume. Some execution systems are faster than others.

However, at the time of this writing, Nasdaq Level III does not offer #Best and several other important informational items. The NASD is working on it, but changes may be a while in coming. If you were a market maker, mightn't you be a little jealous?

Being familiar with all the items on the Level II market maker screen is an absolute necessity. Instant recognition of these items will be crucial to your decision-making process when trading. The Level II screen is the map for your position's entry and exit. A complete understanding means the difference between exiting your position cleanly at a profit and being frustrated or worse and stuck with a loser, wondering why you can't close the position. But Level II would be useless to the trader without the tools of execution.

chapter 6

tools of execution

The tools available for execution fall into three main groups: market systems, electronic communication networks, and exchange facilities. All of the routes work differently from one another, and all have specific advantages and disadvantages in different circumstances. The circumstances may be determined from a quick perusal of Level II, once you understand what to look for. This goal of this chapter is to clarify just how each route works and identify what particular situations will bring out the best and worst in each one. Be sure to check for updates in the routes frequently, as they change their operating structure and add new functionality, and new systems come online.

For each route, I provide a brief historical perspective, and an explanation of how it works. Then we'll look at a summary of advantages and disadvantages, and, finally anecdotal experiences from use of each route. Following in Chapter 7 you'll find a quick reference summary of all the information herein.

Keep in mind that there are no hard and fast rules for what works in all situations. The markets are dynamic and fluid, changing constantly, even as you place your order. What you can do is learn *how* the routes work and *when* they will function in the manner intended. Armed with this knowledge and an understanding of Level II as it relates to execution, you can feel confident in your ability to evaluate in real time what route will best achieve your goal.

Another general note: Different brokerage houses physically connect to their data feed and execution routes in different ways. All the knowledge in the world will only go so far if your brokerage employs last year's technology. It is, in my opinion, a sad fact that very, very few brokerages employ the newest and fastest network architectures. One representative at one of the very largest direct-access brokerages even told me that my concern was unimportant; "We're talking milliseconds, half seconds slower . . ." Unimportant?! If you're number two in a 50-yard dash, you don't win! Likewise, if there are only 100 shares to go, and you get there third in line, what are your real chances for getting done? If your quotes are a full half second slower, what are your real chances of being successful? Of course, if you are not a scalper or "hypertrader," then this may not matter. But keep in mind: All networks are *not* created equal.

market systems

The market systems described here are run by Nasdaq. They consist of SOES, Selectnet, and SuperSOES. At the time of this writing, only SOES and SelectNet are operating. However, SuperSOES should have come online by the time you read this. So it is important to realize that systems SOES and SelectNet will be materially affected by implementation of SuperSOES. Be aware when reading the SOES and SelectNet sections that you will also need to read the SuperSOES section to fully understand how these different systems will work after integration of Super-SOES. Their functionality will be much enhanced by SuperSOES in relation to Nasdaq National Market studies, but their functionality will remain as is for small caps. In other words, you'll need to have a complete understanding of all systems to trade affectively in the SuperSOES environment. So now, execution will become a little more complex from a learning perspective; however, paradoxically, the new environment should really make execution easier overall. Here is a complete description of the systems—as they work separately, and in the new Super-SOES environment.

SOES—the dagger most cruel for the market maker

SOES is the Small Order Execution System. It created the day-trading phenomenon and changed the balance of power in the Nasdaq market. Stories of "SOES bandits" haunt the bars on Wall Street. What SOES does, and why it is so scary for market makers, is that it executes, automatically, instantaneously, against market makers, *without their choice.* If someone makes a market in a SOES-able security, he's accepting the risk that he'll be forced to buy or sell up to 1,000 shares (see "SOES Tier Size," coming up) of the stock at his price any given time. So if he turns his head for a second, he may find himself owning 1,000 shares of Microsoft. At $130 each at the time of this writing, that's a lot of cheese. And if he has auto-refresh checked, his displayed size will automatically be refreshed, allowing him to be SOES'd again and again. That can be one expensive trip to the rest room. But that's as close to sympathy as I'll go, because SOES only executes at the price that the market maker has indicated he's willing to buy or sell at. So he's obligated to buy or sell at that price (the price of his choosing). If he doesn't really have any intention of buying at that price, then he shouldn't be there! Of course, if the market tanks suddenly, or if he is inexperienced, he can get caught. But that is the risk he signed up for.

historical background of SOES

SOES was created in 1984, and updated to current form as a result of the crash of 1987, when some brokers would not answer their phones. It has been said that the phone lines simply could not handle the volume. It has also been said that brokers, being paid on per-share commission, would only take institutional orders, making commissions on, say, 30,000 shares instead of a retail investor's 100 shares per phone call, for example. Whatever the reason, new regulations were enacted that say that small investors—defined as transacting less than 1,000 shares—must have access to the Nasdaq market equal to the institutions. SOES was the first product of these new regulations. And though many people now consider SOES useless, that is far from true. Most who think that simply don't understand how it works and the specific rules for using the Small Order Execution System.

how SOES works

SOES is offered as a point-and-click routing option on all serious direct-access platforms. It accepts market orders and marketable limit orders (limit orders placed at the current inside market). All or none, fill or kill, good till cancel orders are not accepted. And SOES will only execute against market makers; it won't execute against electronic communication networks.

An individual may buy or sell up to 1,000 shares (depending on tier size, discussed next) on either side of the market in a five-minute period using SOES. An order may be limit or market. The individual trader simply designates SOES as the execution route. Due to NASD policy, SOES-able securities have three tier sizes, discussed below. The trader may buy and/or sell up to the maximum number of shares on either side of the market permitted by the tier size—within a five-minute period. Note that the trader may buy and then sell, but not buy and buy again within the five-minute period. All Nasdaq National Market securities are available for SOES transactions; however, small caps may or may not be, depending on whether the market participants have decided to participate in SOES (this will be discussed shortly). In no case will SOES execute against ECNs.

SOES tier size

Pre SuperSOES integration, participation in SOES is mandatory for all Nasdaq National Market securities. After SuperSOES comes online, however, SOES will only work in small cap stocks. For Nasdaq small caps, however, participation in SOES is (and will be, even after Super-SOES implementation) not mandatory but is an optional choice for the market maker. Over-the-counter bulletin board non-Nasdaq securities are never SOES eligible.

NNM (Nasdaq National Market) securities are divided into three SOES liability categories—the so-called tier size. These securities will be subject to SOES orders up to the maximum number of shares in their tier size. The tier sizes are 200, 500, and 1,000 shares. That means that a trader may transact any number of shares up to the tier size maximum (200, 500, or 1,000 shares) on each side of the market in a five-minute period.

So, you can *both* buy and sell 1,000 shares of DELL within a five-minute period (at this time of writing, DELL is a tier 1000 security). But you *may not* buy 2,000 shares of DELL (first 1,000 shares, then an additional 1,000) of DELL within a five-minute period.

It is important to know the tier size of the stocks you are dealing with if you plan to use SOES to exit. I have received calls from traders who've watched in panic as order after order placed by them auto-deleted while the stock tanked. On many occasions the security was a price-inflated small cap where none of the market makers elected to participate in SOES. And in others, only ECNs were bid or offered, rendering their SOES limit orders useless. Remember, SOES will *not* transact against an ECN. So, in these cases, SOES wasn't even a possibility.

For full, up-to-date information on tier size and whether an issue is a NNM or a small cap, go to the Nasdaq Trader Web site. The SOES tier size list appears at www.nasdaqtrader.com/trader/symboldirectory/ definitions.stm#soestier. You will need to check each symbol individually for its tier size "qualifier." Go to this site for a symbol directory: www.nasdaqtrader.com/trader/symboldirectory/symbol.stm.

SOES Advantages
- Instantaneous execution against market makers in NNM (Nasdaq National Market) stocks prior to SuperSOES. After Super-SOES is in place, it will auto-ex against participating market makers in small caps only.

- Limit or market orders.

- Odd lots (any number of shares, up to tier size).

SOES Disadvantages
- Small order size (any number of shares, up to tier size).

- Won't execute against ECNs ever.

- Orders are handled by the Nasdaq in the order in which they are received, and in a fast market, SOES market orders may get you out at a price you're not happy with.

- Market makers in small caps may not be SOES-able.

general notes on SOES
If you need to liquidate fast and there are market makers on the bid, then SOES is the light-speed alternative. When you are first in line with a SOES limit order, you can be executed before your finger even leaves the keypad. However, if you are in an extremely volatile and active security, keep in mind that the Nasdaq will execute your order in the order *in which it is received.* So if a number of other similar SOES orders are entered ahead of you, your limit order may not be executed, as these prior orders may soak up all available liquidity.

When there are very few shares bid in an extremely volatile stock, an SOES limit order may not get executed at all. Because someone probably put an order in ahead of you and was executed ahead of you, and then the market maker moved his position, your order gets canceled because the market moved away. (In other words, the price changed, your limit order gets automatically canceled.) And, furthermore, if you place an SOES market order, the order will be filled in the order it is received, so it may get executed at a price you really don't like. The few shares bid for will be automatically traded, and the market makers, faced with such supply, will lower the price/size of their bids. Just imagine an SOES 1,000 tier size security where, at each price level, only 200 or 300 shares are bid for. Now out comes some bad news, and 10 SOES market orders are entered, each for 1,000 shares. The first order may take out the first three price levels! (See Figure 6.1.)

Just imagine how far down it could move in seconds as those SOES orders execute for 10,000 shares total! The price could spike down dramatically, and you could get the worst print of the day. So you must be careful when using SOES market orders, especially in fast markets—situations characterized by extreme volume and rapid price fluctuation. However, if volume is just starting to pick up, you think the stock is going to rocket higher, and you are willing to buy at the of-

figure 6.1   what can happen with SOES market orders

EFNT		49	↓	300	Ot	t 11:23		49	100
High	50 1/4	Low	43	Acc. Vol.	2374400			49	300
Bid ↓	49	Ask	49 1/16	Close	0			49	100

Name	Bid	Size	#Best	Name	Ask	Size	#Best	
DKNY	49	2	8	ARCHIP	49	8	1	49 100
ISLD	48 5/8	1	25	ARCHIP	49	5	0	49 3/16 100
SHWD	48 1/2	2	8	ARCHIP	49	3	0	49 1/32 100
AGIS	48 1/8	2	2	ARCHIP	49	1	0	49 1/16 200
SLKC	48 1/8	1	20	ARCHIP	49	1	0	49 1/8 300
INCA	48	20	2	RAMS	49 1/16	1	12	49 1/16 200
BRUT	48	1	0	ISLD	49 1/16	1	22	49 11/16 100
MASH	48	1	10	AGIS	49 3/16	1	12	48 5/8 100
HRCO	47 15/16	2	1	HRZG	49 3/16	1	13	49 200
AXCS	47 13/16	2	15	REDI	49 1/2	3	2	49 3/16 100
HRZG	47 3/4	1	13	FBCO	49 1/2	2	6	49 1/32 800
NITE	47 1/2	2	32	ARCHIP	49 9/16	3	0	49 1/16 100
RSSF	47 1/2	1	1	ARCA	49 9/16	3	3	49 100
RAMS	47 1/16	2	5	NITE	49 5/8	1	18	49 5/8 100
								48 1/2 100
								49 100

fer or higher, you might want to place an SOES limit. If you miss it, then you're faced with opportunity cost. Keep in mind that if you place an SOES market order to buy and everyone else does so at about the same time, you could get executed much higher.

When market makers receive an SOES execution that exhausts their tier size obligation, a 17-second period will ensue during which they cannot be executed against. During these 17 seconds, they will decide whether to refresh their size and make themselves available for another execution, or they will move their market. Realize that if you place an SOES order when a market maker is on the bid, he may be unavailable; during that time your SOES limit order will "hang," looking for a market maker to execute against. If the unavailable market maker moves his market and no other market makers show up at your limit, the order will eventually come back canceled "unexecutable." And if you've placed an SOES market order, SOES will simply skip over the unavailable market maker and execute against the first available one, irrespective of price. This is one reason for sudden price spikes. How can you know if a market maker who looks available is really available? You can't for sure.

The bottom line for SOES is this: Given normal market conditions, if you need to be out at any cost and the security is SOES-able, and if you have less than the tier size of shares, and if market makers are on the bid, the SOES market is going to be one of the fastest ways out—if you're first. Usually it is at electronic speed. But in a fast market where there is not much liquidity, you simply *must* be first—or risk your market order staying live for several moments as the price races away from target, and you get a fill far, far away from your intended price. SOES limit orders are great for instantaneous trades. But again, in that fast market, your order may be killed by the Nasdaq as the price moves outside your limit and the order expires as unexecutable. Then you might try another SOES limit or get out to one of the ECNs.

is SOES dead?

The late 1980s and early 1990s were amazing times for day traders. Spreads were big, market makers' minimum display size was 1,000 shares, ECNs were new, and market makers didn't know to protect themselves against the SOES bandits, who prowled the virtual floor of the exchange like alligators, searching for an out-of-line price, an unusually large spread, anything to snatch. The new technologies and rules permitted this. Call it retribution for the stranglehold market makers had kept on the industry prior to the crash of 1987. Traders like Harvey Houtkin, the SOES Bandit, made fortunes *in months*. You didn't need to know much about the stocks traded or even anything about the market at all; the skills of the day were intense concentration, fast typing, and, generally, access to a Level III machine through a local hedge fund or broker dealer willing to let individuals in on the markets. The modern PC-based front-end order entry systems did not exist yet.

It's not so easy anymore. The new order-handling rules, which allow market makers to display actual size, with a minimum liability of 100 shares, and the growth in popularity of the ECNs, which are not SOES-able, have changed the landscape. The playing field now is truly more level, with a balance stuck between the execution ability of SOES and the "vulnerability" of market makers.

What this has done is made it harder to make a buck scalping. Players who move in and out of the markets hundreds of times a day picking up a sixteenth, a thirty-second, an eighth are largely gone. But the opportunity for profit still exists, even greater than before, due to the advent and effects of SOES, ECNs, online brokerages, and electronic brokerages offering direct access to the securities markets. These factors have created huge new liquidity and volatility. Now the best traders ride the trades for 3, 5, or 10 points, and on thousands of shares. Their tools include those in the market maker's arsenal, SOES, ECNs, and sophisticated software. Nowadays, it's not as easy to scalp, but a thorough understanding of all the tools at the traders' disposal, along with a basic understanding of the markets, makes the opportunities greater than ever.

SOES experiences
As a professional in the brokerage business, I am no longer permitted to use SOES for my own account. This is an NASD rule and one I wish didn't exist, because SOES is such a valuable tool. But many a time I've used SOES on the behalf of clients.

In one recent situation, a client of my firm had been partially filled by some market maker with only 93 shares. Subsequently, when he wanted to sell, he found he could not. He "preferenced" (see the Select-

Net section following) several market makers with SelectNet (declined), tried offering the stock out on the Island ECN (it would not appear in the montage, for it was less than the minimum "unit" number of 100 shares), Archipelago ECN (won't accept odd lot orders), and finally called in frustrated beyond belief. This was a $240 stock that moved 20 percent a day. After learning that he just wanted out, at the bid, and *fast*, I entered a limit order on SOES. I saw that there were several market makers on the bid, and knowing that there the SOES tier size was 500 shares, and that each of the market makers was showing at least 500 shares, I felt confident the order would be executed. Sure enough, before my finger left the keyboard, he was filled, for 93 shares. His response was "*@#!! how did you do that?!" The answer: SOES. If you have an odd lot of shares (less than the SOES tier size) and are willing to sell or buy at the inside market, and market makers are there (as opposed to ECNs; remember, SOES will not execute against an ECN), try SOES. It won't always work, because in a fast-moving stock it's altogether likely stock will trade ahead of you, but SOES is often lightning fast. In the right situation, it's as close to instant gratification as it gets.

Warning: Be very careful using SOES market orders. A friend of mine tells me that he bought ONSL (Onsale.com) at $107 using an SOES market order—*entered when the price was $97!* You may remember the day in 1998 that ONSL went from $46 to $108 in one day, only to close the day back down at $56. In an extremely fast market, using an SOES market order is just plain crazy, in my opinion. Think about it: a huge volume, tremendous demand, little to no supply, and an SOES market order. A recipe for disaster! When a stock trades like that, consider sitting it out! Better to not engage and miss a potential opportunity rather than get the highest print of the day and see the stock tank like a pile driver.

In a ridiculous, fast market, *beware the SOES market order*. Of course, under normal market conditions, the SOES market order may be just what you need, particularly if there are numerous market makers with huge size, and you just want to be done with the order quickly.

SelectNet—the market makers' tool

SelectNet is an order-routing option available to all market makers and customers of the better direct-access electronic brokerages. It is run by Nasdaq Market Systems, as is SOES (the Small Order Execution System). Both SelectNet and SOES are order-execution systems, not ECNs. SelectNet is currently the preferred method of execution for market makers, for a number of reasons. First, it enables market makers to trade stock without picking up the phone, dialing, and holding: It is fast. But more important, it removes any confusion that could arise from telephone conversations. It is a vehicle for swift, decisive, transparent transactions. Another reason SelectNet is used so widely is that market makers generally do not have access to the ECNs available to day traders, though this is changing. They *could* have access and in the near future probably *will* have access, but large institutions are slow to change. For the moment, day traders have the edge over market makers regarding ease of execution.

A SelectNet order works like an instant message; it does not deliver an execution. When an order is entered via SelectNet, the market participant will receive notification that some other market participant wishes to buy or sell a certain amount of stock at a particular price. But SelectNet orders take two forms: SelectNet Broadcast and SelectNet Preference. And neither creates execution; the "instant message" must be responded to. The execution comes with the response.

broadcast orders
SelectNet Broadcasts are orders that are "broadcast" to all Level III participants who have an interest in the particular stock. Generally, market makers configure their workstations so that broadcast orders in the stocks they follow appear as one-line messages on their screens. This lets market makers know that some market participant wishes to buy or sell a specific amount of particular stock at a specific price. It is important to realize that since the order was *not directed at him*, unless it is at their price/volume, they are under no obligation to respond. For traders, this order may or may not generate a response.

preference orders
SelectNet "preference" orders are orders directed to a specific market participant. Many market makers configure their Level III workstations with a pop-up window to let them know when they are being preferenced. During market hours, if the order occurs at the current price and size of the market maker's bid or offer, it will be designated

an "Incoming Liability Order," and the market maker is obligated to respond, by accepting, declining, or partially filling the order.

Both process orders on a first-come, first-served basis; thus, if a market maker is holding out to the world a firm quote that he will buy 1,000 shares of ABCD at $38^{1}/_{4}$, the first order to sell him 1,000 shares at that price will be executed; that is his liability. Beyond that, he can decide to buy more there, change his quote size, or move his market altogether.

So, if you preference a market maker or an ECN, at his price and volume, and somebody else preferenced him first, for his total size, he is under no obligation to fill your order because the stock "traded ahead" of you. And likewise, if he is bidding 1,000 shares and receives two preferences, one after the other, one selling 300 shares and the other selling 1,000 shares, he is obligated to fill 300 shares on the first order *and only 700 of the next* (300 + 700 = 1,000, his quote size). This may happen so fast that watching Level II won't give an adequate view of the transactions, so if you feel that a market participant "backed away" (backing away is the NASD's description of not fulfilling the number of shares he is liable for), you must examine time of sales to determine just how many shares traded at that price.

"Backing away" does occasionally happen—sometimes by plain error and sometimes for other reasons—but much less frequently than you'd think if you listened to the banter in the chat rooms. The penalties are aggressive for that sort of activity; any potential gain is far, far outweighed by the penalties imposed.

Additionally, pre- or postmarket SelectNet Preferences do not carry the obligation of a response. You may indeed get an execution, but it is just like pounding on the doors of a bank after hours. Probably you won't even be acknowledged.

However, SelectNet has one massive disadvantage for the trader, especially in high-volume stocks. Market makers are given 30 seconds to respond to a liability order. In a fast market, 30 seconds can seem like eternity. And when you realize that after the wait, the transaction can be outright declined ("the stock traded ahead") SelectNet loses much of its luster.

However, SelectNet does possess several big redeeming qualities for the trader. The first is use of SelectNet as a link to the ECNs. When a SelectNet preference is placed to an ECN, it is a near-automatic, instantaneous execution, up to the size currently available. So if you want to transact with an ECN, SelectNet may be an excellent choice.

A SelectNet Preference to a market maker can also help move a large amount of stock in a volatile market. This involves finding out who the current axe is and preferencing him with your entire order. For example, say you are long 5,000 ABCD. If you offer 5,000 shares, it might weight the market down, and you might not be able to sell your stock at a good price. Suppose also, that all the market makers are bidding small size, 100 or 200 shares each. If you can locate the axe and offer the stock to him and him alone as a SelectNet Preference, he may buy all of your stock, and, in rare circumstances, even if the price is slightly higher than his quote. He might be willing to do this for a variety of reasons, but the most obvious one is that he has proven to be a size buyer on the day. You won't know how much stock he has yet to buy, but you might assume he's got a lot more to buy since he's been buying so heavily so far. And keep in mind that he has to write a ticket for each and every transaction he does; so if he's going to buy 5,000 shares in 100-share lots, that's 50 tickets he has to write and possibly enter into the system. Couldn't it be in his best interest to pay a little more and write only one ticket, particularly if he's only got 5,000 or 10,000 more shares to buy on the day? In any case, the worst that can happen is he declines you and moves his market. The market at large won't be aware that you are trying to sell size, and you are free to pursue other options.

SelectNet Advantages
- Any size order up to six figures.
- Preferencing an ECN can mean near-instantaneous execution.

SelectNet Disadvantages
- Market makers have 30 seconds to respond to preference orders, and a broadcast order may generate no response whatsoever.

SelectNet experiences
Once a client called in and wanted to sell his stock. The problem was that he had 10,000 shares of an illiquid stock, and the market makers were all bidding small size; most were bidding only 100 shares. If he of-

fered it out on ARCA ECN, the world would see his order (offer) and might lower their bids. Selling 10,000 shares into that illiquid market could conceivably hammer the price. But I noticed one of the market makers priced at one-sixteenth lower than the inside bid (who was also showing 100 shares bid) had been on the best bid *63* times that day! Consulting #Best further, I saw that the next market maker in line had been there only eight times. A quick glance at the chart suggested there was a buyer of size somewhere in the jungle, and I suggested to the client that it might be the guy who'd been there 63 times.

The client said he would be more than happy to get out at one-sixteenth below the current bid (as he'd had a large profit on the position). I suggested preferencing the market maker who'd been a buyer at least 63 times that day, who was at one-sixteenth below the best bid with 5,000 shares. My thoughts were that more than 5,000 shares might scare him away and result in a partial fill of 100 shares.

So he did, and several seconds later, received the fill: for 5,000 shares. And the market maker stayed bidding where he was, still showing 100 shares (even though he just bought 5,000!). I suggested sending him another preference, for the balance. This time, he took 3,000 shares, and moved his market. The client just wanted out, and he now had 2,000 shares left, so I suggested putting the rest out on ARCA with a limit at his price. His trade was executed for the remaining 2,000 shares; 1,000 at the same price (and that market maker moved his market) and 1,000 at one-sixteenth above (at the inside market!); that market maker moved his market as well. I checked on that stock later on in the day, and the buyer of size had never reemerged; in fact, the price dropped approximately five-sixteenths from where he sold. All in all, he sold 10,000 shares into a fairly illiquid market at a decent price. Had he gone out on the Island (ISLD), showing 10,000 shares, he might never have gotten filled, and probably would even have driven the price down. Recognizing the axe, and using SelectNet, he got out quickly, and at a better price than might have otherwise been gotten.

the new NNMS (SuperSOES) system

These days it seems that everyone is talking about the new Super-SOES. Will getting the perfect fill finally be easy?

Major changes have been designed for the Nasdaq's execution systems. These changes should, in theory, benefit both market makers and traders alike. If the changes work as planned, it will mean much more transparent transactions without the same level of thought being required to execute. The result should be a faster, easier (in terms of execution), more efficient market.

SuperSOES is scheduled to come online starting November 20, 2000. However, as we've seen before, these dates are often more speculative than practical. The release has been postponed before, and there are reasons why it might be postponed yet again. But rest assured: Like a night train, moving carefully, inexorably, and unseen, the long-awaited upgrade of the Nasdaq's execution systems will arrive—and soon. With this in mind, let's take a look at just what SuperSOES is, exactly how it will work, and the reasons why it may be postponed.

No discussion of SuperSOES would be complete without at least a mention of SuperMontage, the proposed upgrading of the Nasdaq's Level II quotation system. The two systems are designed to work in tandem, enhancing functionality overall. At this point SuperMontage is only a proposal, with an anticipated roll out after the move to decimalization is complete, sometime in the second quarter of 2001. However, SuperSOES is scheduled to roll out before SuperMontage. And though its functionality will be enhanced by SuperMontage, by itself SuperSOES represents a significant improvement over the current legacy systems SOES and SelectNet.

That being said, some things never change. The way SOES and SelectNet work with respect to small cap stocks is one of them. There will be no changes to the operations of SOES and SelectNet with regards to small-cap stocks. The systems will continue to operate just as they do now for small caps. For the Nasdaq National Market stocks, you'll have to use the new system, and the change will be marked. Unfortunately, now you'll have to know all of the systems—SuperSOES, SOES, and SelectNet—in order to execute effectively in all stocks.

For National Market stocks, SOES (the Small Order Execution System) and SelectNet will cease to exist in their current form. However, much of their functionality will be preserved and improved. The new system is to be given the name Nasdaq National Market Execution System (NNMS). It is also known as SuperSOES. It will consist of an automatic execution facility as well as revamped SelectNet.

In the new system, there will be classes of orders; "nondirected orders" and "directed" orders.

nondirected orders: auto-execution for orders less than 1 million shares

Nondirected orders are orders entered into SuperSOES that are not directed toward any specific market participant. Under the new system, you will not be able to auto-execute against a specific market participant. These nondirected orders, which during market hours may be market or limit, may automatically execute against multiple market participants who have agreed to accept automatic execution, up to 999,999 shares or the market participant's size—whichever is less—until your order is filled entirely, or canceled (if you enter a limit order that becomes unmarketable because the market moved, the balance of your order will remain live for 90 seconds, after which, if still unfilled, it will be canceled). Market makers in the Nasdaq National Market stocks are all required to accept automatic execution. However, ECNs have the choice of either agreeing to accept automatic execution or opting to have orders routed to them only a "directed" basis. Nondirected orders will execute in price/time priority against any market makers and ECNs (but again, only ECNs that have agreed to accept automatic execution) automatically—that is, without their choice or discretion. The participant will simply receive an immediate report that an execution took place—on any size, up to the total number of shares available or 999,999.

directed orders—orders directed to specific market participants

You may also send orders directed toward specific market participants, subject to certain restrictions via the restructured SelectNet. The limitations for placing directed orders follow.

directed liability orders

In NNMS, SelectNet is reestablished as a *nonliability* order delivery vehicle. However, there is one exception: market participants who do not participate in auto-execution. As stated earlier, market makers in the Nasdaq National Market stocks are required to accept automatic execution, but ECNs have a choice. Those that do not agree to accept automatic execution will receive orders directed to them via SelectNet. For the ECNs that do not participate in SuperSOES auto-execution, these directed SelectNet orders will be liability orders, in accordance with the Nasdaq's firm quote rule. So, as is the case currently, the

ECNs are obligated to fill these orders immediately upon receipt, if marketable.

directed nonliability orders

Participants in SuperSOES auto-execution may also be sent directed orders. However, since SelectNet is now reestablished as a nonliability order delivery system, market participants in SuperSOES have no liability to respond to these orders. In fact, directed orders may be sent to these participants only on a nonliability basis. Liability under SelectNet was removed in order to eliminate the dual liability that market makers used to face. The pre-SuperSOES execution systems SOES and SelectNet operated separately and independently. This created a separate liability for market makers under each system. This dual liability has been eliminated in order to encourage market makers to enter larger size into the market, since now their exposure can be more readily controlled. You may send a directed order to an auto-execution participant provided that order is either:

a. For a number of shares at least 100 shares greater than the participant is quoted. In this case, the order must be either "all or none," or it must have "minimum acceptable quantity" (MAQ) specified. The MAQ must be at least 100 shares greater than the size quoted by the participant.

or

b. The order must be for more than 999,999 shares.

For those of us most likely to execute under the first of these provisions, it is important to note that since these orders are nonliability, the market participant to whom the orders are directed is under no obligation to respond. In fact, in order to conserve network bandwidth, they are encouraged not to respond at all. How rude!

Example: Say you wanted to transact with an ECN that is quoted at the best bid but does not accept automatic execution. You would send a directed SelectNet order to the ECN, and the ECN would be required to fill it, provided the quote is still good and the order has not yet been filled. And if, for another example, you wanted to send an order for 5,000 shares to a specific market participant who is at the inside market quoting 1,000 shares, you would direct it to the desired market participant with SelectNet. You would have to specify a MAQ, and you could, if you wanted, designate the order as all-or-none. All-or-none orders are by definition nonliability as are orders for size of at least one unit (100 shares) greater than quoted. Again, it is important to note that these orders will be nonliability orders if sent to a market maker and that the market maker would have no obligation to respond, if even to decline.

Active ECNs that use SelectNet in their routing protocol, like Archipelago, for example, should receive some real benefit from Super-SOES. Since market makers were allowed 30 seconds to respond to liability orders directed to them via SelectNet ("preference" orders), in the past the ECNs utilizing SelectNet could really be hobbled when attempting to transact against multiple market makers. Market makers could take the full response time allotted to them, and the ECN would be left waiting for a response. Many traders have told me of their experiences waiting on the edge of their seat for a fill . . . and waiting. Of course, these ECNs were lightning fast when executing against other ECNs because ECNs provide near-instant execution of SelectNet preference orders, which the active ECNs would send them. Unfortunately, these sophisticated systems were at the mercy of human market makers—but no more. The auto-execution feature of Super-SOES should make the systems lightning fast when transacting with both market makers and ECNs alike. However, you have to weigh the value of going through an active ECN to get to the Nasdaq, when you can enter orders directly. Time is of the essence, and if you can enter an order in SuperSOES yourself, why would you want to go through an ECN? One reason is that many active ECNs have, in addition to a direct connection to the Nasdaq, direct connections to the other ECNs. Therefore, you should be able to execute not only in the Nasdq via active ECNs but also in other ECNs themselves, which should save time. And of course, if the majority of ECNs agree to participate in auto-execution, then the active ECNs will benefit even more. However, in that case, entering an order in an active ECN as opposed to entering it in SuperSOES would have no benefit other than the possibility of added liquidity by transacting in the ECNs order book. The biggest ECN book of all, that of the Island, has hands-down the most liquidity of all ECNs in the current market. But the Island does not utilize SelectNet to route orders. So if the ultimate draw is liquidity, the Island will certainly continue to be incredibly popular. The ECNs, which use SelectNet, will no doubt need to rewrite their execution algorithms, and one can only speculate as to the ultimate result at this point.

reduced time between auto-executions
Here's some really good news: Once market makers receive a NNMS (SuperSOES) execution, they will be allowed a greatly reduced "stay of execution" of only five seconds. During this time-out, the market makers must decide whether to stay where they are with respect to their bid/offer or whether to move their market. In contrast to the current 30-second response time allowed for received SelectNet orders and the 17-second stay-of-execution period for SOES, this new system should really speed things up. Additionally, tier sizes and the "five-minute rule" will no longer apply for the Nasdaq National Market stocks either. Of course, the old rules will apply, without any changes, for small-cap securities.

These are the basics of the new SuperSOES. Additional enhancements to the NNMS will come with SuperMontage as well.

elimination of no-decrement feature
A feature on market makers' workstations allowed them to show a quoted size and allowed for that size to remain constant until the market makers either transacted that number of shares or moved their market. This feature has been eliminated; now market makers' quoted size will decrement (go down, i.e., 1,000, 900, 800, 700 with three consecutive 100-share executions) with each transaction. Beware, however, that this does not address "reserve size" orders. These orders will display without decrementing until the actual size of the reserve is less than the displayed size.

Sounds pretty good, right? Well, in theory, this system will be a real improvement once the ECNs sign up to participate, and every market participant is available for auto-execution. But there are strong arguments against the ECNs agreeing to participate in auto-execution at this time. And one of the biggest obstacles blocking their desire to participate is not something that cannot be easily remedied.

network nonsense
There is an inherent delay in the processing of information in any network. In some networks this may be a matter of milliseconds, if there is very little data involved. But the Nasdaq is a massive system, and even the best processors in the world need time to crunch data and send it on its way. The Nasdaq has, arguably, the very best number-

crunching machines and most advanced network in the world. Its capabilities are astounding. Nevertheless, there is a delay between the time that market participants update their quotes and the time those quotes are reflected in the montage. Add to that the fact that the ECNs are separate "exchanges" linked to the Nasdaq, and you've got problems. The Nasdaq says the delay between the entering of an order and the reflecting of an order may be three to five seconds, under heaviest load situations. But then you have the ECNs, which are separate from the Nasdaq and must process their orders themselves. The combined effect could possibly delay total communications closure (an order is sent, an answer is received) by up to seven seconds. That this may seem a very long time is not really the point; in practice the process may seem instant. But here's the problem: Let's say an ECN is signed up for auto-execution and has a best bid reflected in its book and in the Nasdaq Level II quotes montage. Now, a client of a brokerage somewhere with direct access to the ECN sells to that bid, using the ECN directly and bypassing the Nasdaq. Let's also say that shortly thereafter (milliseconds later), the Nasdaq receives an order that would hit that bid and presents the ECN with the report of an execution. Keep in mind that if you are a market participant who has agreed to auto-execution; you are responsible for *all* executions you receive. So, we have two near-simultaneous orders, in effect presenting the ECN with dual liability.

The procedure for the ECN in SuperSOES environment would be to send a cancel order to the Nasdaq to remove its bid when it receives the subscriber's execution. But now, in saunters network latency. The cancel order is sent, at light speed, and processed instantly by the most advanced computer system in the world—and it is too late. The ECN has bought stock from a subscriber and also from a participant in SuperSOES. The ECN is liable for both orders. The ECN now has an erroneous but real proprietary position. Considering the volatility of the market these days, and further extrapolating that any such errors would probably occur in the busiest stocks (the most volatile ones), it doesn't take a rocket scientist to see what a tremendous risk auto-execution represents to the ECNs. Consider how many transactions ECNs process on a daily basis; in June of 2000, for example, the Island ECN alone transacted 2,048,807,082 shares, according to the Nasdaq. Imagine the seemingly limitless liability an ECN would be exposed to if it were to participate in auto-execution. If you were CEO of an ECN, would you participate?

SuperSOES without ECN participants in auto-execution
Like it or not, ECNs might choose not to participate in SuperSOES. This is one reason why the Nasdaq has appended to the SuperSOES system to allow the continued use of SelectNet for directed liability orders to ECNs. It seems that the Nasdaq is intent on upgrading its systems whether the ECNs participate in auto-execution or not. It would be a real shame if the ECNs don't participate in this long-awaited update. Few would argue against a system that fully integrates all market participants on an equal basis. However, this is a mechanical problem and not one to be easily overcome. So a true centralized marketplace may have to wait.

If the problem with the ECNs can be worked out, the new system will be fantastic. It will provide faster, easier executions with less work and skill.

And this in turn might provide additional liquidity and facilitate a more efficient market. On balance, I think SuperSOES is great news for traders. If only the system for small-cap stocks could be updated as well! I can imagine trying to sell and getting nothing done, while the stock is tanking, only to suddenly realize that the stock is a small cap, for which SuperSOES won't work.

As it is, SuperSOES represents major improvement to the Nasdaq's execution systems. One can only hope that the ECN question will be solved prior to the advent of SuperMontage, when and if it is approved. Right now, I'm happy that I'm a trader, and not one of those Nasdaq programmers quietly coding into the night.

SuperSOES Advantages
- Auto-execution against multiple market makers and ECNs that have agreed to accept auto-execution for up to 999,999 shares.
- Liability "directed" orders may still be sent to those market participants who have not agreed to accept automatic execution.
- Odd-lot and round-lot orders accepted.
- Market makers receive only five-second break between auto-executions.

- SOES and SelectNet preserved in present form for the Nasdaq small-cap securities.
- Overall ease of use.

SuperSOES Disadvantages
- "Directed" nonliability orders may be sent only to those participating in auto-execution in either of the following cases: the order is for a number of shares at least 100 shares greater than the market participant is quoting (in this case, the order must be designed either "all or none" or minimum acceptable quantity, with the MAQ being at least 100 shares greater than the quoted size of the market participant to whom you are directing your order) or, the order is for one million shares or more.
- New SelectNet is nonliability, except against market participants who have not agreed to participate in auto-execution.
- ECNs may refuse to participate because of network latency, which would cause them dual liability and potentially huge errors.
- Will affect active ECNs that utilize SelectNet in their order execution protocol. It may radically increase their effectiveness, while at the same time rendering them superfluous.
- Will affect software solutions that utilize SelectNet in their order-routing protocol. Of course, at this point it is impossible to say what the effect will be other than that they should work much faster.
- Will not work for small-cap securities. The Nasdaq National Market System (NNMS) will work only in Nasdaq National Market securities.

SelectNet and SOES will remain unchanged for Nasdaq small-cap securities
Currently, SOES participation is a choice for market makers in Nasdaq small-cap securities. Market makers can simply choose whether they'd like to participate and therefore be open (liable) for SOES executions, or not. As you might imagine, many market makers balk at the very idea of SOES, and decline to participate. So the system works as

it did before SuperSOES; SelectNet, SOES, and ECNs will continue to be the available routing options.

electronic communication networks

Note: Please read "Market Systems" before proceeding to this material. It will be necessary to have a good understanding of the Nasdaq's execution systems (SuperSOES, SOES, and SelectNet) to understand much of the following material.

An electronic communication network (ECN) is defined as an electronic system that widely disseminates to third parties orders entered by market participants and permits such orders to be executed against in whole or in part. ECNs appear in the Nasdaq Level II screen montage just like market makers; indeed, market makers desiring anonymity often place orders in them. For example, a market maker may have an institutional order to buy a large amount of stock, but he doesn't want the rest of the world to know his intentions. (If everyone knows he's going to buy a huge amount of shares, everyone will raise their prices in anticipation.) So he might sit on or near the best offer, in order to look like a seller, when in fact he's on the inside bid through an ECN, buying everything he can get his hands on.

So an ECN allows market participants to both bid and offer stock anonymously. However, ECNs are also available to individuals, through electronic brokerages offering direct access to the markets. The best brokerages offer execution systems with all the major ECNs to individuals as a point-and-click route to use when buying or selling stock.

On the order entry system, you specify which route you'd like to use when buying or selling stock; you might choose SOES, but as SOES will not allow you to buy at the bid, you might want to use an ECN. An ECN will allow you to sit on the bid or offer, enabling you to participate in the Nasdaq Level II quotes montage *just like a market maker.*

So, through ECNs, you can both buy at the bid and sell at the ask. If the stock is bidding 10 by $10\frac{1}{4}$, you can join the bid, at 10, and buy the stock at 10. And, given the right circumstances, you can offer it out right away, at $10\frac{1}{4}$. If done correctly, you may have a profit of one-quarter in several minutes or less.

Now, that may not sound like much, but when you consider that one-quarter on 1,000 shares is $250 and that the best scalpers are do-ing just that dozens of times a day, it all adds up quickly. But scalping as a bread-and-butter technique is rapidly losing appeal. The order-handling rules instituted by the NASD in July 1998 have made scalping considerably more risky, and generally an uneconomic activity. In my opinion, scalping for one-eighth or one-sixteenth is an uneconomic ac-tivity. Several years ago, when spreads were wide and order-handling rules were different, it was a different story altogether. Scalping worked, though, even with the lower level of risk, still benefiting the so-called brokerages as much as it did the individuals who scalped. But now there are numerous brokerage houses teaching (for an extor-tionate fee) outdated techniques (scalping), and offering huge "mar-gin." I put margin in quotes because Regulation T of the Securities Act of 1934, which governs use of margin, has set the rate at 50 percent. "Brokerages" that offer 10 to 1 "margin" are not offering margin at all, but using sophisticated techniques of equity participation in the firm to lend you the money, as long as you abide by their rules, which usu-ally are: (1) scalp only and (2) hold no positions overnight. These sort of "brokerages"—really day-trading shops—are not only designed to separate you from your money, but they may be operating in violation of the law.

historical background of the ECNs

The first ECN was InstiNet. InstiNet appears on the Level II screen as INCA. Only in certain situations is InstiNet legally required to show its bid and offer through the Nasdaq Level II quote system; frequently it does not. InstiNet is so liquid—so much stock trades on it (both listed and OTC stocks)—that it is known as the "Fourth Market," after the NYSE and the Nasdaq. (The "first" market is the primary distribution.)

Trading goes on in InstiNet continuously, 24 hours a day. When you see a Level II screen looking static, but time of sales is showing a lot of activity, those trades may be happening on InstiNet. And when you see INCA in the Level II montage, what you are seeing reflects only the very best bid and offer currently available on InstiNet; who knows how many limit orders may be in the InstiNet book? The Level II mon-tage may show only the tip of the iceberg.

InstiNet was once the domain of traders and institutions that wanted to trade large blocks of stock anonymously, without appearing on Level II. Recently InstiNet was all but unavailable as an option to nonprofessional traders, because it would not allow individuals direct access to the INCA order book. Now, as more and more savvy individuals ask their brokers for quotes on InstiNet, and as forward-thinking electronic brokerages are getting InstiNet terminals, additional liquidity is appearing from nonprofessional traders.

However, InstiNet has major, crushing competition. Several years ago, some guys came up with an idea. Why not create an ECN that is specifically geared toward individual traders and open the order book to them as well? With that concept in mind, the Island was created. Most traders know and love the Island, as by its very nature it is designed to provide the electronic trader direct access to the market. At the time of this writing, the Island (seen in your Level II as ISLD) has such tremendous volume and liquidity that it is considering becoming an exchange unto itself. Total share volume traded on the ISLD exceeded that of InstiNet for the first time recently. This can only be a harbinger of what will come. And since the coming of ISLD, more and more ECNs are opening for business each year. A few of the ECNs are offering exciting, additional options and ways of routing orders, such as Archipelago (ARCA). ARCA uses artificial intelligence algorithms to actively "work" your orders for you. Of course, the future operational performance of ECNs that use the Nasdaq's execution systems in their order-routing protocol will be determined by how they incorporate the new auto-execution features of SuperSOES into their routing algorithms.

list of ECNS

Below is a list of the ECNs currently in use. *Memorize them.* Knowing that a market participant is an ECN as opposed to a market maker will influence your choice of route.

Company Name	*Symbol*
InstiNet	INCA
The Island	ISLD
Speer, Leeds and Kellog	REDI
Attain	ATTN

NexTrade	NTRD
The Brass Utility	BTRD
Bloomberg's Trade Book	BTRD
Archipelago	ARCA
The Brass Utility	BRUT
MarketXT	MKXT

In the years to come, many more ECNs are likely to start or merge operations, as the Nasdaq evolves toward a 24-hour auction system open to anyone who wants to buy or sell stock.

how ECNs work

A standard ECN allows you to bid and offer stock anonymously in the Nasdaq market. Additionally, ECNs offer subscribers access to their order books, and add liquidity and speed to the traders' arsenal. Most ECNs post in the Nasdaq montage in the same manner as market makers. This is just like placing an ad in the paper (the Nasdaq montage) displaying your firm intention to buy or sell a specific amount of stock at a specific price. If you want to buy stock and appear at the best bid, *someone must sell stock to you.* Conversely, if you are appearing at the best ask, *someone must buy stock from you.* In a fast-moving market where there are virtually no sellers and numerous buyers, your chance of buying at the best bid is limited, at best. It's like waiting in line for a movie; eventually the movie will be sold out and no tickets will be left (at your desired price). Conversely, if you are trying to sell at the best offer when there are numerous sellers and virtually no buyers, again, chances of quick execution are limited. Keep in mind the fact that the Nasdaq is a real market, where buyers try to buy cheap and sellers try to sell dear. Sometimes posting to the best bid or ask may not be the fastest route.

In any case, ECNs do not receive SOES executions and, after full rollout of SuperSOES, may not receive auto-executions either. Remember, ECN participation in SuperSOES auto-execution is a voluntary choice; many ECNs may simply decide not to participate. So if you've placed a bid or offer using an ECN, you will have less opportunity for execution because you'll miss out on all SOES-driven liquidity and potentially SuperSOES nondirected liquidity as well. This is not to say that ECNs aren't useful—quite the contrary. Many active traders swear by ECNs and transact a majority of their orders through them. But it is something to keep in mind. Knowing all possible outcomes is important. Surprises may be nice—just not when it comes to execution.

Though no ECNs are SOES-able and others may not participate in auto-execution, some offer much more than simple "passive" ways to display orders. Some have terrific features beyond just posting in the ECN book and the Nasdaq quotes montage. These are called "active" ECNs, because they will actively work your order for you. For example, Archipelago is a cutting-edge ECN with an attitude. Archipelago acts like a great big dragnet. It will not only post to the best bid/offer, but it will first match stock with all the other ECNs. If your order is still not completely filled, it will then go to market makers (using Select-Net or SuperSOES, after rollout) for the remainder of the order. Finally, if your order is *still* not completely filled, it will then post to the best bid/offer and wait passively for someone to execute against it, just like a standard "passive" ECN. Additionally, only *one* aggregate commission will be charged for the entire order. And all of this happens in real time, with *one* mouse click! Several other ECNs offer similar capabilities: Attain ECN and Redi ECN, for example. However, after SuperSOES has completed its rollout, these ECNs may work differently. In all likelihood, their performance will be enhanced by the new system.

Below you'll find an individual look at the functionality of all the ECNs currently available. But first, it is necessary to mention a potential problem—a very typical mistake—that traders attempting to execute using passive ECNs make all too often.

If you don't have full access to an "active" ECN's order book, you may only be able to bid or offer using that ECN. In other words, you are using the ECN in its passive capacity. In these circumstances, the problem of locking or crossing the market may arise. (Note that the Island doesn't have this problem; it is the only ECN to program around this issue.)

Locking or crossing the market is one of the most common mistakes in placing a "passive" ECN order. It results in the order being immediately canceled and deleted. When an order is deleted from the trading system, it obviously never goes live, and nothing is done. During the half minute or so while you are trying to figure out why your order was deleted, the market can move away from the price desired. (The market could also move in your favor—but experience tells me

figure 6.2   locking or crossing the market

TOOLS OF THE TRADE								_ □ ×
ODETA	Last	11 3/8					13:55	----13:55---
High	11 3/8	Low	11	Tot Vol		22800		11 3/8 200
BID ↓	11	ASK	11 3/8	Close		11 3/8		

NAME	BID	CHG	SIZE	#BEST	NAME	ASK	CHG	SIZE	#BEST
RILY	11	+1/16	500	1	NITE	11 3/8	+0	500	1
NITE	10 7/8	+0	100	0	FAKE	11 3/8	+0	100	1
SLKC	10 7/8	+0	100	0	BRUT	11 1/2	+0	1400	2
ALLN	10 7/8	+0	100	0	BTRD	11 1/2	+0	1000	1
CRUT	10 3/4	+0	100	0	MASH	11 1/2	+0	1000	4
HRZG	10 3/4	+0	100	1	ALLN	11 1/2	+0	100	1
BRUT	10 5/8	+0	100	1	SLKC	11 5/8	+0	100	0
CWCO	10 5/8	+0	100	0	HRZG	11 5/8	+0	100	0

that it always goes the wrong way in this situation!) Figure 6.2, a Level II screen, is a simple illustration of what it means to lock or cross the market. The inside market of 11 by 11⅜, with FAKE (fictitious market maker) offering 100 shares at 11⅜.

Usually locking or crossing the market occurs when you try to execute against another market participant with a "passive" ECN. Remember, passive ECNs will not execute against other market participants, although others can execute against them (hence the term "passive").

Were we to place an order using FAKE (our fictitious "passive" ECN) to buy 100 shares at $11, in a few seconds, the order would appear in Level II as shown in Figure 6.3.

Note that in placing this order, you are showing to the world your intention to buy 100 shares at $11, not unlike placing an ad in a newspaper. You are waiting for someone to sell the stock to you. Note again that FAKE is also on the offer, at the limit price of 11⅜.

Now, if instead you placed an order to buy 100 shares at 10⅜ using FAKE, the order would be executed in the FAKE order book (since there is already an order in the FAKE order book to sell 100 shares at 10⅜). In a few seconds the Level II montage would look like the one shown in Figure 6.4.

You would be the proud owner of 100 shares. However, were the

figure 6.3   buying 100 shares at $11 using FAKE

NAME	BID	CHG	SIZE	#BEST	NAME	ASK	CHG	SIZE	#BEST
RILY	11	+1/16	500	1	NITE	11 3/8	+0	500	1
FAKE	11	+0	100	1	FAKE	11 3/8	+0	100	1
NITE	10 7/8	+0	100	0	BRUT	11 1/2	+0	1400	2
SLKC	10 7/8	+0	100	0	BTRD	11 1/2	+0	1000	1
ALLN	10 7/8	+0	100	0	MASH	11 1/2	+0	1000	4
CRUT	10 3/4	+0	100	0	ALLN	11 1/2	+0	100	1
HRZG	10 3/4	+0	100	1	SLKC	11 5/8	+0	100	0
BRUT	10 5/8	+0	100	1	HRZG	11 5/8	+0	100	0

ODETA Last 11 3/8   13:55
High 11 3/8 Low 11   Tot Vol 22800
BID 11   ASK 11 3/8   Close 11 3/8
----13:55--- 11 3/8 200

Level II montage to look like that shown in Figure 6.4 *before* you placed your order, and if you tried to place an order to buy 100 shares at 11³/₈ on FAKE, the order would be automatically deleted, because it would lock the market. In other words, it would cause the best bid to equal the best offer, a condition where the market is locked. NASD fair market practice rules will not allow a locked market condition to exist. The bid price must be at least one thirty-second below the best offer in order to post on the Nasdaq Level II montage.

Additionally, if you wanted to place an order to buy 1,000 shares at 10¹/₂—that is, post to the Nasdaq montage an intention to buy (bid) the stock at 10¹/₂—this order would also be deleted, because it would create a situation where the bid price is higher than the offer price. This condition is referred to as a "crossed" market. Nasdaq fair market practice rules will not allow a crossed market condition to exist.

A locked market condition occurs when the bid price is equal to the offer. A crossed market condition occurs when the bid is higher than the offer. Both locking the market and crossing the market are violations of NASD fair market rules and orders that would create a locked or crossed market condition will be deleted.

InstiNet

InstiNet recently acquired a brokerage and plans to start offering direct-access–style brokerage services to retail investors in early 2001. Re-

figure 6.4 buying 100 shares at 10⅜ using FAKE

NAME	BID	CHG	SIZE	#BEST	NAME	ASK	CHG	SIZE	#BEST
RILY	11	+1/16	500	1	NITE	11 3/8	+0	500	1
NITE	10 7/8	+0	100	0	BRUT	11 1/2	+0	100	1
SLKC	10 7/8	+0	100	0	BTRD	11 1/2	+0	1400	2
ALLN	10 7/8	+0	100	0	MASH	11 1/2	+0	1000	1
CRUT	10 3/4	+0	100	0	ALLN	11 1/2	+0	1000	4
HRZG	10 3/4	+0	100	1	SLKC	11 5/8	+0	100	1
BRUT	10 5/8	+0	100	1	HRZG	11 5/8	+0	100	0
CWCO	10 5/8	+0	100	0	RAJA	11 11/16	-1/16	100	0

TOOLS OF THE TRADE — ODETA Last 11 3/8 13:55; High 11 3/8, Low 11, Tot Vol 22800; BID 11, ASK 11 3/8, Close 11 3/8; ----13:55---- 11 3/8 200

portedly it will offer retail traders full access to the InstiNet order book. This is major news, because at this time InstiNet does not make its order book directly available to individuals. It is still primarily the domain of institutional order flow; you must be a brokerage house or an institution to use the InstiNet order entry terminal. Some firms have gotten around this by purchasing InstiNet terminals and making them available to individuals by proxy: Traders can phone in and ask for "looks" at particular stocks, then place InstiNet orders with their brokers. Other brokers have an order entry button on their order entry system for InstiNet, but an InstiNet operator still has to execute the trade, so it may be faster to use a broker with phone-in service. Phone-in allows you to get a real sense of what's going on in the stock; also, you can modify your order in real time by speaking with the executing InstiNet trader.

InstiNet may appear in Level II as INCA. When INCA appears, it may be preferenced like any ECN. However, you should know that there are certain circumstances when INCA will not post its bids and offers to the Nasdaq Level II quotes montage. And since, at this time, retail traders do not have access to the INCA book, there is no way for retail traders to transact against these orders. But generally speaking, INCA will post its orders to the Nasdaq quotes montage.

effects of SuperSOES rollout

InstiNet is a "passive" ECN. A description of how it works follows. However with the advent of SuperSOES, InstiNet will have a choice: to participate in auto-execution or not to. Whichever way it decides to go, operation will continue as described below, at least until InstiNet launches its product for retail traders and gives them access to its or- der book, or decides to participate in auto-execution.

how InstiNet works

Premarket, postmarket, and during market hours individual can call the InstiNet trader and ask for a "look" in a particular stock. In this case, let's say the call is premarket, at 8:30 A.M. The trader may re- spond something like "300 shares bid for at $128, 1,800 offered at $131." The large spread is typical, since InstiNet is a pure auction sys- tem; nobody makes a market; people just show up, anonymously, with stock to buy or sell. So theoretically, if you believe your shares of INTC are worth $1 million apiece, and you are the only person offering at the time, the quote would be "INTC is currently offered at $1 million a share on InstiNet." During market hours, prices on InstiNet often closely match prices on the Nasdaq or listed exchanges.

However, InstiNet has additional information available nowhere else. The trader in the above example may *also* say "The $131 offer is an accumulating seller, he's sold 161,000 shares in the past two weeks. Additionally, there are several other accumulating sellers of *size*. There are no accumulating buyers of more than 2,000 shares in the past two weeks." This information, when compounded with news of an analyst's downgrade of the stock, which came out after the market closed yes- terday, at 4:15 P.M., and yesterday's closing price of $133, may give the individual the idea that the stock is being heavily sold, and that it is trading down premarket. If the person has been considering going short the stock, this information might be of serious interest.

Figure 6.5 shows what an InstiNet quotes montage looks like. On the left is a current read of the Nasdaq quotes montage. On the right is the InstiNet order book. It is quoted in eighths. Only prices and size are mentioned; market participants transacting in InstiNet are guaran- teed anonymity. So, as currently reflected, the best bid is at 13⅜ for 500 shares. (On the INCA screen the 13⅜ bid is quoted as "13/3." Re- member, quotes are defaulted in eighths.) There is no current offer.

figure 6.5   InstiNet quotes montage

```
 INSTINET                                                          ▨▣▨
▐▌▟  File  Functions  Orders  Messages  Settings
‚

‚09:21 ATHM&RSSFp 40/2x41/0 1x10 CL    ATHM&RSSFp 40/2x41/0 1x1 CL
‚09:21 ATHM&INCA 40a9x41/0 4x10 CL

‚09:20 ATHM&PERTp 39a15x40/6 10x10 CL   ATHM&PERTp 39/7x40a11 10x10 CL
‚09:20 ATHM&PERTp 39/7x40a11 1x1 CL    ATHM&SLKCp 40/4x41/6 1x1 CL

‚GRIN   GRAND TOYS INTL INC         Last&S      100 13/6-       Up 0/3     C
‚Intr-207  Pres-3    WP 14.218              H&S 14/7   L&S 13/4   V 944,100
‚Age.E....Bid.3..Ask.3..Size   Buy................   Sell.............USD
‚CL    S    13/6' 13a13'  2x5  ▊13/3     500        13/7   4,600 A 09/03
‚CL USCT  12a13  13a13'   1x1  11/0=     500        14/3   5,000 A 09/03
‚CL CIBC   13/6'  15a3   2x10  14/3   2,000 A 09/03 14/3   3,000 A 09/02
‚CL SHWD   13/1  13a13'   5x5  14/2   2,000 T 09/03 15a5   7,100 A 08/31
‚CL NFSC   13/6'  14/4    1x1  13a15  2,000 A 09/02 15/0   2,500 A 08/31
‚CL MASH   13/6'  14a5    1x1  15/1   2,000 T 08/31 17a3   4,000 A 08/27
‚CL NITE   12/2  13a13'   1x1  17/3   5,000 X 08/30 17/5  15,000 A 08/27
‚CL HRZG  13a11   13/7    1x1  17/0   4,400 A 08/27 15a1   3,600 A 08/27
‚CL SHRP   13a9  14a1     1x1  17a9  10,100 A 08/27 14/6  22,500 A 08/27
‚CL REDS   13a9   14/2    1x1  17a15  5,000 A 08/27 14/6   4,000 A 08/27
‚09:22  DJI 11078.4 +235.2   V&N 666.6m (798.3)  TIC +728    CLOSE  (c) INSTINET
```

Also note the presence of dates (09/03, for example) and the designations "A" and "T." The date refers to the last time that this particular market participant bid or offered, while the "A" refers to "accumulating," and the "T" refers to "timed out"—in other words, the order was good until a certain time and is now defunct.

So, you can see that as recently as 09/03, someone sold 4,600 shares for $13\frac{7}{8}$, and there are numerous accumulating buyers and sellers. Many times you will see accumulating buyers in a stock that is up significantly. Obviously, given the laws of supply and demand, continuous buying demand will tend to create a rise in price.

You may buy and sell stock before, during, or after the market closes through InstiNet. During market hours, InstiNet prices are generally reflective of the current market. In other words, contrary to what you may have been told, the bids and offers in InstiNet are generally less favorable than in the other exchanges during market hours. If the prices were better on InstiNet than on the other exchanges, a cottage arbitrage industry would be devoted to scalping InstiNet and other exchanges. No such industry exists, though from time to time InstiNet may offer a more favorable price.

InstiNet Advantages
- Substantial pre- and postmarket trading happens in InstiNet, particularly in listed stocks.
- Provides information on accumulating buyers and sellers.
- Offers pre- and postmarket indications of a stock's direction.
- May be preferenced through SelectNet when quotes appear in the Nasdaq montage. (Additional charges may be incurred.)

InstiNet Disadvantages
- At the time of this writing, there is no direct individual access to order book. (InstiNet is promising to soon grant retail traders access to its order book.)
- Extra charge for use: InstiNet currently charges $.015 per share for any trade executed with InstiNet. This per-share charge is passed along to the individual.

general notes on InstiNet
If you want to trade before or after market hours, InstiNct often has available buyers and sellers. Additionally, during market hours, INCA is often in the Nasdaq montage and can be preferenced through Select-Net or Archipelago (another ECN, which utilizes SelectNet).

Some electronic brokerages have begun to offer an "InstiNet Key" on their platforms. At this time, however, *InstiNet does not offer individual access to its order book.* When you use the "InstiNet Key," you are not necessarily placing an order directly to InstiNet; *you may be sending the order to the brokerage house, where an InstiNet operator will, it is hoped, see the order and hand-enter it into the InstiNet system.* In other words, an intermediary may have been added to the transaction, and you may have given up the ability to get "looks" into the InstiNet order book. As mentioned before, some of the better firms offer InstiNet on a phone-in basis only, where you have the benefit of "looks" into the InstiNet order book.

Please refer again to Figure 6.5, the InstiNet quotes montage. (InstiNet wouldn't show me its brand-new retail platform yet but rumors say it is fantastic.) It is divided into two main sections, right and left. On the left side is a version of the current Nasdaq quotes montage; on the right is the InstiNet bid and offer quotation. Note that orders with an "A" or "T" are not current quotes—and therein lies the interesting information. "T" simply stands for "timed out"; in other words, the order has expired. But "A" stands for accumulating. At the time this shot was taken, there are a number of accumulating buyers and sellers. This fact can be of particular interest during a trading day. For example, say you notice that the volume of trades in a particular security seems unusually high. Is it due to day-trader–generated liquidity, or is an institution a buyer or seller of size? If you can call your broker and ask for a "look" at the security, including any accumulating buyers or sellers, you might be surprised at what you hear. Suppose you find that several institutions (they will be anonymous) have bought 200,000 shares so far on that day and, further, that there are no accumulating sellers. Then, in looking at Level II, you notice one particular market maker seems always to show size on the offer but keeps moving away whenever things get close. You might come to think that he is really a buyer, not a seller. While a look at InstiNet is not necessarily the very best of indicators, it does help clear the picture.

InstiNet experiences
More times than I can remember, clients have called in and bought stock on InstiNet premarket, only to see it gap up several points on open, at which point they sell it for a handsome profit. I've also seen clients, upon hearing adverse news come out shortly after the market closes, sell their stock in InstiNet, beating the selling rush that follows the next day.

Warning: Just because a price trades up on InstiNet premarket doesn't mean the price will keep rising once the Nasdaq or NYSE opens. Many times a price trades artificially high as traders bid it up premarket on InstiNet, to the highest print of the day, but the price falls right from the open. In my experience, the fact that a stock is up on InstiNet doesn't truly indicate its coming price in the markets.

the Island
The Island appears in the Nasdaq montage as ISLD. ISLD is hands down the most liquid of all ECNs. Because it was designed for use by all, it is readily accessible at any electronic, direct-access brokerage worth its salt. As mentioned earlier, so much volume is transacted on ISLD that it has considered becoming its own exchange. ISLD func-

tions like a standard ECN, in that it allows you to place limit orders of specific price and quantity in the ISLD order book. When the price of the stock reaches the limit of the order, the order appears in the Level II montage, allowing you to buy at the bid or sell at the ask. Market orders are not accepted, since the ISLD posts to the Level II montage, and someone must either buy or sell stock to you at your specific, "firm" price.

Another advantage of the ISLD is its order book, which you can view for free in real time on the World Wide Web. Go to www.isld.com and follow the link to VIEW ISLD BOOK. It is available in HTML or in a nifty java applet that you can download. For free, again, of course. Also check out the link to the 3-D ISLD BOOK at the address just given. The order book simply lists the orders that individuals and institutions have placed in a particular stock. By checking the order book, you may see a partial listing of the world's interest in a particular stock. For example, very few orders to buy and a great many orders to sell may be indicative of weakness. In any case, the order book tells you where resistance and support lie, at least in the ISLD. Some less-than-scrupulous electronic brokerages advertise the ISLD order book as part of their software setup (which they charge for), so it is again important to note that the ISLD order book is freely available to all, at no cost, at the ISLD Web site.

One of the reasons for ISLD's tremendous liquidity is its relationship with Datek Securities, a revolutionary online brokerage. Both ISLD and Datek were founded by the same forward-looking guys. Datek uses ISLD extensively in its daily brokerage activities. You can buy at the bid and sell at the ask through Datek, via the Island. The Island is, on a share volume basis, the ECN of choice for active traders.

how ISLD works

ISLD is available as a point-and-click routing option through most of the electronic direct-access brokerages. The trader simply designates ISLD as the route, enters the limit price and number of shares, and hits ENTER. The order is immediately placed in the ISLD order book. If the order is executable in the book (if there are enough shares bid/offered at the price), the order is executed instantaneously and is "printed" to the ticker tape. If the order is not executable in the ISLD order book, it is automatically displayed in the Level II montage. Then the trader waits for someone to fill the order. Like all ECNs, ISLD is not executable via SOES. The trader must wait, and either buy shares from or sell shares to another market participant. One characteristic of a limit order is that it may *never* be filled. The Nasdaq is a market; there may be nobody who wants to buy or sell at your limit. *If it is a fast-moving stock on its way down, and there are many sellers and few buyers, an offer at best ask may not get filled. Conversely, in a fast-moving stock on its way up, an order to buy at the best bid may not get filled either.* If you absolutely need to be in or out of a particular position, there may be faster routes. However, if a stock is on its way up, offering through ISLD may be just the ticket to get you in or out at your price. Scalpers often exit their positions through ISLD.

ISLD can also be a speedy alternative to SOES in certain situations. As mentioned earlier, SOES orders are processed and executed in the Nasdaq system in the order in which they are received. In a stock with major volume and volatility, especially on a day when the Nasdaq is experiencing high volume, SOES orders may hang out there for what seems like ages. Because ISLD is an ECN, SOES will not transact with it. ISLD has its own order book, separate from the Nasdaq. If there is an ISLD offer or bid already out there at an acceptable price, choosing ISLD as the route often fills the order almost instantly. The order will transact in the ISLD order book and the transaction will then be printed to the tape. Transacting in the order book of an ECN often means faster results, particularly in high-volume stocks. For similar reasons, an ECN execution within the ECNs order book will often transact faster than a SelectNet preference.

An ISLD routed order may result in partial fills. However, many brokerages charge only one commission per order, regardless of the number of partial fills. If the order partially fills and then is killed by the exchange, traders can be left holding an odd lot of shares—say, 5 or 10. When this happens, at many brokerages you have to place another order, and sometimes you have to pay additional commissions. Note: An SOES order is often a great alternative here, since SOES will accept odd-lot orders and generally will execute immediately.

special ISLD features: subscriber and hidden orders
The ISLD also offers a feature called "subscriber-only orders." (Some brokerages offer this as an optional feature.) A subscriber-only order

is exactly what it sounds like. It will fill in the ISLD exchange *only* and never post to the Nasdaq quotes montage. In the ISLD order book, subscriber orders are designated by a little "s." Without access to the book, you'll never see them at all.

ISLD also offers "hidden" orders. They are just that; they show up nowhere at all. These are useful if you really feel that showing your stock to the market at large would cause the market to move unfavorably. Since hidden orders are, in fact, hidden, they don't invite people to transact with them. Additionally, because they are placed only in the ISLD exchange (and invisibly at that), you have to wait for someone to transact in the ISLD book for the order to be matched. The net effect of subscriber and hidden orders is that they remove liquidity from the market. If nobody can see your order, how do you get filled? That question notwithstanding, some people swear by subscriber and hidden orders.

I personally see both merits and problems with hidden orders. The problems are: You must wait for ISLD-based liquidity in order for your order to be filled. (Nobody can SelectNet preference you, since nobody can even see you are there.) In addition—and this is a philosophical protest—subscriber orders hide liquidity from price discovery in the open market. But there are some strong benefits to them. For one thing, there is the argument that "what the market doesn't see won't hurt it," and placing subscriber orders may indeed lessen volatility by dampening the effect of additional liquidity. It will be interesting to see if subscriber-only orders gain market share or lose it over time. My bet is they'll lose favor in the long run. However, I'd still like the option available in my software. I want the choice! And it's still pretty cool that ISLD offers this as an option, whether I use it or not. Note: Ever seen 100 shares offered on the Island, where it looks like the stock may trade up if only somebody takes out those 100 shares? Then *you* decide to take them out yourself? And you execute in the ISLD direct because you know it'll be faster—but something funny happens: the 100 shares offered remain, unaffected by your buy, and then you notice the print is 1/256 *lower* than it should have been. While you're puzzling over this, 100 share prints are going off like mad.

Then you realize that somebody clever offered size (who knows how much? 4,900? 9,900 shares?) but *hidden*, and then baited you and other traders with a display of 100 shares. Then you (and dozens of others) tried to take that stock out, 100 shares at a time, accomplishing the savvy day trader's goal: liquidating his large position. You see, he couldn't just offer it in plain view; that would risk a little selloff and he'd have to compete for stock. No, what he did was bait you, and then got rid of his entire size, at only 1/256 below the best offer! As a postscript, guess what happens next? All the buyers are done, and the seller's last 100 shares disappear. Then, almost as soon as traders were buying, they begin selling. And you, with your 100 shares, realize you've been suckered. But now you know the trick. As they say, "give a man a fish and he's fed for a day."

Keep in mind that brokerages enable different levels of functionality to their routing architecture. Some brokerages may offer access to execute in the ISLD but not to see the book. Others may offer the book but not allow subscriber/hidden orders. Others still may offer the highest level of connectivity by hard-wiring into the ISLD and offering all services that ISLD has to offer. You'll need to check with your brokerage to find out just how connected it is. Few brokerages understand the utility of hidden orders, and fewer still offer them.

ISLD is trading listed stocks now, pending a vote on whether to allow ECNs to trade them. In all likelihood, ISLD will eventually become a tremendously liquid vehicle for NYSE stocks too. As I said, they're forward-thinking guys.

Island Advantages

- Can post to the Nasdaq montage; buy at the bid or sell at the ask.
- Tremendous liquidity in the ISLD order book, which may be viewed for free.
- ISLD order book execution is often faster than routing through the Nasdaq market. (Trades occurring in the ISLD order book are reported instantly to the tape.)
- Can trade any number of shares; keep in mind, however, that an order of less than 100 shares will not post to the Nasdaq quotes montage.
- No extra charges for doing business with ISLD. (While ISLD *does* charge a fee per order, most brokerage firms pick up this cost and do not pass it on to the individual.)

- The ISLD order book is available to all, at no cost, over the Internet.
- ISLD trades after market; orders will stay live on ISLD until 8:00 P.M. EST.
- Hidden and subscriber orders.
- Orders won't lock or cross the market.
- ISLD will trade NYSE (listed) stocks as well.
- The Island is open for business both pre- and postmarket. Orders may be entered starting at 8:00 A.M. EST. Orders will stay live until 8:00 P.M. EST. Orders entered on ISLD pre- and postmarket are visible in the Nasdaq montage.

Island Disadvantages

- Only limit orders accepted.
- Sometimes makes pesky partial fills.
- ISLD posts only to the montage; it will not actively execute against other market participants. It is important to note, however, that other participants may transact with the Island. (They may buy stock from or sell stock to it.)

the ISLD order book

As mentioned, the Island order book is freely available in real time on the Internet. However, since it is so very useful, many brokerages offer it as part of their software package. Figure 6.6 is an example of the ISLD order book for DELL; Figure 6.7 presents the Level II montage for DELL. Both screen shots were taken at the same time. The ISLD book is elegantly simple in design, with bids prices and sizes on the left and offers and prices on the right. Note that it is always priced in decimals, not fractions. Only the very best of the ISLD bid/offer will show in the Level II quotes montage at any given time.

    The Level II quotes montage screen shot shown in Figure 6.7 was taken simultaneously. Note that there is a fair amount of liquidity at all levels that simply won't show in the Nasdaq quotes montage.

general notes on the Island

Many traders do much of their trading on the Island. Executions in the ISLD order book are near instantaneous; bidding for or offering stock

figure 6.6   the Island order book for Dell

Island Book - Microsoft Interne... _ □ ✕

island home	system stats	help

ⓡ DELL   GET STOCK [DELL] go

LAST MATCH		TODAY'S ACTIVITY	
Price	46.9375	Orders	8,386
Time	14:45:56	Volume	1,532,375

BUY ORDERS		SELL ORDERS	
SHARES	PRICE	SHARES	PRICE
100	46.8945#	300	47.0000
1,000	46.8906#	5	47.0000
1,790	46.8789#	1,000	47.0000
400	46.8750	400	47.0000
100	46.8750	1,000	47.0000
200	46.8125	500	47.0625
100	46.7600	5,000	47.0625
12	46.7500	5,000	47.0625
100	46.7343#	100	47.3125
100	46.6250	1,000	47.3750
100	46.5625	100	47.5000
50	46.5000	300	47.5000
100	46.5000	100	47.5000
105	46.5000	200	47.5000
500	46.2500	600	47.5625
(142 more)		(486 more)	

As of 14:46:34

may take longer, since someone must either sell stock to or buy stock from the Island. This is particularly important in fast markets; as noted, when there are tremendous amounts of buyers and few sellers, trying to buy stock by posting to the Nasdaq bid may be slow and ineffective. The same goes for selling when the market is tanking.

Note: Island orders won't lock or cross the market. The Island has a bit of programming unique to the industry. Orders placed by

figure 6.7   Level II quotes montage for Dell

DELL Level-2 :2			
2	redi	46 7/8	10	HMQT	46 15/16
1	inca	46 7/8	27	brut	46 15/16
32	isld	46 7/8	1	LEGG	47
10	PRUS	46 13/16	8	GFIN	47
8	MASH	46 13/16	4	inca	47
1	SLKC	46 13/16	28	isld	47
10	MSCO	46 13/16	1	PWJC	47
9	NITE	46 13/16	1	SLKC	47
5	mwse	46 13/16	10	SBSH	47
10	MLCO	46 13/16	10	GSCO	47
10	RSSF	46 13/16	10	DLJP	47
10	INGC	46 3/4	10	BEST	47
10	SBSH	46 3/4	6	MASH	47
5	MADF	46 3/4	10	KCMO	47 1/16
10	LEHM	46 3/4	10	MONT	47 1/16

traders that would, in other ECNs, lock/cross the market, won't do so if placed in the Island.

Say a stock is bid at 10, offered at $10^1/_{16}$. You place an order using the Island to bid at $10^1/_2$. Normally, placed with any other ECN in passive capacity, this order would be deleted for the reason that it would cross the market; in essence, you are attempting to place a bid into the Nasdaq quotes montage that is higher than the current offer, a violation of Nasdaq fair market practice. What the Island will do, however, is accept the order into its order book where it will display at the price you entered, $10^1/_2$, and send it to the Nasdaq at the best price allowed given the current inside market: in this case, 10. So it will display as a bid in the Nasdaq quotes montage at 10, while appearing in the Island book at $10^1/_2$. If the market moves up, the Island will reenter your order at higher and higher prices, until your limit is reached. So, in theory, your Island bid may appear to chase the stock up. However, should you receive an execution, you'll buy stock at the limit you requested: $10^1/_2$, even if the current Nasdaq inside market is $10 \times 10^1/_{16}$. This feature works because the Island is a separate "exchange" from the Nasdaq. It's a great idea—cutting-edge functionality like this is what keeps the Island the most liquid ECN. The feature makes entering orders easier. However, if your fingers run wild on your keyboard, you may want to enter these orders carefully: You'll get what you ask for, even if you made a mistake.

Be careful. This is a double-edged sword. Here's a kicker. You *can* enter an order that on face value would seem to cross the market and get it filled, substantially away from market, often to your detriment. Here is the way it works. Remember again that ISLD operates like an exchange unto itself. You can and will transact in the ISLD book often, and ISLD's speed can be a great benefit.

However, let's say a stock—ABCD for example—is bidding 99, offered at $99\frac{1}{16}$. Now let's say further that you are a seller of 1,000 shares, and that ISLD is not bidding or offering at the inside market. And looking at Level II, you do see an ISLD bid for 100 shares at $99\frac{3}{4}$. But the current inside bid is 99. But say, by accident, you were to place an order to sell 1,000 shares at 9. *Whammo*. The order *could* take place, because there *may* have been liquidity in the ISLD book at a price above your limit of 9. In fact, considering that the Island is the most liquid of ECNs, there probably are many bids above 9—but how many, and at what price? If there is liquidity in the ISLD book at a price that is better than your "low" ($9 here), your order will be treated as a limit order to sell with the price entered as a low, to be executed entirely in the ISLD book irrespective of the Nasdaq market. So, just for giggles, let's say that in the ISLD order book, there were bids at the following price sizes: 100 shares bid at $99\frac{3}{4}$, 100 shares bid at $98\frac{1}{2}$, 100 shares bid at $98\frac{1}{4}$, and 700 shares bid at 97. When your sell is treated as a limit order to sell with a low at 9, to be executed in the ISLD book, you would receive the following prints: 100 at $99\frac{3}{4}$, 100 at $98\frac{1}{2}$, 100 at $98\frac{1}{4}$, and 700 at 97. As far as ISLD is concerned, you have just received a price improvement over your order to sell at 9. Lucky you. (But ISLD has good reason for doing this.)

Lets say the same stock, ABCD, is bid 99, offered at $99\frac{1}{16}$. And ISLD is, in the Nasdaq Level II quotes montage, the only market participant on the bid (at 99), and for only 100 shares. And at the next price levels below, few shares are bid. But now you take a look at the ISLD order book. (Remember, it is free and available at www.isld.com. In the ISLD order book, you see a bid for 2000 shares at $98\frac{15}{16}$. Keep in mind that ISLD will only show its best bid and offer in the Nasdaq Level II montage, so you won't even know that this size bid exists unless you have the ISLD order book. But you know what you're doing, and so you have it handy. And you know the time has come to sell, and sell now. So you enter your order: Sell 1,000 shares ABCD at $98^{15}/_{16}$ on ISLD. And whammo, you're done at the following prices: 100 shares at 99 and 900 shares at $9^{15}/_{16}$. And now you watch Level II with a grin as everyone else panic sells and chases the stock down, more desperate to sell with every moment.

So the ISLD book can be a good tool. But like all good tools, if misused, somebody winds up getting hurt. What happens if you accidentally enter an order to sell on ISLD with a ridiculously low price and get filled? Well, the ISLD governors are very fair and will sometimes break trades if they clearly are erroneous. This means that a ruling is made based on the general liquidity, trading pattern, market conditions, and other relevant information about the stock. They will, in good faith, decide if the trade occurred at a price so far outside the norm as to be considered clearly erroneous. Note that this does *not* mean that a ruling is based on the fact that you made a whopping, clearly accidental trade. When the ISLD governors weigh the facts, they will make a fair decision based on the market—not on your situation. So be careful not to make this error.

Bottom line: Be very careful what you ask for; you may get it.

ISLD experiences
Many times a client has called in with this sort of situation: In an extremely fast, overly liquid market, she has been trying to sell her shares. The problem is that the price bounces around so much, before she can point and click to enter her order, the stock has moved. Again and again, up and down, down and up, and all within one or two points. ISLD and many ECNs appear on the bid for a moment, only to disappear as fast as they show up. Enter the genius ISLD.

In cases where a stock is not really going strongly up or down but just rapidly bouncing up and down like a superball in a box, I'll ready an order to sell or buy on ISLD, and wait, finger on the trigger, till ISLD shows up best bid or offer at the price I have entered. In stocks like these, the wait is usually only several seconds. As soon as I see ISLD there, I execute. I call this "the Island Magic Trick."

Amazing result: I usually get an instantaneous fill! I've often wondered why this works so often, and I believe it is a combination of two factors. First, most market professionals (market makers) will preference ISLD using SelectNet. This results in the order routing through the Nasdaq computer first, then going out to ISLD. This takes time! If you have direct access to ISLD, use it. You might just beat everyone else by a few milliseconds. And the early bird gets it, every time. Second, I believe that the ISLD computers run a little quicker than those of the Nasdaq, probably because an unimaginable amount of data is racing around the Nasdaq. It is a wonder its computers don't fail more often. Nevertheless, whatever the reason, if you've got direct access to ISLD, and the opportunity to use it strikes, use it!

Warning: ISLD has the pesky, infuriating habit of partially filling orders, with weird partials, like one share. Try selling one share! One share becomes like a hot potato, getting passed from hand to hand, market maker to market maker. Nobody wants it! It is damn hard to sell one share.

There is nothing you can do to avoid the occasional weird lot partial fill from time to time. And to add injury to insult, every time you place an order, you pay a commission.

Once, very early on in my ECN trading career (right around the time the ECNs started operations), I placed an order to buy 1,000 shares on ISLD just below the current bid. There was good volume in this stock, and the spread was one-eighth. This was thought to be a scalping-type play (poorly done!), the unsound economics of which will become clear: I bid for 1,000 shares, hoping to turn right around and sell it immediately at an eighth profit. The stock traded down to my price, and I watched, as first 53 and then 130 shares traded. And that was it!

So there I was, long 183 shares, and the axe, who *had* been long gone, went and reappeared on the offer, with size. Other market makers began to drop their bids and shy away immediately, and I knew there was no way I was going to be able to get my eighth now, and so all I could think was *retreat!* I canceled the remainder of my bid and silly, greedy me, offered the 183 shares out at the best offer. Maybe, I thought, I'll still make my eighth.

I got one partial, of *one* share, and the market maker who was offered dropped his offer. Now my offer was no longer on the inside market. So now I had 182 shares of this stock, which was about to make a new low, and I had racked up *two* commission charges already! So, silly, silly, greedy me, what did I do? I lowered my offer to the inside best. The stock traded down even lower for a moment, then back up to my price, and I was filled again: *Six shares this time!* And then it dropped again. Now I had 176 shares of a stock I didn't want, and *three* commissions!!! So what did I do next? I offered out one more time. My mother used to say "Fool me once, shame on you. Fool me twice, shame on me!" I wonder what she would say if I told her that fully five commission charges later, demoralized, humiliated, and with an additional loss of approximately three-eighths a share, I was done. Well done, burned, and stuck to the pan, actually. But I had learned a lesson: I didn't know S@#*! about buying or selling stock! This trade began my ECN learning curve.

(There were any number of ways I could have gotten out; SOES is the one I probably should have used.) Remember: There is a learning curve. And as the trader on the account, you are responsible for all trades, stupid or not. And stupid rarely gets paid.

the Archipelago

The Archipelago ECN (ARCA) is a very popular "active" ECN. Many active traders swear by it, some decry it for its part institutional ownership, and still some complain of terribly slow fills in certain circumstances. One thing is for sure: ARCA, properly used in the right circumstances, is pure white lightning. And just like all other routing systems that work great in certain situations and poorly in others, ARCA has its Achilles' heel. If you understand just how to use it properly, the Archipelago is a very powerful execution tool.

SuperSOES effect on Archipelago

Archipelago is an "active" ECN—meaning that it will actively work orders for you. You are not limited to simply bidding and offering with ARCA; active features do much more. Essentially, ARCA currently (and until SuperSOES is completely rolled out) uses the Nasdaq's SelectNet to work your orders. But before I cover the specifics of how it works, you must recognize that its functionality may change with SuperSOES, at least with respect to the handling of orders in Nasdaq National Mar-

ket stocks, because SuperSOES has auto-execution that provides instant fills. (In the current SelectNet system, market makers who are
"preferenced" have 30 seconds to respond.) So, overall, it should really speed Archipelago up, at least in regard to executions against
market makers in Nasdaq National Market stocks. But, of course, the
question remains as to whether Archipelago will decide to accept
auto-executions or not. If it does, then it will be enhanced even more.
If it doesn't, then you'll just have to realize that your bids and offers
placed into the ECN will receive orders sent to it via SelectNet, which
will be near instant, as compared to the truly instant "automatic execution" feature of SuperSOES.

Archipelago's features
The Archipelago ECN is similar to the Island (ISLD) in that it will allow someone with direct access to it to execute orders within the
order book and, additionally, to post to the Nasdaq quotes montage
if no liquidity is found elsewhere. However, that is where the simi-
larity ends. Archipelago does several additional powerful and exciting things that make it an amazingly powerful tool. It is the first of a
new generation of ECNs—what I call "active" ECNs. More on that
shortly.

For now, it is important to understand that Archipelago has its
own order book, like INCA or ISLD. Archipelago's order book is
available for viewing on the Internet, at www.tradearca.com. A curious and sometimes confusing feature of the Archipelago order book
is that for those who have full direct access to it, *the order book is
displayed within the Nasdaq Level II quotes montage.* So, if you have
full access to the Archipelago, your Level II quotes montage might
look like Figure 6.8.

Users with direct access to the Archipelago ECN see many
"ARCHIPs" in the quotes montage. These ARCHIPs are the individual
orders that comprise the total liquidity available in the Archipelago
book. Seeing all the individual orders is invaluable, since it gives you
insight into what other traders are thinking. If suddenly there are 25
individual orders to buy on ARCA, you may assume that, for whatever
reason, suddenly there is increased demand. Additionally, if there are
very few shares offered, and you see many "chippies" bidding at the

figure 6.8   Level II quotes montage for someone with access to ARCA

AMPLIDYNE INC									_ □ ✕
AMPD		8	↓	+4 7/8	300	Os	15:08		
High	9 23/32	Low		3 1/8	Acc. Vol.	10485900			
Bid	8	Ask		8 1/16	Close	3 1/8			

Name	Bid	Chg.	Size	#Best	Name	Ask	Chg.	Size	#Best ▲
ARCHIP	8	+0	15	1	FAHN	8 1/16	+0	1	7
REDI	8	+1/1	10	42	INCA	8 1/16	-5/1	1	39
ARCHIP	8	+0	7	1	ISLD	8 1/8	+0	10	469
ARCHIP	8	+0	5	1	NITE	8 1/8	-11 7/8	4	88
ARCHIP	8	+0	3	1	REDI	8 1/8	+0	2	73
PGON	8	+1/8	1	2	HRZG	8 1/8	+0	1	34
ARCHIP	8	+0	1	1	ARCHIP	8 1/8	+0	25S	1
ISLD	7 15/16	+0	45	422	MASH	8 1/4	+0	20	44
HRZG	7 15/16	+0	10	39	ARCHIP	8 1/4	+0	1	1
ARCA	7 7/8	+0	15	120	SLKC	8 1/4	+1/4	1	24
ARCHIP	7 7/8	+0	10	0	PGON	8 1/4	+0	1	7

offered price, you can bet you won't get those shares. You might even be influenced to place a buy order slightly above the inside market. Sacrificing one-sixteenth here often may be better than chasing the stock, wondering why you aren't getting filled.

Note the many ARCHIPs in Figure 6.8. These frames in Figure 6.9 were frozen simultaneously.

Now take a look at the screen shot in Figure 6.9. This is what the rest of the world (those without full ARCA access) sees—*with an aggregate size reflecting the total of all the individual Archipelago orders added up.*

For example, if there are individual orders to buy 100, 500, 400, and 1,000 shares on Archipelago, and you have access to the Archipelago ECN, you will see all of the orders displayed individually, along with ARCA which reflects the aggregate size of all the individual orders: 2,000 (100 + 500 + 400 + 1,000). If you do not have full access to the Archipelago ECN, you will see what the rest of the world sees: ARCA with a size of 2,000. This feature can be confusing, but once you are used to it, it can be very helpful, since any insight into current market sentiment is always going to add value

figure 6.9 Level II quotes montage for someone without access to ARCA

** AMPLIDYNE INC									_ □ X
AMPD		8	↓	+4 7/8	300		Os	15:08	
High	9.23/32	Low		3 1/8	Acc. Vol.		10485900		
Bid	8	Ask		8 1/16	Close		3 1/8		

Name	Bid	Chg.	Size	#Best	Name	Ask	Chg.	Size	#Best ▲
REDI	8	+1/1	10	42	FAHN	8 1/16	+0	1	7
PGON	8	+1/8	1	2	INCA	8 1/16	-5/1	1	39
ISLD	7 15/16	+0	45	422	ISLD	8 1/8	+0	10	469
HRZG	7 15/16	+0	10	39	NITE	8 1/8	-11 7/8	4	88
ARCA	7 7/8	+0	15	120	REDI	8 1/8	+0	2	73
SLKC	7 7/8	+1/4	1	12	HRZG	8 1/8	+0	1	34
MASH	7 13/16	+0	37	73	MASH	8 1/4	+0	20	44

when making buy or sell decisions. You will also be able to see more clearly areas of support and resistance. If you note, for example, a tremendous amount of liquidity in the ARCA book at say, $30^{1}/_{16}$, when the stock is on its way up and currently is at $29^{7}/_{8}$, this might add value to your exit strategy.

how Archipelago works

Archipelago is available as a point-and-click routing option in the order execution platforms of the better direct-access electronic brokerages. And the way Archipelago works is what makes it so interesting. Archipelago makes use of the SelectNet execution system (run by Nasdaq market systems) to facilitate its order handling, external to its own order book. When a limit order is entered to buy using Archipelago, the following operations occur almost instantaneously (with the push of *one* button):

1. ARCA checks its own order book and matches as much stock as is available "in house." But keep in mind—if an order entered at your price is currently in the ARCA book, but ARCA is preferencing someone—you may not be able to transact against it. More on this later.

2. ARCA then goes out to all the ECNs, and transacts as much stock as is available. ARCA has direct connections to many of the ECNs, and will execute directly with them in their book. Since these are direct connections, it is faster than going through the Nasdaq system first to get to the ECNs. It also will use SelectNet to link to the ECNs that it doesn't have a direct connection to, like a great big dragnet. As mentioned earlier, a SelectNet link to an ECN is a *near-instantaneous execution at electronic speed*, provided the stock hasn't traded ahead. Also note that ARCA will attempt to "work" your order, first tapping the inside market and working toward your limit price, potentially providing price improvement along the way. But let's say for the sake of explanation that there is no liquidity available in any ECN at the current inside market.

3. Then ARCA will SNET preference each market maker individually, taking as much stock as possible. It uses a proprietary algorithm to dynamically decide which market maker to preference first, then sends a preference to him. Reportedly, Archipelago's routing algorithm seeks out those market makers who have transacted the most volume in the stock (the axes). This is a highly effective protocol. But if you're still not completely filled, turn to the next step.

4. Finally, ARCA repeats its process and keeps actively working the order until it is filled or until the limit price is reached. This is why you can enter market orders as well as limit orders on ARCA. If a limit order becomes unmarketable, or if it was entered as a limit outside the market to begin with, ARCA will post the order to the Nasdaq quotes montage, just like a standard ECN.

All of this happens faster than your eyes can track, with a single mouse click. Archipelago can fill massive orders nearly instantly. I have personally had an order of 10,000 shares fill in less than 10 seconds on Archipelago.

But one gaping hole in the armor of Archipelago renders it nearly useless in certain circumstances. The utilization of SelectNet, which makes Archipelago so powerful, is a double-edged sword.

You will recall from the section on SelectNet that a SelectNet preference against an ECN works at electronic speed. However, you will also recall that when a market maker receives a SelectNet preference, he is obligated to respond immediately *but is given a 30-second grace period.* Thirty seconds in a fast-moving market might as well be a lifetime. The stock can run like a freight train right past you while you wait for your order to be . . . to be . . . to be . . . *declined!* Then, as the stock continues tanking like a pile driver, the process repeats again and again and again.

Its creators were aware of this "chink" in the armor, and so made Archipelago work like this: When preferencing a market maker, ARCA will give the market maker only 30 seconds to respond. Whatever the reason, the market might move so much in this time as to make the execution unfavorable when it happens, so after 30 seconds, the preference to that market maker is canceled, and ARCA then preferences the next market maker.

But even with this operating method, however, ARCA can be rendered near useless. (Please note that once SuperSOES is completely rolled out, this problem should disappear.) Here is how it happens.

Let's say that ABCD stock, of which you own 4,000 shares, is a very active stock trading 10 million shares a day. Some major, terrible news just came out, and you need to sell now. You look on Level II, and you see very few buyers and many sellers queuing up. You can tell this in advance, because you have full access to the ARCA order book. On the bid there are all market makers, showing measly 100 share bids, to boot. And no other ECNs in sight. Now the stock starts trading down. Having had many near-instantaneous executions with Archipelago, you enter your order to sell 4,000 shares at market . . . and you wait. The stock goes crazy as everyone panics to get out. The price drops like a pile driver and you wait for your fill . . . and wait . . . and wait.

Finally, a seeming eternity later, you get filled, three points below the price when you entered. What happened? Well, there was a tremendous, extraordinary amount of supply, and very little demand. And into this market, you preferenced market makers and gave them the ability to decline you. And on top of it all, you gave them 30 seconds each!

Selling a large amount of a "crazy" stock into a tanking market requires finesse. This chapter is designed to give you just that. Thankfully, most stocks do not behave in the way just described. But it is just as well to know the possibilities and therefore not get caught unawares.

If you are long in a crazy, fast market stock (which I hope you aren't in too often; common sense tells you that these episodes of pure madness contain far too much risk), and there are no ECNs to be seen, the price is dropping fast, and you need to get out now, there is no single, simple solution. A very effective way to sell your position in this circumstance may be a SelectNet preference to the axe, at a price *lower* than the current best bid. You may find yourself saving time and money by forgoing one-sixteenth or one eighth in these circumstances and just plain getting out, rather than chasing the stock over hill and dale into the valley of the damned.

But what if, in the previous scenario with ABCD stock, you wanted to sell and there were no market makers at the bid? What if there were five or six ECNs on the bid (which, by the way, is very typical of such situations) and the ECNs show an aggregate total of shares well in excess of your 4,000? You place your order on ARCA, and . . . *wham*. You're done. Practically before you can move your fingers off the keypad!

Remember, a SelectNet Preference against an ECN fills nearly instantaneously, as long as there is available stock. And ARCA goes out to all ECNs automatically.

In many situations, Archipelago executes at light-speed; yet certain scenarios can render it nearly useless.

Archipelago also will not work with an odd lot of shares. It only accepts round-lot orders—orders placed in multiples of 100. So if you have 193 shares of ABCD stock, SOES or ISLD will be better alternatives, as ARCA simply won't accept your odd-lot order.

One of the most striking features of ARCA is that it often price-improves your order. Say you want to sell a stock, and you enter a limit price of $58\frac{1}{8}$. If the current bid is *higher* than $58\frac{1}{8}$, ARCA will "work" the order, hitting bids all the way down to your limit level. This is convenient if you want to sell the stock now, but you don't want to offer it and wait for someone to come along and buy it from you, and you have a limit price you feel comfortable with. ARCA also works this way on the buy side.

ARCA accepts market orders too but I advise against using them unless you're sure there is adequate liquidity at the price you like. The reason is this: A sudden onslaught of market orders can whipsaw a price down, only to get filled with a lousy print. The concept here is similar to a SOES market order.

ARCA's use of SelectNet creates some interesting situations and points of confusion. A common misunderstanding is as follows.

You see a stock like one pictured in the Level II screen in Figure 6.10. You see all these "chippies" bidding much higher than the current market and want to transact with them; so you place an order to sell at that price, and wait. Nothing happens. In frustration, finally you cancel the order and sell some other way, at a reduced

figure 6.10   a common misunderstanding through ARCA's use of SelectNet

	E-NET INC										_ □ ✕
ETEL			5 11/32	↑	+2 11/32		500		Os	9:46	
High	5 1/2		Low	4			Acc. Vol.	1370800			
Bid	5 23/32		Ask	5 3/4			Close	3			

	Name	Bid	Chg.	Time	#Best		Name	Ask	Chg.	Time	#Best
p	ARCHIP	5 3/4	+0	9:47	1	P	ARCHIP	5 1/2	+0	9:47	0
P	ARCHIP	5 3/4	+0	9:47	1	O	HRZG	5 3/4	+0	9:47	0
P	ARCHIP	5 3/4	+0	9:47	1	O	USCT	5 3/4	+0	9:47	2
P	ARCHIP	5 3/4	+0	9:47	1	O	SLKC	5 13/1(	+1/8	9:47	0
O	ARCHIP	5 3/4	+0	9:47	1	O	INCA	5 7/8	-3/8	9:47	0
P	ARCHIP	5 3/4	+0	9:47	1	O	MASH	5 7/8	-1/8	9:47	3
P	ARCHIP	5 3/4	+0	9:47	1	O	BRUT	5 7/8	+1/8	9:47	0
O	ISLD	5 23/3:	+0	9:47	14	O	ISLD	5 7/8	+0	9:47	7
O	NITE	5 23/3:	+0	9:47	1	O	FAHN	5 7/8	+7/3	9:47	4
O	REDI	5 11/1(	+3/1	9:47	2	O	GRUN	5 7/8	+0	9:47	1
O	ARCA	5 5/8	+0	9:47	9	O	ARCA	5 15/1(	-7/1	9:47	2
O	ARCHIP	5 5/8	+0	9:47	1	O	ARCHIP	5 15/1(	+0	9:47	0
O	ARCHIP	5 5/8	+0	9:47	0	O	REDI	5 15/1(	+0	9:47	0
O	ARCHIP	5 5/8	+0	9:47	0	O	BACH	6	+1/8	9:47	0
O	ARCHIP	5 5/8	+0	9:47	0	O	WIEN	6	+0	9:36	0
O	SHWD	5 5/8	+0	9:47	1	O	HILL	6	+0	9:43	0

price. Why did this happen? Those "chippies" bidding higher than the Nasdaq bid are actually using SelectNet to preference market participants at those higher price levels—they're *not* bidding in the Level II quotes. Remember, SelectNet preferences never show in the Level II quotes because they are like "private messages." So how can you see them? Access to the ARCA book enables you to see what is going on in ARCA's order book. ARCA shows what it is doing. (It may be utilizing SelectNet, but ARCA still will let you in on what the individual ARCA orders are.) But you cannot execute against someone's preference order to a third party. All you can do is wait and hope that he doesn't get his stock and that when ARCA runs through its progressions again, it'll match with you. In practice, it is nigh impossible to execute against these bids.

ARCA offers some interesting order capabilities, including reserve size, conditional orders, and stop orders. Of course, your brokerage house may or may not enable this additional functionality.

- *Reserve size.* ARCA will allow you to "show" a chosen number of shares to the market at large while you really have a much larger order "in reserve." An example: You show 200 shares in the quotes montage, but you really have a reserve size of 2,800. What you are trying to do is offer some small amount of shares out, which won't scare the market, while you really are offering many more. Repeated executions get you done. Ever seen a market maker sit on the bid with 100 shares but watch in confusion as 10,000 go by while he still shows 100? This is what's happening. Use reserves with caution, as some brokerages charge a commission every time a trade equal to the "shown size" executes. Check with your brokerage and determine if it supports reserve size orders, and, if so, find out how much it charges for commissions for this kind of order.

- *Conditional orders.* These offer a unique and unprecedented breakthrough in the retail brokerage business. Conditional orders allow you to create a set of conditions and then set up "if/then" orders based on those conditions. A conditional order might be: If the Dow drops 100 points intraday, place order to buy 1,000 AOL at 62½. Since the conditions are programmable and infinite, you are limited only by your imagination.

- *Stop orders.* ARCA offers stop orders.

ARCA trades in the aftermarket

You can use Archipelago to buy or sell stock pre- or postmarket and on weekends too. Orders entered in Archipelago during market hours expire at 4:02 P.M. EST. However, you may enter orders after 4:02 that will stay live, viewable in the Level II quotes montage until they cancel at 5:00 P.M. EST. And at 5:01 you can enter the order again, and it will stay live until midnight PST. In addition, your orders may be placed before market, starting at 8:45 A.M. EST. Archipelago intends to become the 24-hour trading vehicle of choice, open round the clock to all who have access to its ECN.

ARCA Advantages

- Accepts market and limit orders.
- Will actively "work" the order using Nasdaq's order systems as well as passively post to the Nasdaq Level II quotes montage, allowing for quick multiple fills in certain situations.
- Order book appears right in the Level II montage.
- Buy or sell before or after market hours.

ARCA Disadvantages

- Accepts round-lot orders only.
- Archipelago's utilization of SelectNet when only market makers are present can cause slow to no execution, particularly during fast market conditions. However, once SuperSOES is totally rolled out, this problem may be alleviated, at least with regard to Nasdaq National Market stocks.

general notes on Archipelago

Many traders do the majority of their trading through Archipelago. Trades executed in the Archipelago order book are often near instantaneous, as are trades executed when ECNs are on the inside bid or offer.

You can move large amounts of stock in minimal time through judicious use of Archipelago. Additionally, you often pay only one transaction charge per order on Archipelago, regardless of the number of partial fills.

In selling 5,000 shares of stock, it is easy to imagine getting 10 or 20 partial prints as the order is being filled. On Archipelago, the charge may be . . . only *one* transaction. However, if any of the executions are against ECNs that charge per share for doing business with them, those ECN charges would be passed along to the individual. Those charges (recall $.015 a share for trades with InstiNet) are not insignificant, and must be weighed against the benefits of holding the position or using alternate routes.

ARCA experiences
As mentioned before, I've had near-instantaneous fills on orders of up to 10,000 shares. You will have to try ARCA when many ECNs are on bid/offer to fully experience its potential. So here I'll concentrate on the danger of ARCA: its speed.

The setup: I was going to execute an order for 10,000 shares of a very volatile stock. I was a bit nervous because of the size, but I'd decided the moment was now, and for the full amount. So I'd been watching carefully with my finger on the trigger (my order entry screen filled out completely, and my finger on the mouse button, ready to strike) for enough ECN liquidity to appear at the inside price to fill the majority of my order. As you may have noticed, in really volatile stocks, often a tremendous, fluttering ECN-driven liquidity appears at the inside market. The key was to wait (seconds) until enough ECNs lined up to fill most of my order. Suddenly things resolved: ISLD, INCA, REDI, BRUT, and BTRD all appeared at the inside best. This was an ideal situation. I "clicked" automatically, without hesitation, instincts primed and honed, milliseconds after recognition. Within seconds, partial fills started covering my order entry screen.

But something was wrong, terribly wrong! I wanted to *sell*, not *buy*! I had clicked the *wrong button*, and partial buys were filling my screen with a vengeance! My entire erroneous order filled right before my eyes! In slow motion I saw my hand drive the cursor over the cancel button, but by the time I clicked it, I had my total complete fill: 10,000 shares of a stock I not only didn't want, I wanted to sell!

The lesson is: ARCA truly is a fast vehicle, given proper circumstances and use. Use it wisely; it *will* do what you ask.

Speer, Leeds and Kellog (REDI)

Speer, Leeds and Kellogg (REDI) is an "active" ECN that is rapidly gaining favor and market share among active traders. Redi is also a front-end order execution system used by institutions and individuals associated with institutions. It operates in a very similar fashion to Archipelago but differs in one very important respect (this is why it is rapidly gaining favor): In its order routing protocol, when it uses SelectNet to send orders to market makers, it does not go to the axe (as ARCA does). It goes to whoever has the most size available first. This may seem like a commonsense winning situation, but there are valid reasons for going to the axe. It is all a matter of choice. Many active traders have told me that this small change makes all the difference. Transacting with the REDI ECN costs $.015 a share, buy or sell, and REDI will not transact with odd-lot orders.

effect of SuperSOES on REDI

REDI is an "active" ECN—meaning that it will actively work orders for you. You are not limited to simply bidding and offering with REDI; its active features do much more. Essentially, REDI currently (and until SuperSOES is completely rolled out) uses the Nasdaq's SelectNet to work your orders. But its functionality may change with SuperSOES rollout, at least with respect to the handling of orders in Nasdaq National Market stocks. Because SuperSOES has auto-execution, its use should provide instant fills—as compared to the current SelectNet system, where market makers who are "preferenced" have 30 seconds to respond. So, overall, the new system should really speed REDI up, at least in regard to executions against market makers in Nasdaq National Market stocks. But, of course, REDI may decide to accept auto-executions. If it does accept them, it will be further enhanced. If it doesn't, your bids and offers will receive orders sent to it via SelectNet, which will be near instant, as compared to the truly instant "automatic execution" feature of SuperSOES.

general notes on REDI
All "active" ECNs have similar attributes and differ mostly in smaller details—and, of course, in overall liquidity. I chose to describe one active ECN—ARCA—fully. With that example in mind, look at the small differences between the "active" ECNs: REDI brings tremendous liquidity to the table, mostly from institutions. But as more and more day traders are discovering just how much of a difference a small change in the execution algorithm can make, active trader-driven liquidity in this ECN is increasing by leaps and bounds.

Attain (ATTN)

Attain (ATTN) is the active ECN owned and operated by the electronic brokerage All Tech Securities. Founded by electronic trading revolutionary Harvey Houtkin, author of the seminal book *The SOES Bandit*, the ECN is part of a complete trading platform offered by the brokerage of the same name. ATTN tries to match stock in its own order book; if it hasn't completed the order, it uses SelectNet to link all ECNs at the price specified. If it still hasn't filled the order completely, it will preference market makers at the inside market. Finally, if it still has not transacted, it will post to the Nasdaq quotes montage. Similar to Archipelago, during fast market situations or when no market makers are on the bid, ATTN's efficiency is greatly reduced, making it especially susceptible to partially filled or canceled orders.

effect of SuperSOES on ATTN
ATTN is an active ECN—meaning that it will actively work orders for you. You are not limited to simply bidding and offering with ATTN; its active features do much more. Essentially, ATTN currently (and until SuperSOES is completely rolled out) uses the Nasdaq's SelectNet to work your orders. But its functionality may change with SuperSOES rollout, at least with respect to the handling of orders in Nasdaq National Market stocks. Because SuperSOES has auto-execution, its use should provide instant fills—as compared to the current SelectNet system, where market makers who are "preferenced" have 30 seconds

to respond. So, overall, the new system should really speed ATTN up, at least in regard to executions against market makers in Nasdaq National Market stocks. But, of course, ATTN may decide not to accept auto-executions. If it does accept them, it will be further enhanced. If it doesn't, your bids and offers will receive orders sent to it via Select-Net, which will be near instant, as compared to the truly instant "automatic execution" feature of SuperSOES.

Even if you have direct access to its order book, ATTN is not enabled to show it. Having access to view the limit orders in the book is arguably a great advantage, one that ATTN currently does not support.

Another interesting feature that ATTN has that the other ECNs don't is called "Hit the Street." You'll have access to it only if your broker has enabled this function. This feature *preferences all market makers at the inside market with the* full *size of the order.* Obviously, this may result in a more than complete fill, since all market makers will have an incoming liability order and must respond by accepting in full, partialling, or declining. This function is available only to the better traders and for good reason: If all market makers accept, you may wind up owning who knows how many shares. However, if there are only one or two market makers at the bid/offer, and the combined size is much less than you've got to transact, you can achieve a fast and favorable fill with minimal effort using "Hit the Street." The risk, of course, is that you will overfill; however, if your experience and observation tell you that the market makers at the inside market are not size buyers on the day, then you might just get a great fill with minimal effort. *"Youse pays your money, youse takes your chances!"* Clearly a cutting-edge feature, not recommended for the inexperienced or faint of heart.

ATTN will accept orders and post them in the Nasdaq montage after hours, much like the other ECNs.

ATTN offers point-and-click order changes, if your broker has enabled this functionality. (It was the first to offer this money-saving feature.) In using other ECNs, you must first click on the live order to cancel it, wait for the cancel to be confirmed, then reenter the order at a new price. ATTN has a nifty feature that will cancel the order for you and automatically reenter it. It works in the following way: you "click" the order, then "click" on a little arrow button to raise or lower the price, and then hit ENTER. The old order will be canceled and the new order entered. This feature saves time and aggravation when changing an order. In reality, the order still has to be canceled by the Nasdaq in the same way as if you just pressed CANCEL. But in a fast-moving stock, seconds count, and this, I'm told, is a very useful feature which may save you money.

ATTN Advantages

- Accepts market and limit orders.
- Will actively "work" the order as well as post to the Nasdaq quotes montage; can buy at bid or sell at ask.
- Preferences other ECNs and market makers through SelectNet.
- Buy or sell before or after market hours.
- No extra charges for doing business with ATTN.
- Point and click raise/lower price.
- "Hit the Street" function.
- After-market trading.

ATTN Disadvantages

- Accepts round-lot orders only.
- No visible order book.
- ATTN's utilization of SelectNet when only market makers are present can cause slow to no execution, particularly during fast market conditions.

general notes on ATTN
ATTN has suffered lately from a comparative lack of liquidity. ISLD total volume and REDI total volume have surpassed ATTN by huge leaps and bounds. It's hard to say why; it may be due to more effective marketing plans by competitors. Users of ATTN swear by it. Clearly, it is a good system, created by a true market reformer. It is said that Harry Houtkin has single-handedly changed the markets. I

believe it. His influence on the day-trading phenomenon is truly unique.

Bloomberg Trade Book
Bloomberg Trade Book (BTRD) is used by mainly institutions and individuals associated with institutions (money managers, etc.).

It is run by Bloomberg, the incomparable news/analysis/research provider. Generally only institutional clients have access to Bloomberg terminals due to the high price. However, you often will see BTRD bidding or offering in the Nasdaq montage, ready to be executed against. And through SelectNet (and Archipelago as well) you may transact with BTRD. At the time of this writing, BTRD charges a fee of $.015 a share to those who do business with it (both buys and sells).

Brass Utility
Also used mainly by brokerage houses and institutions, the Brass Utility (BRUT) is more than an ECN. It is a full-featured, position-minding, front-end order execution system. However, now BRUT is confining itself to institution-originated business. Rumor has it that it may open its doors to individual traders in the near future; a market can be ignored only for so long. For now, the cost of transacting with BRUT is $.015 a share, both buy side and sell side. You may transact against it through SelectNet and the active ECNs as well.

BRUT will not transact with odd-lot orders.

NITE Securities
I've included NITE Securities (NITE) here since there seems to be some confusion as to whether it is an ECN or not. NITE is reportedly the very largest market maker in the Nasdaq. It trades staggering volume and is gaining in volume daily. NITE runs an internal ECN of sorts; it uses Brass Utility (BRUT) as a front-end order matching and entry system. If you were an institutional client, it is possible that you would be filled within NITE's book. If not, NITE would bid or offer in the Nasdaq as "NITE" (market maker) or "BRUT" (ECN), or through any of the other ECNs available.

Since NITE is a market maker, it can be executed against through SOES, SelectNet, and the active ECNs.

Midwest Stock Exchange

Midwest Stock Exchange (MWSE) is not an ECN, nor is it a market maker. MWSE is a facility of the exchange, as described next. Because of its unusual status—and despite the fact that it makes de facto markets in so many issues—MWSE is able to avoid the obligations of normal market makers. I do not know what the actual statistics are (and I think the Securities and Exchange Commission should do a study), but my personal experience and that of many traders I talk with is the following: MWSE is unlikely to give a good print. Maybe it is just that it plays the game better than I do and is always one step ahead. Since MWSE is a facility of the exchange, it technically may not be guilty of backing away; I don't know. All I know is that if I have a choice, I'll try to trade with someone else.

SuperDot: the order execution facility of the New York Stock Exchange

Unlike the Nasdaq, which is a negotiated system in which many market participants bid and offer competitively, thereby theoretically creating a fairer, more efficient market, the listed exchanges utilize the "specialist" system with a centralized order book. The order book contains all of the buy and sell limit orders placed in the particular stock as well as all the market-on-close/market-on-open orders. The orders drive the market; supply and demand rules, with an administrator in between: the specialist.

One person, the specialist, controls the order book and sets the prices according to supply and demand. America Online (AOL) traded nearly 100 million shares in a single day recently; how could one person oversee so much volume? (In the future, people will probably read this and say 100 million; that's *it*?)

Since the specialist knows where all the limit orders are (i.e., many sellers at 30, many buyers at 28½), he is in a unique position to manipulate the market to his advantage—which he does. When a huge order to buy comes to him from a floor broker representing a large mutual fund, say a mutual fund that is a buyer of 100,000 shares of GE, the specialist says, "What a coincidence; I have these stocks too," and participates along with the buy, maybe even selling shares back to the buyer as the price rises. Being a specialist is special indeed. It is a license to make nearly risk-free money, and gobs of it. This is one way that the specialist is compensated for managing the huge risk involved in creating an orderly market.

To be fair, the real risk a specialist faces is a downturn or crash, where an inordinate amount of sell orders come in, and he is forced to make a market and take the other side all the way down "to the mats," as they say. In this case he may quickly run through all his capital and be forced to mortgage everything he has, but *fast*, and then borrow to the max from all of the investment houses. During the crash of 1929 and again in 1987, the markets came precipitously close to not opening again because the banks (which were contractually obligated to back the specialists) refused to come up with the necessary cash. But I digress.

The SuperDot is the proprietary, electronic link to the specialist's order book. It is available as a point-and-click routing option on all the better trading platforms. Orders entered and executed through it are said to go through "the machine," as opposed to one of the floor brokers, who also bring orders to the specialist. Many times large institutional players prefer to engage the services of floor brokers, as those brokers are in a unique position to see what's going on in a stock (even though nobody but the specialist gets to view the order book).

Since the order book for each stock is centralized (there is only one "market maker"—the specialist—whereas in the Nasdaq, many market makers possess various orders and negotiate openly for the best price), market and limit as well as stop orders and stop limit orders are accepted, as are GTC (Good Till Cancel) orders; all may be entered via SuperDot. If orders are for more than 1,000 shares, they may be automatically matched and executed by the machine. Note that there is only one true market participant, the specialist; the price he sets is the price where the stock trades. Unmarketable orders will sit in the order book and await the stock to trade to a marketable level. However, you can bid or offer stock; the specialist is required to display your size along with his.

Several traders I know who like to scalp often find NYSE stocks with high volume, but little to no volatility, that trade within a certain established range and buy at the bid and turn around and sell at the offer. One trader I know employs this as a regular strategy, scalping an eighth or three-sixteenths a dozen times a day on 900 shares. This is an odd strategy, and one that I believe the specialists are relatively unprepared for, when compared with market makers on the Nasdaq. It is not, however an m.o. that I would seriously consider.

Specialists often fill smaller-size bids and offers without moving their market. Remember, specialists get paid by the exchange on a per-share basis for the number of shares transacted; and if they see small orders long enough, often they'll fill them.

According to studies regarding price improvement on the exchanges, small orders (less than 300 shares) done on the NYSE tend to receive price improvements a small majority of the time.

Figure 6.11 is a screen shot of AOL, a listed security. For all intents and purposes, you really don't need to pay too much attention to the regional exchanges—likely, you won't be able to transact on them anyway. The NYS (short for NYSE) is the one you need to watch. The regional exchanges generally follow the NYSE's pricing cues. However, if you can execute on the regionals in a timely manner, occasionally arbitrage opportunities do exist—a listed exchange may

figure 6.11 AOL

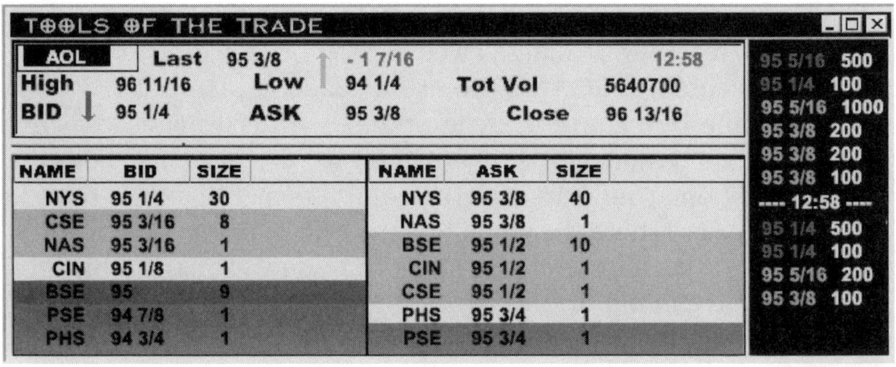

be slow to update a price and you may be able to profit from an offer that's lower than the current New York bid. But these cases are few and far between. Figure 6.11 shows what the listed quotations look like; they look basically the same in any software package. Please keep in mind that SuperDot is not the only way to transact NYSE stocks. The ECNs have recently begun to trade listed stocks. Over time, ECN-driven liquidity may grow to the point where there is a ready market in the ECNs for the trading of listed stocks, just as there currently is for Nasdaq stocks.

chapter 7

order routing grid

In this chapter I present graphical representations of information in the previous chapters. Please use the figures for reference only. For ease of representation, I've broken market conditions into four categories: slow market, normal market, fast market, and crazy market. It is hoped that this sort of breakdown will facilitate understanding the mind-set you must have when executing—market conditions are very relevant. And, since the nature of the negotiated markets is constant change, there is no single sure-fire route. You must analyze all relevant factors and make the best choice based on your knowledge and interpretation of the situation. The following charts do not represent the be-all and end-all to routing. Your comprehension of the situation at hand does. Also, keep in mind that SuperSOES is often going to be your best bet, especially if the ECNs decide to participate in auto-execution. The following grid supposes you cannot use SuperSOES. Please read it with this in mind. Furthermore, don't attempt to use these grids while executing. These are for review purposes only; and any time taken away from the screen when you need to execute will be time poorly spent—or worse, expensively spent.

fast market conditions

Fast market conditions exist not only when the Nasdaq advises all participants of a "fast market condition," but also all the time in certain stocks. If you are trading a stock with an average daily volume in the several millions, and the volume available at the inside market usually is on the order of several hundred shares (not the many, many thousands of shares that tends to limit volatility), you are trading a stock that I call a fast market stock. Such stocks are much more difficult to trade, given their general lack of liquidity at the inside market and the volatility that they also generally exhibit. Often the price/size of participants will change before you can even enter an order. In trading these stocks, consider strategy first. It may be necessary to accept the loss of an eighth right away (and just get out) rather than offering stock out repeatedly, chasing the stock down, and finally losing three-quarters or much more due to greed. Or at least lack of planning. *Note:* If you get stuck trying to liquidate an odd lot (say 932 shares), often it is better to sell the round-lot number of shares first (in this case 900 shares) because a round lot opens you up to many more order-routing possibilities. Of course you will incur an extra commission doing this, and I don't like that sort of slippage . . . but consider: $25 extra commission, plus the loss you will incur when you SOES out of your 32 remaining shares (say $1 on 32 shares, or $32) for a total "charge" of $57 vs. the potential one-point loss on the entire 932 shares ($932!). Common sense will tell you: Get out of the majority of your shares the quickest way possible, then pick up the pieces.

Please review the following commonsense approach in Figure 7.1 fast market conditions diagram. And try to stay away from these stocks until you are confident of your knowledge and on-your-feet thinking. Buying or selling in fast market conditions requires finesse.

slow market conditions

Slow market conditions are the most straightforward conditions in which to trade. Since many slow stocks also have low average volume, several unique situations may be present. One situation is that the axe in the stock may show several thousand shares on the bid/offer at any

figure 7.1   fast market routing

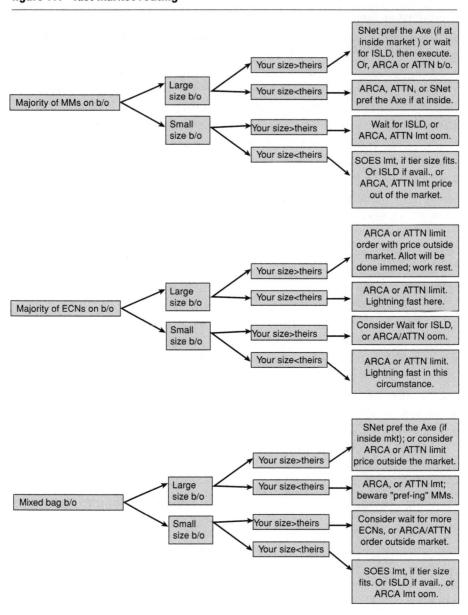

b/o: bid or offered; oom: out-of-market

given time. Often these slow-moving stocks (ones nobody cares about) are not traded actively by day traders; consequently, market makers feel a little freer to show the world what they are doing. Sometimes they wish to attract buyers or sellers by showing size. But beware: The stocks with the smallest float and the smallest average daily volume are often the most volatile ones if there is sudden tremendous interest. So if you've just found out about a stock (because it's launching a new Web site or something) and it normally trades 15,000 shares a day, but today it's already traded 4 million, throw all "slow market" ideas out the window. See the crazy market conditions section if that is the case. But there also may be few shares shown at the inside market as well. If so, it is of real importance to determine who the axe is. In these sorts of stocks, the axe often controls a truly disproportionate amount of liquidity. Watch for him and try to do business with him; he'll have the orders or inventory to facilitate your trade. One note: If the stock you are trading doesn't trade many shares (relatively speaking), beware offering out large size. In a stock that trades 20,000 shares daily, with market makers showing small size (100 to 500 shares), an offer of 5,000 shares can really affect the market. Market makers may lower their bids, and you may get stuck with nothing done. One more thought: Often in slow-moving, low-volume stocks, there are few ECNs to be found. This is another good reason to know the axe. Take a look at Chapter 4 for how to find the axe in a stock that doesn't trade. (Because no shares may have traded today, Level II information like #Best or Hammer may be useless.)

With thinly-traded stocks, it may be difficult to trade size without affecting the market. Always think strategy first, if trading large size. Figure 7.2 is written with an interest in transacting as opposed to offering out or bidding out and waiting. Keep in mind that this discussion is not meant to encourage trading these sorts of stocks—it is simply meant to help you facilitate execution, if you do.

normal market conditions

Normal market conditions are what we experience every day in the vast majority of stocks. Unfortunately, many times we find ourselves trading "crazy" stocks, in crazy market conditions. (See the next section for an explanation.) If you are wondering if the stock you are trading falls

figure 7.2   slow market routing

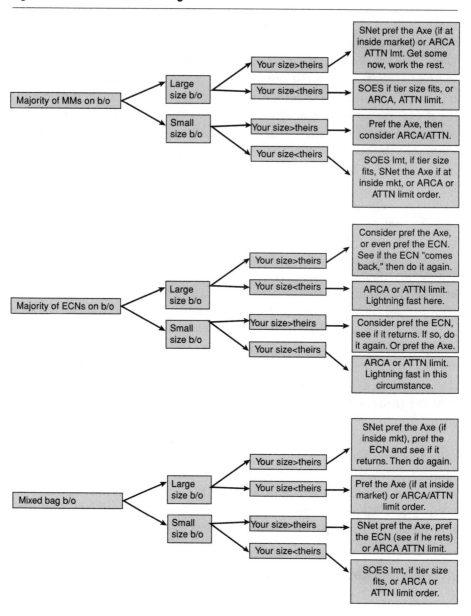

into the "normal" category, ask yourself the following questions. Is the stock an initial public offering? Has major news with huge consequences for this stock just hit the market? Is this a thinly-traded security on an average day? Is this stock a "high-flying Internet" stock? If you answered yes to any of these questions, chances are you are not trading a normal market condition stock.

My definition of normal market conditions is an arbitrary one. For ease of discussion, I've divided the market into several "conditions" that will affect your trading. Normal conditions are those in which there is a typical amount of volume trading in that stock (typical for the stock on a month-to-month basis) and the events of the day are devoid of any major news concerning the stock. So it may be that Dell computer has traded 10 million shares today; this is normal. It is a volatile stock, but there is enough liquidity to dampen the moves. There is almost always enough liquidity in this stock to enter or exit a position of small size (under 1,000 shares) at one price. There are almost always several thousand shares bid or offered at any given time. This is in contrast to the high-flying Internet stocks, which often have so few shares bid/offered that often the price changes before you can even type in your order. (Thank goodness for macros and hot keys.) In trading normal market condition stocks, you really need to consider the amount of liquidity available before entering an order. For example, in a stock with big volume, offering out when trying to sell might be a great idea—as long as 100,000 shares aren't offered alongside yours. With a huge amount of volume trading and relatively few shares offered alongside yours, chances are that your inside market offer may get taken. But if the stock is tanking hard, and there are 100,000 shares offered already, you might want to reconsider and actually sell your stock now. In the language of chess, you must always consider the efficacy of sacrificing your pawn (the one-sixteenth more you might make—or *not* lose) to save your king. In other words, when you need to be out, don't make the mistake of offering out over and over while watching the stock plummet. REDI, ARCA and ATTN will work the order for you by placing it with a price below the current market. Consider accepting the loss of a sixteenth or an eighth in order to just get out and be done with it. Bottom line: If you decide you need to sell now, do it. Don't mess around and put yourself at risk for a sixteenth. Please examine the routing chart in Figure 7.3, and try to

figure 7.3   normal market routing

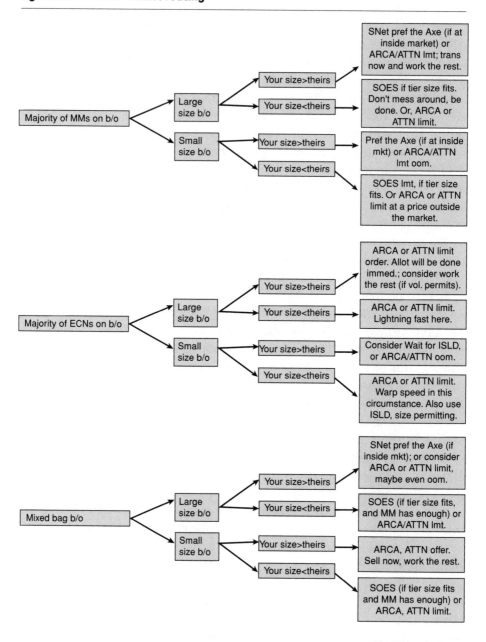

understand the reasoning behind it. Once you understand the reasons, you won't need to look at it again.

crazy market conditions

There is no "diagram" for crazy market conditions. In crazy market conditions (which occur everyday), the price and market participant field will change faster than you can possibly type in an order. Finesse with a capital F is required in these situations, and a simple chart just won't do it. You'll be busy trying to read a diagram and remove your focus from the market, where it needs to be.

Try not to trade in this condition until you have fully mastered Level II interpretation and all the execution systems. To do otherwise is to accept huge, crushing risk with negligible upside.

In a crazy market situation, you will need crystal-clear concentration. You will need to anticipate the "local move" in advance, and enter your order with the next 30 seconds in mind. You will need to watch and plan your strategy in real time, maybe even sitting with an order ready, finger "on the trigger," waiting for the market participants on screen to resolve into a situation favorable for the sort of order you are placing, before executing it. You may have to sacrifice a pawn to save a king here. Countless times I've heard from traders who have, because of ego and greed, chased a stock down, placing order after order—offering out—in a stock that was dropping like a rocket-powered pile driver, only to be repeatedly passed over and declined until they sold at the very bottom (when buyers finally came back in and bought the stock at the very low), losing several points on large orders. In trading crazy markets, you must be "pound wise. . . ."

Remember your size: On 99 shares the loss of one point isn't really significant, but on 6,000 shares it's crushing.

Don't sweat the "tiny" shares. If you have 932 shares, and this is a stock where you can't use SuperSOES, do yourself a favor and sell 900 first; 900 is a round lot and you open yourself up to many more routing opportunities this way. If you sell your 900 right away, you won't really sweat a loss of one point on 32 shares. Get out of the majority of your position, then consider SOES for the rest. (Just be done with it!)

In crazy market situations, market maker size will almost always be smaller than you've got—and it requires skill and finesse to sell even 100 shares into a crazy, tanking market. In these moments, you must function exactly like an athlete; your responses must be automatic and conditioned.

- *RE: Market Maker Size in a Crazy Market:* If this is a Nasdaq National Market stock, and you can use SuperSOES, it is an important consideration. However, in small caps, where you can't use SuperSOES, it is irrelevant, unless a market maker is at the inside market, or you have very few shares (100, for example). Why? Because there is so much volume and confusion in the fray that in all likelihood you will be declined.

- *RE: ECN Size in a Crazy Market:* Disappears right before your eyes. Consider the ISLD trick of getting an order ready and keeping your finger on the trigger until ISLD appears, then execute. Your execution, routed through the ISLD system, will trade ahead of all the others trying to "link" to ISLD through SelectNet (as well as any of the ECNs that don't participate in auto-execution, too). Or wait for the field to resolve into many ECNs gathered there at the same time, then hit the ARCA or ATTN button and be done.

- *RE: Odd Lots in a Crazy Non-SuperSOES Market:* Worry about odd lots *after* transacting the majority of your shares. Always keep a calculator with big numbers beside you to keep your positions clear in your head, then use SOES or an ECN.

Understand Level II. Go over the routing system explanations in earlier chapters. Know what they do and in what situations to use them. Use the charts as handy references to remind you. But please, don't use them too much. You really have to learn how the tools work, as every situation is different, and in the end it is your own knowledge, judgment, and experience that will make the day.

chapter 8

complete guide to selling short

He that sells what isn't his'n
must get it back or go to prison

Short selling is the converse of buying long. When you buy a stock (go "long"), you hope for appreciation in price. At some point you would sell the stock and keep the profit—the difference between the cost basis (purchase price) and the sell price. The phrase "Buy low, sell high" is often heard.

But buying low and selling high is only half the story. Suppose you found a stock that is a real loser, one that is going to go down (depreciate) in price. It is possible to take a bet on this too, by "selling high, *then* buying low" and keeping the profit. This is the difference between the price the stock was sold for and the price at which it was purchased to cover and close the position.

In a nutshell it works like this. First, you *borrow* the stock from a willing lender and sell the stock, receiving cash. Later, when the price has dropped, you simply buy the stock back and *return the stock to the lender*, keeping the profit: the difference between the sale price and the purchase price. The aspects of borrowing and returning the stock will be covered later.

Selling "short" is basically the same as selling stock you own; the key difference is that you don't own the stock to begin with; you borrow it. The designation "short" simply refers to this fact. When you sell a stock you own, it is called a "long" sale.

So, you can profit not only by the price of a stock going up *but also by the price of the stock going down.*

For example, a global cell phone communications provider traded as high as $57 last year. Fantastic ads showed a picture of Planet Earth with the words "Welcome to your new calling zone." Being a technogadget nut, I had to have one of these phones. I checked on the company and found that it incurred mind-boggling debt in order to finance the launch of its many satellites and had tremendously optimistic goals for new subscribers. But again, being the technogadget nut that I am, I had to have one of these phones—even though at $3,000, the cost of the phone was admittedly steep. And that didn't even include airtime, which also was priced amazingly high. But I figured "Okay, so the phone's extortionate, and the airtime is just as bad, but, hey: It's a global phone! People will eat this up!" And then I tried to buy the phone. And tried. And tried. Not once ever, could I get an account rep on the phone—the regular old $25 version I keep at home. Nor could I reach them by e-mail! I sent literally dozens of e-mails, and only received one response: from an account rep in Indonesia! My opinion of this company began to change. "Okay," I said to myself, "this *is* an expensive product with a limited potential subscribership. And okay, the company could conceivably go bankrupt if it misses their skyscraper-high debt payments. But what a product!" Of course I'd never seen one, because apparently, the company didn't want my money! And then I talked with friends. They had received exactly the same response as I—nothing! We talked jokingly about how we should "short this piece of crap company that doesn't want our business." But because we were still in love with the idea, none of us did. Silly me.

Invariably it is bad to let business decisions be motivated by emotions. Add this one to the list of missed opportunities, because one year later, the company has missed all its subscription goals. Wonder why? And it has missed its debt payments, and it has filed for bankruptcy. And the stock halted trading, at about $4 a share.

what selling short means

There are a few things you must know in order to sell short. Understanding the concept of short selling is very important, since once you do, you will be able to identify and understand potential situations as they arise. So now the hard stuff.

First, you must find a stock that is available for borrowing. Not all stocks are available for this purpose. Your brokerage house will keep an updated list of those stocks that are borrowable. If the brokerage house is doing its job, it will have a list that updates frequently, maybe even changing daily if the brokerage is really on the ball. The best brokerages have a person in charge of aggressively pursuing shares of otherwise unavailable stocks. At some brokerages, you can even call in and request a stock for borrowing, and they will try and locate some shares for you.

What makes a stock borrowable? Well, first of all, all stocks available for borrowing are marginable. (See Chapter 11 for a complete explanation of what margin means.) When a stock is marginable, it essentially means that the Federal Reserve has decided that brokerages may make loans toward the purchase of these stocks, in a special kind of account called a margin account. Please note that the Fed has in no way passed on the merits of these securities, it has simply given the banks permission to make loans toward the purchase of these stocks subject to Regulation T (Reg T) of the Securities Exchange Act of 1934.

The clearinghouses themselves determine which stocks they are willing to lend for the purposes of short selling. Often clearinghouses *sell* their lists of borrowable stocks to banks and brokerages. This is why it is so important to use a brokerage that aggressively pursues short "inventory."

All short sales *must* take place in a margin account. When you are attempting to *borrow* stock, someone must *lend* the stock to you. *Therefore, only marginable stocks may be sold short.* (See Chapter 11 for some good rules of thumb for determining which stocks are marginable.)

One more very important rule: Short sales must be affected on up-ticks. This makes the game a little more difficult, since you can't simply wait till the stock is tanking and then place an order to sell short. And shorting over-the-counter (Nasdaq) stocks is different from shorting listed (exchange traded) stocks (NYSE, AMEX, etc.).

- *Shorting Nasdaq stocks.* You may only short stocks on the Nasdaq subject to the bid test rule. This rule asks: "Is the current bid higher than the last bid?" If so, then you can sell short. You can also offer stock out short *at a price at least one-sixteenth higher than the current bid.* If the stock is bought from you, you have legally effected your short sale. For example, say the fictional Nasdaq National Market stock ABCD is currently bid $10, offered $10\frac{1}{8}$, and is on a down-tick. You can offer out stock "short" for sale at $10\frac{1}{16}$, or $10\frac{1}{8}$, or any price higher. If someone buys it from you, you have effected your short sale. You cannot legally sell the stock "short" at 10, since it is on a down-tick.

- *Shorting listed stocks.* You may short a stock on the listed exchanges subject to the zero-plus tick rule. This states that you may short a stock on an up-tick or a zero-plus tick: The stock is on an up-tick if the current bid is higher than the last bid. A zero-plus tick means that the stock was at an up-tick but has since traded at the current offer without the bid having moved. So, in other words, the stock was on a plus tick, and since then has traded but not moved price-wise.

Keep in mind that, just like a long position, a short position can be held indefinitely. You have no more obligation to close a short position than a long one, except under extremely unusual conditions. More information on closing a short position is found later in this chapter in the section on the risks of selling short.

how to sell short

The best order execution platforms have a button or a box that you check to designate that the sale will be short. Basically, you are telling the brokerage house that you don't own the stock; you're going to borrow it. Once you check the box, you *simply sell the stock.* The clearinghouse takes care of the borrow automatically. Keep in mind that selling borrowed stock is the same as selling stock you own, except you are subject to margin rules and short sale rules—and you *must* designate the sale as short. To make things easier, most better day trading platforms have an error window that pops up if the stock is not borrowable; it will say something like "order deleted—for the reason: the security is not borrowable."

So let's say this stock is a borrowable one. You check the "short" box on your order entry screen and place a sell short order on the Island one-sixteenth above the bid. Several moments later you receive a transaction confirmation: *Sold Short 1000 ABCD stock.* Several minutes after the sale, more sellers come in, and soon the stock's price starts tanking as fewer market participants are willing to pay top dollar to purchase it.

The price continues its drop, and after a few moments, the several-point drop causes the price to drop below its 50- and 200-day moving averages, where it's been hovering and testing for the last several days. Now the mutual fund managers see what's happening and begin to liquidate their holdings. Volume suddenly spikes up, and massive trades print to the tape. The price plummets with a vengeance as panic sellers come in, liquidating now to avoid margin calls or to preserve what little gain they've got left. Volume skyrockets, 10 times higher than average.

Now, finally, after many pullbacks, toward the end of the day the price begins consolidating. Not many more sellers here. The volume evaporates. Several minutes go by in which there is not a single trade. Market makers jockey now, trying to put over head fakes, trying to figure out what's going to happen next. Goldman Sachs offers 10,000 shares at the best offer, trying to scare the few that haven't yet sold out of their stock. But no more sellers emerge. Salomon Smith Barney bids 5,000 shares, but nobody sells. Goldman lowers the price to within a one-sixteenth of Salomon Smith Barney's bid but doesn't sell any stock to the latter. Nor does Salomon Smith Barney buy any from Goldman.) Several more moments go buy, with no more trades. Sensing a tidal change, you decide to cover your position, right here, right now.

To close your position, you simply buy the stock, without designating anything special at all. Your brokerage house, aware of your short position, *automatically* closes your borrowed (short) position out. In fact, you buy from Goldman Sachs, ignoring all the rules that say never buy from the axe while he's selling. Because you gather he's not really selling anymore; you believe he's just fading the trend. (See Chapter 10.) Your guess was right, because after selling your 1,000 shares to you, *Goldman Sachs disappears from the offer!*

A moment of silence goes by, as the market digests what's just happened. Then, suddenly, your time of sales ticker literally explodes with trades. Buyers rush in, taking all the offers, driving the price right back up. You notice Goldman Sachs on the bid with every pullback and smile because you know that firm is covering its shorts too.

You are now out of the market. All in all, a great day. Things went as well as they could. You didn't sell the high, and you didn't buy the very low. And you got out with a 14-point gain on 1,000 shares. You could have gone long and bought the stock as well as covered your short and rode it up again, but you decided not to get too greedy. You go for a walk instead.

At the local coffee shop you hear people talking about their three percent return—per annum—on Wilshire 5000 index funds and how 95 percent of mutual fund managers can't beat the S&P 500. Others wonder why they "just can't play those high-flying Internet stocks. Why, ABCD dropped 21 points in a day!" You don't engage. They wouldn't believe you anyway, and at best they'd label you a gambler who got lucky.

At $3.75, that coffee is a bargain.

real risk of short selling

The risk of short selling is, of course, that the stock goes up in value. Keep in mind that if it goes against you, eventually you will need to cover the short position. So if you shorted Yahoo! at $27, or Amazon at $8, you'd have been positively killed if you didn't stick to strict money management skills and closed the position at a small loss right away.

Theoretically, there is no limit to how high a price can go, but there is a limit to how far it can fall: zero. So if you go long, your maximum loss would occur if the stock went to zero. You would lose everything you had in it. However, *if you are short, it is important to realize that the potential loss is unlimited, since the price can climb infinitely high.*

Additionally, on occasion, a company's stock will suddenly, for various reasons, become nonmarginable. Any outstanding short positions will be required to cover by a specific date. The real danger here is that this can lead to a short squeeze, as people try to cover. If you are at a loss in a short position and the stock is called (i.e., all borrowed stock is required to be returned to the owner) take the loss. Remember, all great losses started small.

advantages of short selling

Fear can be a beautiful thing. The fact is, people often sell positions out of panic and buy only after careful consideration. Translation: *Stocks often drop much quicker than they rise. Many times a stock will tumble several points in several minutes, only to slowly rise throughout the day to a high above the open.*

Stocks tend not to close at their high or at their low. I've heard statistics quoted that say 8 out of 10 times a stock will close lower than its high or higher than its low. Personally, I've not conducted any serious study, but I believe empirical evidence is a little less encouraging—something more along the lines of seven out of eight. Still, more often than not, stocks tend to close higher than their daily low and lower than their daily high. Selling short is simply taking advantage of the other side of the "buy low, sell high" mentality. If you are in the market and only playing half the game, you may be missing some opportunities.

Another interesting point is that most investors—I'd even say most *traders*—don't have a firm understanding of what short selling is. It is still perceived as some mystical devil's alchemy that requires special knowledge and ability. Nothing could be further from the truth. Maybe this chapter will get the word out; maybe not. In any case, having read this, perhaps you will consider playing both sides.

more risks: beware the dread short squeeze

The so-called short squeeze is real and it is a killer. Beware the short squeeze. This section will explain what a short squeeze is; more important, it will tell you how to avoid being crushed to death and how to profit enormously from a short squeeze.

A short squeeze is a situation where there is a very large percentage of short positions in a stock relative to the number of long positions and the number of shares outstanding. If and when the price goes up, many shorts will try to cover their positions. This increased buying drives the price up higher, attracting more buyers.

And as more buyers buy, the price shoots up higher, fueling more interest and driving the price even higher. And all the while, the shorts are losing money at accelerating speed. Eventually, the shorts must cover—at any price. The results can be dramatic.

the scenario

Some stock, like K-Tel Records, for example, is largely considered a joke. For months, maybe years, people have been taking short positions in K-Tel Records every time it trades up a little. Now, this is a real example, and it happened in February 1998. K-Tel Records (Nasdaq: KTEL) had a huge portion of its stock in short positions. The consensus was that the record was played out, and the music was over. People figured this company was going to zero. And so they shorted it whenever they could.

Now, what made this so dangerous was the fact that KTEL had a very small float, something like only 700,000 shares outstanding. (In contrast, Dell Computer has 34 billion shares outstanding!) With such a tiny float and supply so very limited, you can only imagine what would happen to the price if someone decided to buy 100,000 shares.

Well, worse happened. KTEL, whose rumors of demise were greatly exaggerated, came out with a news release. It was going to sell its records over the Internet! According to gossip, KTEL would become the Amazon of the record industry. Day traders and people savvy to Internet stocks jumped in immediately and bought. The price of KTEL, which had started the day near $7, began to shoot upward.

But remember: There was no supply! There were no more sellers of this stock.

the squeeze

Everyone who was short this stock got word of the news and checked on the price. I can only imagine the utter astonishment of people calling their brokers for a quote and hearing "KTEL is $15\frac{1}{8}$ by $15\frac{1}{4}$." So, many hesitated, for sure in astonishment, thinking "15 and $\frac{1}{8}$?!" then asking "Well . . . what is it now?"

"KTEL is $17^5/_8$ by $17^3/_4$."

"WHAT!??" Well, you can imagine what followed; several failed attempts at limit orders, followed by abject desperation, and finally: market orders to cover, at any price. By midday, KTEL saw $40 a share.

- *How to avoid a squeeze.* When there is no float and everyone in the world is short, don't you short it too!

- *How do you find the float?* How do you find the "short interest"? Go to your broker's fundamental analysis information section, or if your brokerage doesn't have one, go to Yahoo! Finance or a similar page. Look at the number of shares outstanding, then look at the float. ("Shares outstanding" refers to the number of shares the company has issued, but "the float" refers to how many are actually in the market.) Note that by regulation, stock owned by the corporation or control persons cannot be liquidated readily, so the float refers to the actual number of shares out there that can be readily bought or sold without restriction.

  The company may own the majority of its shares, or control persons may own a majority of the shares, and by law they are limited in how many shares they are permitted to sell in a given time. There are important restrictions on selling control stocks, so for near-term trading, you need to look to the float to see how many shares are actually available. The fewer shares available, the less supply there is, and the more volatility possible.

In addition, you need to look at the short interest *relative to other companies in the same industry.* Brokerages are required to report the number of shares customers "hold" short in every stock quarterly. Since this is only a quarterly indication (and a lot can happen in a quarter), it is not a fail-safe indicator. But it is good, and certainly bears looking into, especially before shorting a company relatively unknown to you.

Of course, if you find a KTEL situation, or a SIEB (Muriel Siebert Inc., a short squeeze initiated rise in February 1999, from $7 to $30 a share, with only a 600,000-share float) or a JBOH (J.B. Oxford Inc., $5 to

$25, March 1999, 700,000-share float), or any of the many others, you might consider a buy-and-hold approach.

Yahoo! (YHOO) was trading at $27 dollars a share in November of 1997. I personally used to trade it daily for $\frac{1}{2}$- to 1-point profit everyday. I didn't pay any attention to the fact that at that time the float was only about 700,000 shares. Shame on me. Never again. (Split adjusted, YHOO is about $1,000 a share now.)

shorting all the way to zero

As a licensed broker, I am unable to recommend the following situation. But as many people do abuse this loophole in the law, I'll discuss it here—as a warning.

I pay a lot in taxes. I pay the least I can according to the law, but I am proud to be an American and consider myself fortunate and blessed to be able to contribute my fair share to this country. I'm the grandson of immigrants who came here for many reasons, among them the desire to pay fewer taxes on their earnings than they did in Europe. Two hundred years later, taxes in European countries are still massive, sometimes up to 60 percent of income, and salaries are often lower than ours too, relatively speaking. I think I'm pretty lucky as it is and don't press my luck by availing myself of the following loophole that the Internal Revenue Service has been trying rightfully to close for the past 60 years.

If you short a stock in your margin account, and it depreciates in value, your account equity will increase. But until you close the position—that is buy it back to cover your short—you have no actual taxable profit. If you were to close the short position at a profit, you would obviously be subject to short- or long-term capital gains taxes.

Yet, before you close the position, you *do* have an increased equity in your account (see Chapter 11) that can be withdrawn from your account in cash as a loan, lowering your equity and increasing your debt balance. This equity, held in your Special Memorandum Account (SMA), may also be used toward the purchase of or the short sale of additional securities.

Suppose you shorted a listed stock that slowly but surely went to zero. But you never closed the position. Instead, you used the equity created in your SMA to short other stocks that went to zero as well.

Now you have a lot more equity than you started with, and it is withdrawable as cash or usable for purchase or short sales of other securities. But let's say you never closed those positions; instead you used the created equity in your SMA to short more stocks that also went to zero . . .

As I mentioned, the IRS has been trying to close this loophole for the past 60 years, and eventually it will have its way. So if you are abusing this loophole, beware: Only two things in life are inevitable: death and taxes. While it is possible you will achieve the former before the latter while abusing this loophole, someday, somewhere, someone will have to pay the taxes.

Right?

one more warning

Always make sure to designate a stock you intend to sell short as "short." Many software programs will allow you to sell a stock not in your portfolio by simply selling it (not designating it "short"). The reason for this is that you may have the stock long in another account and may be in the process of transferring it in. If you do this with a stock that is not shortable (not borrowable), you will have created an *illegal short position.* You will have sold the stock without owning it and without borrowing it either. The important thing to know here is that, while you probably will not be criminally prosecuted for this, the NASD and listed exchanges reserve the right to break bad trades. The situation could be this way: You sell the stock short illegally and buy the stock back, covering your position. Later on, who knows when, the NASD realizes what you did and breaks the illegal short sale. Well, since now the sale never happened but the buy to cover did, you'll find yourself long the stock. Now suppose the stock has dropped significantly since then. You own it, and the loss as well. Always be sure to designate a short sale as such, and you won't have trouble.

selling short when you're really long

If you are long stock and you accidentally designate the sale as short, not to worry. Since you cannot be both long and short in any stock in an account at the same time, your clearing firm will notice that you are actually long the stock, and so will sell out your long position to cover the sale. In the end you will wind up flat; that is, you will own zero shares after the sale, provided you sold the same amount of shares as you owned. However, accidentally doing this may create a journal entry error in your account: Long and short positions are segregated from each other; so if you buy long, then sell short, the clearinghouse's system may "think" you are long in your long account and short in your short account. In the end, you will be flat, but you may have to spend some time on the phone with your brokerage in order to clear it up.

moving from short to long or from long to short in one transaction

You can go short from being long, or long from being short, in one transaction but *not* if you're playing by the rules. You *must* designate a short sale as such before executing the trade. If you do not, you may have violated the up-tick rules and may have created an illegal short position. You will also have circumvented your trading platform's "short" function. You may even have sold stock that is not marginable (and therefore not borrowable) without owning it. Many platforms will allow you to do this, since, as just mentioned, you may actually be long this stock in another account and be in the process of transferring it in, anticipating its arrival before settlement. Your trading platform may have no way of knowing this, and in many cases it will allow you to execute the trade, thereby creating an illegal short position.

Not a good situation, especially if you were right regarding the future of this stock and it had continued its downward descent. The quick answer is: Always designate a short sale as such, and you won't have any problems.

What about going long from being short? You can do this also, but at most brokerages, not without problems. You see, short sales are segregated in a special part of your margin account. When you buy stock to cover, it automatically goes into that type of margin account. So, you will wind up being long in your "short" account. Often you can resolve this sort of situation with a phone call to your broker. But it can be a hassle. And some brokerages are difficult to get on the phone. Better to plan ahead and sell your stock, and then follow the rules to sell short. And then cover it, and go long in a separate transaction. Of course, then you might have another commission to deal with, but that's just the cost of playing by the rules.

a final note on selling short

Selling stock short inherently contains more risk than going long, since your potential loss is unlimited. But just as you would never in good conscience and practice of sound risk/money management techniques ride a stock you hold long all the way to zero—losing everything—you would also, in exercising sound money management, close out a short position if you were wrong. Tune out the ego and preserve capital to fight another day. If you abide by the rules of selling short, and research to avoid being caught in a short squeeze, selling short can be another profitable tool to use in the financial jungle.

chapter 9

risk management

In the hall of Great Traders Past, the spirits of the Old Traders of Yore sat in a circle, heads bowed, chanting a quiet mantra. If you listened closely, you could hear murmured, "When in doubt, sell it out, when in doubt, sell it out . . ."

Money Management is the least talked about, perhaps most important aspect of trading. It is the difference between gambling and speculating; it is the difference between winning and losing. Two traders, trading the same stocks at the same time, with the same amount of capital, can have diametrically opposed outcomes. One wins consistently, on balance, whereas the other loses consistently, until he's lost all his chips and is kicked out of the gaming hall.

The comparison to gambling is a valid one, in that a person has a certain amount of money (chips) with which to play, and he buys and sells in the great casino called Wall Street. Fortunes will be made, fortunes will be lost, and the same psychology present at the casino assaults the trader at every turn.

But successful traders take precautions to avoid and be unaffected by the gambler mentality and to structure their "plays" to remove as much risk as possible. Risk is always present; good traders recognize this reality and plan for it in advance. They never roll the dice indiscriminately, never risk too much on one position, and always stack the odds in their favor by studying and finding as many indicating factors as possible, and by utilizing strict, often painful money management techniques in order to protect their ability to survive bad trades and remain in the game for the infrequent, fortune-making, elusive home run trades.

It is possible to make many bad decisions and be crippled by them. With a little planning, it is also possible to ensure that those bad decisions (which everyone makes) are merely instructive learning experiences rather than debilitating, crushing losses.

In this chapter, first we'll deal with the mechanical aspects of risk management and then take a look at some of the psychological ramifications of trading. Trading is a harsh game; it is not to be played for the thrill. Often it is a relatively boring, psychologically grueling endeavor. Care must be taken to remove the emotional highs and lows, to develop a plan of attack that doesn't allow for emotion-based trading. Decisions, based on reason, coupled with sound risk management principles, will save the day; they're the difference between emerging from the jungle big and strong and being eaten alive.

The term "risk management," as it applies to trading, means placing trades in such a way so as to stack the odds toward *on-balance, consistent, long-term wins*, while minimizing losses in the short term and therefore, in the long term, *preserving capital.*

First of all, if you are currently actively trading your account or are thinking about it, please pay careful attention to the following: *Do not speculate with money you can't afford to lose. Do not speculate with a large fraction of your total portfolio. Keep your trading activities limited so as to never risk more than one percent of your trading capital on a single position. If you currently don't possess enough assets to speculate profitably with only a small percentage of your total portfolio, then don't do it. Speculation is a very risky activity, one that requires patience, practice, dedication, and skill; risking retirement monies, or money you need or will need in the near future is plain stupid.*

cover your assets

Watch the pennies and the dollars will take care of themselves.

All things being equal, a stock is either going to go up or down intraday. (If you're not trading volatile stocks, you're not making money.)

However, these odds aren't the most important ones. The most important ones are your odds of winning on a consistent, on-balance, long-term basis. In other words, trade not only to win, but trade to *preserve capital*. Preservation of capital should be your paramount concern.

Start small. So, you've got $100,000 and want to trade. Should you buy 1,000 (or 2,000 on margin) shares of a $100 stock? If it goes up two points, that's $4,000 profit. If it goes down, however, you've lost $4,000, and tomorrow your buying power is down by $8000! (See Chapter 11 for an explanation of buying power.) It is easy to get pulled in by the get-rich-quick mentality and trade big size whenever possible. But it may be much wiser to start well below your capacity. Your profits on the average, everyday, small trades may be smaller, but you might still be in the game for the once-in-a-while windfall grand-slam trade. Everybody knows the WGST (Windfall Grand Slam Trade); it's the one that went up 20 points yesterday, while you were busy losing three-quarters of a point in Microsoft. Being in the game for the WGST is arguably the most important thing you can do. That trade will skyrocket your portfolio, eclipsing all the consistent small profits of the preceding quarter. Preserve capital. *Be in the game.* Suppose you did the following.

Instead of buying 2,000 shares, you bought 100. A hundred. Yes, let's say 100 measly, little shares. Now, if MSFT goes down two points, you've lost $200 plus commissions. If it goes up, obviously you've made $200 minus commissions, and just as obviously, it's not worth your time. However, that's just the beginning.

. . . *and Increase Size.* What if every time you trade, you start small, and as soon as you find you are wrong, you get out? Your losses on bad trades would be very small. But if, on seeing that your thesis was right (the stock goes the direction you bet on), you increase size, say, by buying every quarter point in your direction; say 100 additional shares, then 200 additional shares, then 500, then 1,000 and so on, up to whatever size is comfortable, and then, when the stock is up two points and you figure the party is over, you sell out for a profit on all shares. Over time, including profits and losses, you can see quickly how much larger your gains will be than your losses. Of course, your commissions will be huge, comparatively. So let's look at this situation; say you made five commissionable trades to buy the entire size. Let's say each commission is $25, for a total of $125. This is clearly a sizable amount. But compare $125 with the $4,000 loss you would have sustained had you bought the entire size outright and the position moved the wrong way. And keep in mind, the larger commissions come out of profit. They are not losses.

Buying in slowly, increasing size at an average price (cost basis) well below the market, keeps losses under control.

keep a mental trailing stop loss

A stop loss is the price at which you will liquidate your position, having decided your thesis was wrong or that factors have changed. The practice of starting small and increasing size also serves another function. Since your average price is going to be below the current market, you will also have some built-in downside protection if things turn sour.

But what if the position goes the wrong direction right away? Some traders use extremely tight stop losses, say one-eighth or one-quarter. In the trading of extremely volatile stocks, a quarter-point stop loss may keep you on the edge of your seat all the time and probably will get you "whipsawed" out of your position. Everyone who uses stop losses has at one time or another been whipsawed out of a position only to see the stock go ballistic from there. So, how much is adequate? In extremely volatile stocks, a larger stop loss is warranted (you rarely buy the very low or sell the very high), but on how many shares? A large stop loss on a big position can not only take you out of your position if things go wrong; it can take you out of the game for good. But if your plan includes moving into a trade incrementally— that is, opening the position with small size and increasing size only if you were right—then a larger stop loss may be warranted. You might have been wrong with regard to timing. The only real answer to what constitutes a good stop loss lies in planning ahead and determining your own comfort level. Remember, a day trade is a day trade; it must be liquidated by the end of the day. Many traders have made the gamblers' mistake of holding a losing position overnight in the ego-driven hope that the price will go up the next day. It may, but it might also tank. Stocks bought *for the purpose* of a day trade are probably not the

same as the stocks you own in your swing trading or long-term investment portfolio. Remember the reason you bought in the first place!
Don't justify a losing situation because ego won't let you accept failure. If
you bought the stock for an intraday bounce, then that's what you
own it for. If you were wrong—the stock doesn't bounce but just tanks
from there—admit it quickly and liquidate the trade at a loss. And
above all, don't average down a losing position! If you exercise a strict
risk/money management plan, your loss will be small, relatively speaking. You would not have a large position at this time, since your plan
would include moving in slowly, in anticipation of just this sort of circumstance.

all great losses started small

Small losses are easier to accept than big losses. It's hard enough to
liquidate when wrong, so keep the starting position small. Your thesis
will be either right or wrong. If wrong, the best you can do is accept it,
get out, and keep enough chips to play again. If right, you can only be
more emphatically right; increase size and stay in the race all the way
to finish. But be ruthless with your stop loss. *If the trade goes bad,
close it and move on.* This is one of the hardest and most important
rules in the jungle. If you lose it all today, you won't be around tomorrow to catch the big one. There will be many many small losses and
many many small gains. Approaching your trading from the perspective of preservation of capital will keep you in the game for the
WGSTs—the trades that make all the tedium and admissions of failure
worthwhile. Strive for preservation of capital and consistent profitability. Once you've mastered these, you'll be able to participate in
the WGSTs.

combat the gambler's mentality

"Buy low and sell high" is a great strategy. Unfortunately, human nature in the form of ego often prevents this from happening. Many
gamblers who are down big recklessly hope their "luck" will turn
around and gamble with their losses by doing nothing or, worse, by
increasing size on a losing position. This can lead to massive, debilitating losses. And, most curiously, often these same gamblers will

close a winning position at a small profit, overjoyed finally to get a bone, only to watch, sickened, as the stock they just sold goes through the roof. Recognize the scenario? If not, you must be from a different planet, because this happens to everyone at some point. In the words of the great trader Jesse Livermore's excellent biography *Reminiscences of a Stock Operator*: "I sold the wheat, which showed me a profit, and bought the cotton. . . ." Don't sell the wheat! The mentality for successful trading is the exact converse of gambling: In trading you need to cut losses immediately and ruthlessly and, curiously, gamble with winners.

never gamble with losses

Here's a scenario: the stock you just bought for the anticipated intraday bounce off its low doesn't bounce. Instead, after hovering for a moment near your purchase price, it tanks. In a moment, it drops below your stop loss. You are faced with a choice: Do nothing, get out, or buy more.

Now, in struts ego, in the form of human nature, tempting you to find justification for the loss, supporting your original thesis, in spite of apparent reality. In these times you may be tempted to resort to conventional investment advice (often sound for long-term, fundamentally backed investing) and double or average down (buy more shares to lower the per-share cost basis). This misplaced optimism, really just a form of ego-driven denial, will inevitably lead to disaster. *Remember the plan.* Remember the reason for placing the trade. If the reason was wrong, or is no longer valid, consider liquidating. And stick to the stop loss.

You will make many, many bad decisions. Recognize them and call them what they are. Accept reality and, thereby, keep your losses contained. Trading is a humbling experience; you will do well to accept that fact. Ego is the enemy, and worse yet, *it's already in your head.*

I recently spoke with one of the best traders I've ever known, a man whose trading account has increased from several thousand dollars to over eight figures. I will probably never even approach him in terms of game. Yet even with his track record, he still makes plenty of bad decisions. But he always uses strict, ruthless, highly-developed risk management techniques. And he is brutally honest regarding his trading decisions. He calls 'em like he sees 'em, with no ego-induced denials of reality. Still, over time, even with his stellar track record, he insists (with humility) that he's *lost* much more than he's kept.

gamble with wins

One trader I know keeps a trailing stop loss of 50 percent of his gain. In other words, as the winning position increases, he'll move his stop-loss target up, always preserving 50 percent of his gains. I believe this is an excellent starting strategy. Consider the following.

Suppose you stick rigorously to stop losses, especially when painful, keeping losses contained. And suppose, when having a small profit in hand, instead of closing the position, you were to gamble with it, to say "Gee, I've got a small gain here, and I'm willing to risk some of it on the chance this trade is a home run in the making." And now, instead of closing the position (whoopee, three-eighths!), you were to do nothing. Indeed, you might even buy more, following the upward price with a trailing stop loss. If it turns around, you execute the stop. If it continues upward, you're in the game for the ever-elusive WGST.

psychological ramifications of speculating

Trading can be a thrilling, emotional high when you're right. But it can also be a debilitating, crushing depressant when wrong—especially when you're wrong several times in a row.

It would be well to note here that trading is a business, not a ride in an amusement park. Just as you would not want to go into an important meeting depressed and unable to make decisions, you would not want to undertake any serious decisions when giddy with feelings of invincibility and carelessness.

Many of the biggest losses that once-hugely-successful traders have endured have occurred directly after the biggest gains they ever had.

Keep in mind that a small loss is easily justified as a learning experience. A major loss can make you question your very right to live. Follow strict money management practices, and never let things get out of hand, either financially or emotionally. Understand that being wrong a lot of the time is simply a condition that all traders must deal with.

strategies for emotional stability

A great many books dealing with stress management are available. Read them all. Just kidding; read as many as you can. And practice the techniques. It is of vital importance to your health as well as your trading success that you not be in a constant state of toxic shame-fear-panic-elation. If you are feeling overwhelmed by these types of emotions, please consult a mental health professional for information. I am not qualified to give any advice. Here I just relate things that traders have told me they have done and that have worked for them.

Studies have tracked the physical and mental health of individuals engaged in highly stressful occupations. Results of the studies show that physical health affects mental health. If you are in shape, you increase your capacity to deal with stress. And trading can be highly stressful. But it doesn't need to be. You can do simple things to increase your health and mental stability to the point where you can weather the most grueling situations.

- *Be in shape.* Simple physical exercise is an excellent means of stress reduction. You will need to consult a physician before embarking on a plan of exercise, and I'm not qualified to give any recommendations, other than to say that studies suggest that when you are physically fit, your capacity to deal with difficult situations is greatly improved.

- *Quit when you're behind.* Take a break after numerous losses. Maybe for a day or a few! *Take as long as necessary to clear your mind.* If you can take a walk, do so. That's something simple you can do to relax. In any case, it will get your mind off trading. And take time and do something nice for yourself. This is very important, since a series of bad trades really can infect a person with feelings of desperation and worthlessness. And this is the last mood you want to be in when trading, for these feelings will corrupt your judgment and cloud your thinking. Desperate people make lousy choices and suffer for them. Quit for a while! Reevaluate your strategy. It is not the end of the world! Remember: Just because a penny winds up heads 50 percent of the time doesn't mean it won't wind up tails a huge number of times before turning heads. And every time, the odds increase in your favor.

Reevaluate your plan later when you are calmer. Losses can be very instructional. A win doesn't help you improve: It just teaches you to do the same thing! A loss contains inherent possibility: the chance to grow and improve. Reread the section entitled "Combat the Gambler's Mentality" and always, always use strict risk management: *Never be in a situation where you risk too much capital,* and if you've made a series of bad trades, stop trading. Take a break and clear your head.

- *Quit when you're far ahead.* A long string of winners will cloud your judgment too. It will fill you with feelings of certainty and invincibility—totally inappropriate emotions when trading. Ego will enter, and you may make bad decisions. ("What the heck, I did so well on *X* that I'll try *Y*"—a trade you would never even consider if you were in your right mind.) Ego will say in a calm, reassuring voice, "Average down . . . you *know* you're right." It is truly sad to hear of all the tremendously successful traders who blew out not only all of their recent gains, but all of their savings too, because of a blasphemous, insidious belief that they could do no wrong. Better to take a break, take a walk, and do something nice for yourself. Don't continue until you clear your head. Reread the section on combating the gamblers mentality, and always, always use strict risk management: Never be in a situation where you risk too much capital. Great traders blow up. Believe it. No one is immune. If you've had a series of incredibly successful trades, stop trading. Take a break, you deserve it. And clear your head, because you can be sure that you'll need clear focus to avoid making bad decisions.

chapter 10

games people play

how market makers do what they do

This chapter is all about "game." In any forum where traders chat, we hear comments like "This market maker *screwed* me! Every time I try to sell, he drives the price down. Every time!" "Why won't he just let me sell my 300 shares!?" Everyone who has ever been in a day traders' chat room has heard words like these. The sad reality is that these ogres, these beasts, to whom we ascribe so many tricks and treacherous ploys, are really just like you and me, except that in their case, more money is on the table and the stakes are higher. Some of what you hear is true, but much of it is not. So let's examine what market makers do, and all the myths and fallacies surrounding them, so we can then figure out what it *really* means to "make a market" in this day and age, and understand what gamesmanship inevitably arises from putting everything on the line day after day. We'll examine the tricks and decoys they use to accomplish their goals. This chapter is not going to endear the old school trading community to me, but that's okay, because it's a changing world. And a *rapidly* changing one, at that. I'm not going to say anything outrageous here; it's a shame that some in the trading community view this exploration of what they do and how they do it as "letting the cat out of the bag."

The proverbial "cat" has *been* out, and for some time now. And now the old school traders are realizing the claws are already in— deep. I'm confident the old schoolers will adapt; they always do. But until the market makers are evolved out of existence (what I believe ultimately will happen—in the very distant future), I'm going to shine a light on some of the realities you need to know if you desire to play on the same field and win, taking control and responsibility rather than guessing, gambling, and blaming.

some of the myths

Market makers have so much more information on Level III Nasdaq workstations than we do.

If you read earlier chapters, you will know how wrong that statement is. Market makers have fundamentally the same information that any traders will have if they go through a top-flight, direct-access–oriented brokerage. The only difference is that market makers may be working an order and know the order's size. Market makers *do not* have any special access to or special view of other's limit orders per se. The situation is, of course, different on the NYSE, where "specialists" act as dealers. Each stock on the NYSE has only one specialist, whose job includes maintaining the order book of the stock in which he specializes. However, specialists are under strict legal control with regard to sharing the contents of the order book. No one but the specialist is allowed to see it. I constantly read Usenet posts in which people say market makers can see each other's orders. Ridiculous! No such thing occurs.

What an over-the-counter Nasdaq market maker does have, it is hoped, is a whole bunch of orders which they'd like to execute for third parties. (This is termed "order flow.") If market makers have a whole bunch of orders, or one order to sell 50,000 shares today in a stock that regularly trades one million shares, then they are happy, and they certainly hope the stock trades at a price where they can complete the order. If market makers don't trade, they don't make any risk-free capital at all. More on this later. For now, it is sufficient to realize that market makers *cannot* share the nature of their orders with anyone. To do so would be a gross violation of client interests (as well as the law), because someone with that specific knowledge could "front-run" customers. Front-running, an illegal version of "getting in front of size," refers to the illegal practice of an individual with material inside information (such as the fact that George Soros is going to buy 700,000 shares of ABCD stock by Friday) buying or selling the stock short before customers can effect the trade in expectation that the price will run as the large order is filled. And institutions aren't stupid. They are aware that their intentions can leak out; since they always stand to lose big, they go to elaborate means to disguise their intentions and share their information with a very select few. Often traders/market makers executing the trade are unaware of the size of the total order; they may only be aware that they are selling 30,000 shares for a client. The client may have 800,000 shares behind that but won't let the trader know; the client would be compromising his position if he did! So you can see how it is in the client's best interest to not let market makers in on the full picture. And so clients rarely do.

In fact, there are strict laws covering disclosure of this sort of information. Licensed equity traders must pass a test that includes information on the harsh punishments for divulging such information to anyone. And market makers' trading activity is carefully monitored by StockWatch—the police of the cyber jungle. (More on StockWatch later.) So, market makers know the orders that they personally have, but that's it! They do not, and could not, know the orders of anyone else. Some well-traded stocks (DELL, for instance) often have upward of 60 market participants; it would be nigh impossible for all those participants to collude and share specific knowledge of each other's orders on an ongoing daily basis while their phones are recorded and StockWatch is watching.

Market makers "back away" constantly!

Not so. Yes, it happens. Yes, sometimes it is out of bad intentions, and sometimes it is out of plain ignorance—some neophyte assistant trader incorrectly adds up how many shares the trader transacted, and the trader, thinking he's traded his liability, declines a legitimate liability order. But the main thing is, traders don't do it constantly! Nowhere near as many times as you'd think if you listened to the banter in the chat rooms. Given my background and experience as a market maker, having been the axe in a dozen or so stocks, it has certainly happened to me.

And as head trader at a retail direct-access electronic brokerage, I've heard countless complaints over time. And as a licensed equity trader, when this complaint is justified, I'll call the market maker in question or the Nasdaq and get satisfaction. The Nasdaq takes the prospect of backing away so seriously that it monitors not only the trades, but the very bids and offers of every market participant on a real-time basis. In questionable situations, traders call a special number, and the regulatory body of the exchange checks the records (all time coded) and determines, often in a matter of seconds, whether the accused has indeed backed away.

The penalties for backing away are severe, as backing away would tend to erode the very fabric of a fair and stable market (which is vital to the U.S. economy). The regulatory bodies aggressively pursue transgressors. As a former market maker and institutional sales trader, I've had my share of "back-aways." I've called the special number on several occasions, and I was wrong on all but one. The vast majority of times a customer complains of backing away, a simple examination of time of sales reports reveals the customer's error. Many traders don't realize how important time of sales is in determining the quality of their execution. Especially if you trade through a full-service brokerage house, if you enter an order and receive a crappy print, examine time of sales. It is altogether possible that your order was executed poorly. Time of sales is an irrefutable record of what *actually* happened, regardless of what you think you saw. I'm not taking the old school party line here; backing away does happen, but *really*, not that often.

The vast majority of times, poor trading is the reason why individuals can't close their position. Many individuals engaged in active trading simply don't have a firm grasp of the tools used in trading. Countless hours of conversations (I was recently told that my phone conversations at work, which are recorded, take up almost 10 times as much space as the other traders on a daily basis) finally led me to write this book.

Market makers can short all they want, stopping a rally and beating the stock into the ground.

Not quite. There are stringent rules and regulations concerning short-selling securities in which you make a market. While it is true that market makers are not subject to some of the rules that individuals selling short for their own account are, they cannot indiscriminately short sell a stock and beat it into the ground. If you make a market in a stock, you may only sell short for the firm account in connection with "bona fide market making activity." Keep in mind that as a market maker, you are required to keep a two-sided market at all times; you must stand ready to buy and sell as necessary to create a liquid market. And you will need to put firm capital to use in this endeavor. However, you may not just sell and sell, beating a stock into the ground because it pleases you.

You may, for instance, sell short in anticipation of customer sell orders. You may also work large customer sell orders, which in many illiquid stocks may look as if you are nailing the stock to the ground. Of course, as a market maker, you are usually subject to short-selling rules specific to market makers.

You may, however, sell short for the firm account as an individual would if you do *not* make a market in the stock.

> *Major firms will come out with strong recommendations so that they can sell huge orders (received before the recommendation) into the increased demand or with downgrades for the converse situation.*

There is no denying this sort of activity seems to occur. However, something called the Chinese Wall Doctrine says that the brokerage house must *separate* the analysts from the trading department so completely that the division is impenetrable.

The "Chinese Wall" exists because any trader who trades with advance information concerning a report not yet available to the public would be guilty of insider trading by definition. And StockWatch is not blind to the trading activity of the big firms. Any analyst who is aware of a pending client order is in possession of material inside information; to issue a report under these circumstances would be tantamount to Russian roulette with all chambers loaded. You don't just lose your career for these sorts of crimes, you go to jail.

Nevertheless, I've often wondered when watching various

stocks if this happens anyway. I've seen major buying, followed with an upgrade; I've seen major, major selling by one market maker for days, followed only then with a downgrade. This is certainly an area that bears watching. Much of this could simply be common sense: A company is coming out with earnings, several major stockholders think the report is going to be bad, so they divest themselves in advance of the report. But still, seeing what I've seen leaves me with questions rather than answers. With trading violations, there is an irrefutable record (time of sales), so proof is positive. Maybe the Chinese Wall doctrine is more difficult to enforce. There are always bad apples. But then again, maybe there are real, substantiated reasons. One thing is sure: You can bet these sorts of situations are investigated aggressively. And in a legal system where "if the glove doesn't fit, you must acquit," nothing is perfect 100 percent of the time.

Note: Prior to the Securities Act of 1934, and particularly in the 1920s, this sort of activity was not only legal but was rampant. Just read *Reminiscences of a Stock Operator* for a feel for the Wild West aspect of the markets during that time. Some historians believe that such manipulations had a lot to do with the crash of 1929. The Securities Acts of 1933 and 1934 outlawed most of these practices. The public, having read the seminal stories from that time, and having seen movies like *Wall Street* (but not having read the securities acts, which are sterile and deadly boring) is often under the impression that these same shenanigans still take place.

They don't. But other, more sophisticated ones must. Maybe I'm a cynic, but I believe it is human nature to try to cheat. It is possible that the major institutions do engage in tom-foolery. But given that any games played would be so complex as to fool the aggressive investigations of the authorities, I can't speculate on what they would be! And even if they do exist, I doubt they would be targeted at individual traders. Believe me, market makers don't really care about a sixteenth on our 1,000 shares; they've got much bigger fish to fry. Many people believe that the stock market is a zero-sum game, and that for somebody to win, somebody must lose. This is not the case. You really never know the position of the contra to your trade; you may think you "got over" by selling stock to somebody at the high, but you don't know if the other side isn't purchasing additional shares at an average price well below the current market, or buying the last shares to cover an on-balance profitable short position. Don't think someone is always out to get you. At best, thinking that way is just a waste of time.

what it means to "make a market"

The term "market maker" refers to the over-the-counter Nasdaq market. There are no market makers on the listed exchanges; there are specialists. We'll deal with them later. Market makers are dealers of stock. They buy for appreciation in value, just like you and me, and they buy so they have an inventory, which they may then resell to customers. They buy the stock at a dealer price and mark it up a little. Market makers must stand ready to buy or sell a minimum number of shares, as determined in the NASD's order-handling rules, from any market participant, anytime, at their quoted price, which must be in fair relation to current market. In other words, if you make a market you're required to both buy and sell stock as the situation warrants, and you are liable to sell it at fair market value, regardless of its cost to you. You cannot take the cost of the inventory into account when filling customer orders. You cannot withdraw your market during bad times and enter your market when things are more favorable to you. There are punishments for withdrawal. You, as a market maker, are required to be open for business and ready for liability orders during all market hours. You don't go out for lunch. You don't leave your desk. Your bladder develops superhuman capacity.

And that's on a slow day, when you don't have any big orders to work. When you have big orders to work, or when you are the axe, you are focused, like a fighter, an air traffic controller, a kid playing a video game. But this time it's your ass on the line. Missed opportunities, little accounting mistakes, add up remorselessly. After all, this is *money*, and it is your legal fiduciary responsibility to see that it is handled correctly. Everyone is watching: StockWatch on one side to keep you honest, and on the other the customer, whose very financial life you hold in your hands.

To make matters more interesting, average market makers keep markets in a dozen or more securities. At smaller firms with fewer traders, many times market makers make markets in 40-plus securities. They are required to respond to any liability orders within 30 seconds, or they are in violation of the regulations. And SuperSOES will speed this up even more. There are no excuses. Mutual fund managers aren't going to care if your bladder was about to burst and that made you miss the sale of 5,000 shares at $3 more than current prices. That's a $15,000 loss, and clients deserve nothing less than satisfaction.

The managers won't care that you had numerous simultaneous orders in several securities, that news just came out on two stocks, and that you simply couldn't digest the information and click the buttons at the speed it was coming at you. That's *your* problem. And how many shares did you sell of ABCD? How many shares did you *buy* of ABCD? (You have buy orders too.) And what is your current (the firm's) position? And what about the other two dozen stocks? What about the Dow tanking and the Federal Reserve Board meeting and the earnings reports? And what about SuperSOES and SOES? How many shares have you transacted there (remember, these systems execute against you automatically as a market maker; you receive notification that you just bought or sold stock) while looking after your other stocks? How many shares do you now own that you didn't want, now that the Dow is down 75 points and the tick is just ugly? What is your average price in any of these stocks?

Now don't get me wrong: Traders make money on every share they transact correctly. But not like the old days. In the old days (three short years ago!), spreads were positively luxurious. But now, due to volatility and the liquidity of day traders, generally speaking, there is no spread at all. No margin for error. The first-class luxury coach has been traded for a crowded New York subway at rush hour.

Being a market maker is not an easy job. It's hard enough to trade your own account well, without any of the legal requirements and fiduciary responsibilities of making a market. But that's the career they chose. (No one falls into it; the level of responsibility and the emotional demands are too high, not to mention the work required to get all the licenses.) Market makers are a breed apart. And the world does need them—at least for now.

what market makers want

Market makers want three things:

1. To trade as many shares as possible for others (order flow); they get paid a commission or a markup on every share.
2. To trade for the firm account and create as much value as possible in inventory (buy stocks low and sell them high).
3. To disguise their intentions so nobody knows what they're doing. If they tip their hand, they'll lose big. Guaranteed.

To these ends they will employ several techniques, including headfakes, and fading the trend. Watch for them next time you are watching a stock. The techniques are discussed below.

clandestine operations

Clandestine activity is activity normally hidden from view; but if it is witnessed, it is seen for what it is. There is no trickery involved, you just have to look for it, and there it is. Market makers don't want you to know what they're doing, and frequently they go to clever lengths to disguise what they do. But the vast majority of the time, their intentions are clear. So, seek and you shall find.

You may notice a market maker on the bid, off the bid; on the offer, off the offer, intermittently, at all different prices during the day. This is normal activity. He probably has nothing major to do on the day, and he's simply fulfilling his role as a market maker. If he is the axe, you may notice he's on the bid or offering more than anyone else (see "#Best" in Chapter 4) but not by a massive amount; he's been there 10 times today; many of the others have been there three, four, or five times. This is normal: He's the axe, and people come to him first with their orders because, generally speaking, he'll have the liquidity to facilitate your order quickly. So it is natural that he's just going to do more business on that day than many others. This situation represents the market makers' first desire; to trade as many risk-free shares as possible. Remember, he gets paid a markup or commission for every share he transacts. As a market maker, you generally get a salary plus a percentage of profits (commissions or markup) as bonus; so the more profitable business you do, the more your bonus is going to be.

In the days when spreads were huge, it was easier to make a great deal of money. Nowadays, with spreads smaller (virtually nonexistent, many times), it is much more difficult to make money.

Being profitable now involves more risk, because to really make money, you need inventory purchased at a cheaper price that you can sell to buyers as they arrive. With the increased volatility in the marketplace, it is more difficult to take on positions. Some of the more volatile Internet stocks will drop $30 a share on a bad day. Can you imagine if you were loaded to the gills in one of these stocks, and the price dropped 20 percent in one day? Imagine what that does to your profitability. And if you are loaded to the gills and the price starts to drop, and your clients (large institutions, it's hoped) call in and want to unload all of their huge positions, you can't just put them on hold and sell your own stock out so you don't lose your ass. You must sell their positions first, *irrespective of what's happening to your own inventory.*

In other words, inexperienced market makers can lose their asses, and often their firm's as well. Perhaps you've heard about the trader at Barings, one of the oldest, richest merchant banks in the world? One young out-of-control trader, operating in the Asian derivatives markets several years ago, literally bankrupted the entire company. So, nowadays, particularly in those crazy tech-Internet stocks, firms carry less inventory. This can make it more difficult for you to enter and exit positions, because nobody has much of the stock lying around in inventory; so selling your 5,000 shares may drive the market down a point or two (for a moment) as market makers who don't want to lose money will buy the minimum legally required from you—as little as 100 or fewer shares, depending on current liability requirements—and readjust their market. But ideally, a firm would acquire a lot of stock in a company that nobody is interested in, and as the company's story becomes known, the firm will trade around its position as the stock goes up, making shiploads of money for the firm in the process.

So, you may see market makers on the bid/offer, off the bid/offer much as described. In line with the orders they're filling, they may be buying or selling for their own inventory. This is to be considered normal activity.

But trading the company inventory is a challenging job with the heaviest of responsibilities, both legally and ethically. There is so much risk involved, and if mistakes are made, the money's gone for good. The conflict between the new directions of the job of market makers and the old-school ways may be described as risk-free capital vs. capital gains. In volatile markets, holding inventory for appreciation involves substantial risk. But on the other hand, risk-free capital in the form of simple order flow may pay less.

And when you look at the fast rise of the ECNs, which generally charge $.015 a share whether you buy or sell (meaning that for each share the ECN matches, it receives $.03, *totally free of risk*), and that ECNs operate automatically, electronically, carrying no inventory whatsoever, it is easy to predict at least the partial demise of the market maker system as it now stands. In some ways, it's just like mechanized automation on assembly lines.

If a machine can do the same work, with substantially less human cost, isn't a company obligated to upgrade, at least if it's public? It is interesting to note that Goldman Sachs recently took a 25 percent interest in Archipelago (ARCA), the ECN run by Terra Nova Trading. More on that in Chapter 12. Clearly, with so much at stake and margins so thin, if market makers have a size position or a client order, they're going to do what they can to disguise their intentions.

disguised intentions—covert ops!

In military terms, covert operations are those operations that in execution appear to be something other than what they truly are. Ideally, they are conducted in full public view, with the viewers hoodwinked into thinking they are watching one thing, when in actuality, something very different is going on.

Covert ops are the most fun to watch and the most difficult to figure out. Since we'll never know with certainty just what exactly it is that the market maker is doing, we must use common sense, intuition, a "feel for the markets," and careful observation of the market makers and ECNs involved to try to see just what the market makers try so hard to hide.

Typical tricks are headfakes and fading the trend as well as sudden rash selling or buying to drive the price one way or another, panicking the weak hands into taking or closing positions. The reasons are many, but they all come down to one thing: profit.

headfakes

Probably one of the most common things market makers will do to trick you into thinking the market is going to go one way or another is the so-called headfake. Many "experts" say in their courses that when a market maker (the axe, especially) sits on or near the offer, he's a seller on the day.

I'll bet that every trader has seen a stock that bears all the traditional attributes of one that by conventional Level II interpretation is about to tank: The axe is on the offer, few bids are in sight; heavy selling starts; and so . . . you sell short, only to see the stock rocket up moments later. What few of the "experts" address is the fact that the major firms—the axes in stocks—realize *exactly how they are perceived* by the public and so they disguise themselves to fool you. An example follows.

The axe in a stock you are watching suddenly goes on the inside offer showing 10,000 shares offered. You may also notice, depending how devious the market maker is, several other large ECN offers *at or near* the best offer. Were they there before? It seems that suddenly, there is a lot of liquidity on the sell side; it would take a lot of buying pressure to break through that much stock. Next, on the bid side, the same market maker lowers his price substantially. InstiNet (INCA), seconds later, seeing the added liquidity, lowers its bid slightly. (Was that *really* why the market maker lowered his bid?) Several trades go off at the offer price, but the axe still offers 10,000 shares. By not reducing his size, he says to the market at large: "I have a huge sell order. Nobody can buy as much stock as I've got for sale." And now, as soon as everyone's noticed that his size didn't diminish, he increases his size—offering 12,000 shares! Now whatever market maker was buying at the best bid disappears, sensing in a few moments he might get a better price, leaving a large spread. And suddenly other market participants, seeing what looks like an imminent drop in price, jump in to sell inside the spread, hoping to sell first, before the axe chops the price down. Other market makers at or near the bid change their size to 100 or lower their prices far out of the way. The stage is set; the spring is compressed.

Suddenly a market participant who can't take the anticipation sells to INCA at his bid price. INCA drops its price by one-sixteenth and decreases its size to 100. Other market participants hop on the best offer, hoping to sell. If you have access to the ISLD or ARCA order book, you may see many individual sell orders lining up. Some few more trades go off at the offer, with the nonaxe market participants being the sellers, playing into the axe's hands perfectly, taking his risk upon themselves. (They may be selling short here.) A moment goes by as the market digests what's happening, and suddenly the axe lowers his offer to the inside.

One more moment of palpable tension, with traders everywhere moistening their keyboards, then BOING! They're off. Everyone sells, the ticker fills with trades. INCA sucks up all the liquidity, lowering its bid all the while, then disappears altogether for a moment. This action spikes the price downward, as nobody in their right mind is going to buy in front of that selling pressure. Then INCA's back on the bid, buying every share offered to it. Many, many trades go off, and volume spikes up dramatically. Huge prints hit the tape: 10,000 shares, 25,000 shares. (These are aggregate prints out to the client, whose real order, given to the axe, was "Buy 40,000 shares.") And now, the finish. The axe disappears from the offer and appears on the best bid.

Suddenly the tape goes wild with buys, as the axe takes all the offers, right up to the price the stock traded *before* he offered. Only this time, his offer is nowhere near the inside. And all those ECNs that were offering? They're gone too. There is no supply now in this stock. But now, in comes the *demand*. The market sees the axe buying, and traders, many of whom are now short and realize what just happened, hop on the bandwagon, bidding the price higher and higher. Scalpers, like sharks, smell blood and make lightning-speed trades. The price bids even higher.

The axe, simply using his reputation and the services of an ECN, managed to acquire a substantial number of shares, at an average price well below what was the current market, *just because of a head-fake*. And for better or worse, all those who were tricked into shorting upon seeing his size buy back now, creating a microshort squeeze. The axe's client is happy, because somehow, he bought 40,000 shares of this stock $1 cheaper than it is right now. The fund manager can rest happy, because at least for now, he's up $40,000. Now you can see one of the advantages of using the axe.

Obviously, this was a pretty perfect scenario. The axe had 40,000 shares to buy and did so at a price very favorable to the client. Situations like this happen all the time. However, they're often a little less dramatic. *The extent to which market makers can accomplish their goals without affecting the market is the extent of their success.* If the stock came right back up to where it was, and no further, it would have been perfect. You have to remember that a trader isn't in on the totality of a client's needs; if the client needs 100,000 shares on that day, and the market maker now has to buy the rest at a higher price because the world found out he's a buyer of size, then his games have backfired, and he'll be the loser.

And what about the risk? He was offering some good size. If another market participant was a buyer of size and bought all 10,000 or 12,000 from him, he'd be legally obligated to sell. He'd have to fill the client's order first, without regard for his position. He'd wind up in a bidding war if he wanted to get the shares back. And what about the client's order? A game like this can easily end in tears. If it backfires, a market maker's reputation would be greatly diminished and at the very least he'd lose a bread-and-butter client.

The ethics of this sort of behavior are questionable, and if it was found that the market maker was manipulating the tape, the end result would be disaster. However, watch the 800-pound gorillas of the market-making world, and I guarantee you'll see stuff like this daily. *Beware the headfake:* Misinterpretation of the axe's behavior will separate you from your money. The good thing is that, with practice, this sort of trick is easily identified. It's a little like Simon says: You've got to distinguish what's actually happening from what it looks like.

fading the trend

This happens just before an intraday reversal in price, relating to the next few minutes or hours. The idea is that the market maker is basically done with whatever his orders were, or he is in preliminary exercises to set up a headfake. Essentially what he'll do is try to induce the maximum number of buyers or sellers, trying to exhaust liquidity and prime the market for a price reversal. Keep in mind the market maker may have client sell orders or client short-sell orders (or the converse), or he may be buying or selling for his own inventory.

Say INCA or some other ECN, or even a market maker, has been buying up a stock, driving the price ever higher. The axe has been on and off the offer, and there are very few offers of size out there. To many, it looks like there is a lot of support and very little supply. Volume, which was active before, has largely dried up. The axe, however, keeps raising his price almost every sale, sucking in those few last traders who are convinced the price is going to continue up. As soon as there are no buyers left at the offer for a moment or two, the axe may lower his offer a little bit. But as soon as someone buys stock from him, he raises his offer. As you can see, he's hoping somebody else is going to buy from him. It is important to realize that he may be selling short here or selling the last shares of a client's order. He's trying to reel in the last buyers at a higher price by seeming unwilling to sell. He's hoping all the buyers will disappear and selling will begin, at which point he may run a headfake or otherwise just buy the short shares back. Sooner or later, someone is going to get tired of waiting for what they thought would be a run-up (but disappointingly, the price just hovers). And the more people drawn in at that high price, the harder the price will fall when they all decide they were wrong and try to liquidate. Meanwhile, by creating the impression that the stock is going up, and by luring greedy buyers, the market maker has cleverly sold the totality of his client's order at a very favorable price.

The market maker might also be working a large sell order at a specific price throughout the day. This can be surmised using #Best and a chart, which will have clearly erratic and normal lows, on normal volume, and a flat top price beyond which the stock seems not to be able to pass. The market maker may get on and off the offer price, but every time the price hits that level, he's a seller.

When you identify a market maker who's fading the trend, take a good look at what's happening, and be wary of taking an opposing position. Consider that he has unlimited capital to support whatever he's up to. If you can't tell what he's up to, don't put yourself at risk.

Note: An interesting situation to see is a price that doesn't move at all and has an uncharacteristically static, narrow spread, with good volume, in a stock that usually moves. Check #Best, and you will probably identify two market makers, currently both axes, at least intraday, who both have large buy and sell orders on the day. Supply and demand meet on equal terms, and it is the war of the axes. Though the stock doesn't move, it trades. There are at least a couple of fun ways to play this: by getting in front of size and by participating in line.

getting in front of size

Wait till one of the axes really disappears from either the bid or offer. The key here is that either the supply or the demand has left, and the stock may move strongly one way or the other after the other side is gone. Last year I noticed one market maker in a particular stock bidding all the time and another market maker on the offer all the time, for a couple of days in a row. The stock usually moved 10 percent intraday but for these days, it was static. By my figuring, the two of them had transacted at least 100,000 shares each, and the float on the stock was less than 800,000 shares. While I was eating lunch one day, I noticed the market maker on the offer disappear and reappear, trying to fade the trend, but the bidder wouldn't pay higher. Then a little while later I saw two large prints hit the tape at the bid price (one market maker was printing his aggregate sale or buy to the client), and the market maker on the offer raised his offer way, way out of the way, indicating, at least for the moment, that he was done selling. Then he hopped on the bid; I assumed he was being a greedy little guy and trying to get ahead of the other market maker's size. Well, I wasn't the only one watching, and soon people started taking all the offers. The stock had been trading steadily at 14 by $14^1/_{16}$. By the time I bought in it was $14^1/_8$–$^5/_{16}$. The stock saw \$22 that day, on massive volume; I was out at 18 and change.

"Getting in front of size" is an excellent way of lowering risk. The difficulty lies in two things: (1) after close study of the stock and the market participants, you have to determine that the market maker is a size participant on the day; and (2) you are never going to know when the liquidity you are getting in front of will dry up. When the market maker's order is filled completely, it's time to consider closing the position. Only with careful observation of the market maker's activity and knowledge of the stock will you be able to make a determination. Keep in mind that your best determination is, in fact, an educated guess.

participating in line

Another way to exploit a static market, if there is a large enough spread, is to try to participate by buying at the bid price and selling at the offer. I had just that luck for the first time with Iomega (IOM) in March of 1997. It was bidding $4\frac{7}{8}$–5 for what seemed days. Finally I thought: Why not place an order and see if I can participate in line? So I placed an order to buy 1,000 shares at $4\frac{7}{8}$.

Twenty minutes or so later, I got a fill. So I put the order out to sell at 5. Sure enough, half an hour or so later, I was filled. At about $100 profit after commissions, I figured this wasn't bad. And if I could do it again, even if the price dropped, I'd have at least one-sixteenth ($\frac{1}{8} \times 900$ shares minus commission) downside protection after commission. So I placed the order again and had identical results!

I did this eight or nine times a day, every day, for a few weeks, until, miraculously, my orders wouldn't fill. Opportunities like this abound everyday, if you find stocks that fit the criteria, though I question the economics and ethics of doing this, and don't really do it anymore. Percentage-wise, I think commissions and risk are way too high to make an eighth or a sixteenth worthwhile. And to that end I'll say: Many "day trading" brokerages offer courses in "trading" (to them, "trading" is really scalping) and huge leverage to the trader who agrees to scalp and close all positions by the end of the day. Usually they encourage traders to trade the most active Nasdaq stocks, emphasizing their high volatility. Unscrupulous would be a tender, kindly compliment for those firms, as scalping in today's market is by and large an uneconomic activity, only benefiting the sleazy brokerages that insist on and recommend this activity. In other words, it is very difficult, in practice, to do this. Beginners should probably try a more conservative approach. If you encounter one of these "brokerages," believe me it is in your best interest not to listen to the get-rich talk and steer clear. Remember, brokerages get paid whether you win or lose, and even if you break even after commissions, the "brokerage" gets paid commissions on the 90 or so trades you made. At this point, who are you *really* working for?

rash selling/buying

Sometimes, particularly after news, there will be a sudden flurry of trades on the bid or offer, which will cause a momentary spike in price. If these were trades executed by parties in collusion or by a single market maker with the intention of causing a spike in price, it would constitute "painting the tape," which is strictly illegal. Only StockWatch knows for certain, but it is my opinion that, whether executed by single parties desiring this effect, or multiple parties with natural orders, rash buying or selling will often spark a momentary rally and spike in price.

Watch out for these price movements, as many times the price returns right to where it was before the momentary "spike." The rash of trades serves to shake out the weak hands. It is easy to be whipsawed out of a position (one's stop is hit) this way. Carefully observe these spikes. They can be headfakes, even if unintentionally induced, shaking you out of position at a loss, when success was close at hand.

The realities of a very volatile market make it arguably much easier to be whipsawed out of a position nowadays than in the recent past. You must pay close attention to money management to plan for and mitigate this sort of occurrence.

StockWatch: police of the cybertrader realm

Some people assume fancifully and wrongly that the markets are a Wild West environment where anything goes. Nothing could be further from the truth. A large part of our national livelihood is at stake in our markets, and assurance of fair and orderly markets is a national priority. Equity traders are subject to many laws and are watched carefully. Believe it or not, the staff at StockWatch watches the trading in every security traded on the Nasdaq. They watch and record every bid that is raised, size that is changed, shares that are bought/sold, and traders' phone conversations are recorded. To that end, StockWatch recently pumped approximately $100 million into its surveillance program. In short, equity traders are watched very closely, as anyone with so much responsibility should be.

my totally innocent brush with StockWatch

My brush with StockWatch happened back when I was making markets. The particular stock I was trading, in which I was the axe, was trading near its high, at $8 a share.

A young fund manager (he was 24 years old, and running over $100 million!) owned near half a million shares of this stock, which he had got as a spin-off dividend; in other words, his cost basis was near zero. Over the last month I had been liquidating his entire position and was almost done. I could only sell a little bit of the stock at a time, since the daily volume was under 60,000 shares, and there were few market makers who "made" this stock. (If I sold a whole bunch at once, it would hammer the price.)

Well, we were down to the last 22,000 or so shares when the fund manager called and asked what would happen if I just sold out the rest, right here, right now.

I told him that we would hammer the price and he'd get nowhere near what it was worth. Better to sell slowly into the day, and be done whenever we could.

He said: "Sell it right now. Take it to where it trades."

I said, "But—"

He said, "SELL THE F#%(@ STOCK RIGHT NOW!! I'm curious what'll happen. Hit the bids!!"

He wasn't reacting to any news, he just wanted to be done with this stock so he could buy another one. He'd already profited enormously from it, and he didn't care about price. So I did what he said. He was watching Level II and had a small laugh as all the market makers in this stock panicked and lowered their prices as fast as they could—all the way down to 4\frac{1}{2}$, in about two minutes. And then we were done, so I hung up the phone. About one minute later, my private phone rings, and there is an unfamiliar, goofy-sounding young voice.

"Hey, yeah, is this the trader in ____?"

"Yes . . ."

"Wow, I mean, what's going on, is there some news, or what?"

"Not that I know of. Why?"

"Wow, man, you're . . . um. You just sold so much stock, I just want to know what you know."

Now, as I explained before, nobody can see who's selling stock. That is a confidential matter. One can surmise, but I wasn't even offering the stock, I just preferenced all the market makers on SelectNet. (Note: The market makers whom I transacted with would obviously know that I had sold stock to them, but I had not sold a large block to anyone; it probably took 25 or more trades to sell that stock.) I was mad; and the guy sounded like an idiot, not at all like a trader. (A great many traders are idiots, but something told me he was not of this variety.)

I said, "Who the #&#@!! is this and what makes you think I'm selling stock?"

All of a sudden the voice was clear and serious. "This is John X at StockWatch. I noticed you just sold 22k shares, at a price that doesn't seem reasonable. . . . I'd like to know why." I established his legitimacy by phoning him back at StockWatch and told him it was a natural client order. He again repeated that it didn't sound reasonable that a client would want to sell all that stock that way.

I explained the whole situation, with every detail, and he said that he would look into it. And furthermore, he'd look into *every trade I made for the past six months*. And I was to promptly provide any and all information that he needed, when he needed it, and that failure to comply immediately would result . . .

Thank goodness the money manager was just cocky and young, and not trading with any inside knowledge. Thank Big Brother for recorded phone calls! The situation was obviously uncomfortable, but I hadn't done anything wrong, and I did take away some knowledge from it. StockWatch *is* out there, and does its job, even in the little stocks that nobody pays attention to. And it is aggressive and thorough in its surveillance.

I said at the beginning of the chapter that market makers play far fewer games than you would imagine listening in on the chat rooms. Some people out there are simply unsuited to take on the responsibility of trading their own accounts. These are the ones who are reckless and who won't take time to learn, even when it's their very savings at stake, and these are the ones desperate to blame others rather than do whatever is necessary to get educated. It's not easy. There are very few real overnight zero-to-zillions stories.

There are plenty of success stories, otherwise the speculative markets would not exist: You can make a handsome living at it, but it's not easy. If it were, this book wouldn't be necessary.

Keep in mind, market makers generally have been in the business several years before they are allowed to sit near a desk. They are professionals, skilled at a craft they practice every day. Trading profitably alongside them requires knowledge, cunning, ability, and experience. There is no substitute for these requirements.

chapter 11

margin

Note: Several important changes currently are being promulgated by the Federal Reserve. If enacted, they may materially affect margin regulations—and therefore the contents of this chapter. Always consult your broker to determine the specific rules and regulations that apply to your account and to keep abreast of any changes.

This chapter is *not* intended to be a complete and definitive discussion on margin. It will not serve as a substitute for doing your own due diligence, talking with your broker, and determining any special house rules your brokerage has. As you will see, there may be many. It will, however, give you a general idea of some of what you should know about margin and provide you with the sort of questions you'll need to ask your broker to determine just where you stand.

it's your money

If you were running a movie theater concession stand, you'd make sure you have enough popcorn, hot dogs, soda, and cups before starting your day. If you were running a bakery, you'd see to it that you have enough flour, yeast. . . . You get the point—a daily inventory is essential when dealing in a "commodity"-driven business, like the equity markets.

You must account for your inventory—your money and securities—on at least a daily basis. Common sense will tell you that it's essential. Ask anyone; they'll say, "Darn right it is!" So then why do so many traders rarely examine that most important document, the daily margin report? The only reason I can come up with is that most margin reports look like a bunch of numbers thrown in a bag and spilled on the floor.

But a thorough understanding of margin is absolutely vital to running your business and being profitable. And more important, you need to understand margin to avoid unexpected and unnecessary "calls"—demands to send in more money, often in the thousands, immediately, or suffer your account being closed. The problem is that nothing out there explains margin in an easily understood way. In fact, most of what is written is simply incomprehensible—confounding everyone, including many brokers. And when brokers try to explain margin, they often wind up confusing their clients even more than they were before asking.

So let me throw my hat in the ring. I have a mechanical background, and maybe that is why I dislike things that are not easily understood. Even more, I dislike things that can be broken down and easily understood but that nobody understands! In words once used to describe our Bonnie President Ronnie (forgive me; I mean no offense), "It's not what he doesn't know that bothers me—it's what he knows for damn sure that just ain't so!"

Margin is one of those seemingly complicated things that, when broken down, is easy. I wouldn't say a thing about margin if I didn't think it was so very important or I didn't know it is really simple! This discussion first covers the concepts, then the specifics of understanding margin. I believe that it is more important to understand the general concept of margin—as it applies to standard accounts and "pattern day trading" accounts—than it is to know the specific minutiae of the regulations.

There will probably be terms contained in this chapter for which you don't know the exact definition. I recommend that you know the exact definition. It is worth it to purchase *Wall Street Words*, an excellent source for explanation of stock market–related terms.

For now, here's the basic definition of a margin account: A margin account is a brokerage account that permits an investor to purchase securities on credit and to borrow against securities already in the account. Buying on credit and borrowing are subject to standards established by the Federal Reserve and/or by the firm carrying the account. Interest is charged on any borrowed funds and only for the period of time that the loan is outstanding.

Basic concept 1: Brokers may lend you money toward the purchase of stock. The lending of money toward the purchase of stock is covered by Regulation T of the Securities Exchange Act of 1934 (Reg T). The regulations themselves are very confusing.

For the sake of clarity, I'll deal with the concept as it applies to purchases of stock in a margin account first, then I'll deal with the slightly different rules regulating short sales of stock, and finally, those additional rules specific to day trading. Special regulations have been established regulating accounts designated as pattern day trading accounts. These regulations differ substantially from standard Reg T in several ways, so it is vital to determine whether your account will be coded "pattern day trading," and therefore will be subject to the additional regulations. I'll deal with pattern day trading accounts last, after you have a firm understanding of the basics of Reg T. And please, read that section last. You may think you know this stuff by heart already, but bear with me and read it through. There may be things you are not aware of, and an understanding of the general concepts is absolutely essential if you are considering trading for a living.

By the way, as you may have picked up from Chapter 8, on selling short, any brokerage account in which one is borrowing money or stock is called a margin account. All margin accounts are regulated by Regulation T of the Securities Act of 1934.

It is important to note here that clearinghouses may, at their discretion, establish *more stringent* policies than the standards stipulated in Reg T, but in no case may they be more lax. Brokerage houses must adhere to the standards set forth by the Federal Reserve in the 1934 act, but clearinghouses may decide to create policies that not only adhere to the standard requirements but are in fact and addition more restrictive. This chapter deals first with the standard policies of Reg T. You *must* consult your broker to determine if its clearing rules are "standard Reg T," or more stringent. Additionally, you'll need to know whether your account is a PDT (pattern day trading) account. Otherwise you won't know the policies by which your account (and therefore your money) is regulated. And if you are in ignorance, you risk being surprised in very unpleasant ways. Think of it this way: The federal speed limit on rural highways may be 70 mph, but if a particular community has decided that on the stretch of highway that winds through their community the speed limit will be 35 mph, and you violate this 35 mph speed limit, even if in ignorance of the law, you'll still pay the fine. Ignorance of the law is no excuse. And ignorance of the regulations by which your hard-earned assets are regulated is a shame. An expensive, aggravating, stressful, fully avoidable shame.

purchase of stock in a standard margin account

When you open a margin account, you are giving your brokerage certain rights, in consideration of which you are getting certain things in return. What the broker gives you in return is the ability to borrow money toward the purchase of "marginable" stock. The Federal Reserve Board makes the initial determination of what stocks are eligible for borrowing against, though your clearinghouse will make the final decision regarding whether it wishes to lend on specific securities. For example, the Fed may determine that ABCD stock meets the requirements and is therefore eligible (for loaning against) for purchase on margin. However, your clearinghouse may feel that notwithstanding the fact that ABCD is "marginable" according to the Fed, ABCD is currently too volatile or risky to justify loans against, and so may only allow purchase of the stock using 100 percent cash, for example. After the Fed has made its decision regarding the stock, your clearinghouse may still, at its discretion, decide that the stock is too volatile to loan against. Remember, if you make a purchase "on margin" you are borrowing funds (i.e., getting a loan) to pay for the stock. The stock is "held" by the brokerage to secure the loan.

In opening a margin account, in addition to gaining the ability to borrow money toward the purchase (or short sale) of securities, you agree to several binding conditions. The four more important ones for understanding margin are listed here:

1. You will pay interest charges on borrowed money.

2. You will allow the brokerage to lend your stock out to secure your loan—and for this you will not receive interest—but you will be free to sell your stock anytime.

3. You agree that if the equity (cash value) in your account drops to less than 25 percent of the current market value of your margined positions (positions purchased on margin; i.e., purchased with some of your cash and some lent to you by the brokerage), you will be called (required) to send in money or liquidate enough stock to cover the "maintenance" within a certain period of time. You further agree that if you don't, the brokerage or clearinghouse will be required to liquidate and will do so.

4. You further agree to abide by the regulations set forth in Reg T as well as any additional "house rules" of your brokerage/clearinghouse.

So, how much money will the brokerage loan? The Federal Reserve chooses a maximum margin of money that is allowed to be lent toward purchases of stock. The amount of money a brokerage may lend you toward the purchase of stocks on margin is calculated as a percentage of the total purchase price for the stock, and the percentage is variable. Currently (and since the early 1970s) the rate is 50 percent. So, the maximum amount of money your broker may lend you is 50 percent of the total initial value of the position. Therefore, your purchasing ability is always *double* your excess equity in a margin account in a standard Reg T situation. "Excess equity" will be explained in a moment. Your purchasing ability is referred to as "buying power." So when you wonder how much stock you may purchase, ask your broker what your current buying power is, then divide that amount by the current price of the stock. For example, if you have no positions and $10,000 cash, your cash (all $10,000 is "excess equity" in this case, since you have no positions) equals 50 percent of your buying power. So, $10,000 × 2 equals $20,000—100 percent of your current "buying power." To find out how much ABCD stock you can currently buy (remember, ABCD is a "marginable" stock), you take your buying power of $20,000 and divide it by the current market price of the stock. Let's say that ABCD stock is currently offered $10\frac{1}{2}$, so at that price you could buy 1,904.76 shares, or 1,904 shares ($20,000 divided by $10\frac{1}{2}$ = 1,904.7619, or 1,904 shares since you can't buy a partial share).

The money that you have in excess of the cost of your positions (or your amount of cash, if you hold no positions) is equal to

50 percent—half—of your buying power. So, with $10,000 in cash, you have the power to buy $20,000 worth of stock. This "credit" is available to you anytime you choose in a margin account. In fact, and this is an odd concept, it is always available to you in a margin account: Generally speaking, any purchase made in a margin account will consist of 50 percent your cash and 50 percent borrowed money.

What? What about if you have $100,000 cash and decide to buy only $10,000 of stock in your margin account? What then?

Well, $5,000 (50 percent) of the purchase cost comes from your pocket and $5,000 (the other 50 percent) is loaned to you, leaving you with $95,000 cash (and $190,000 buying power: $95,000 × 2). If you close the position by the end of the day, generally you pay no interest on the loan value ($5,000) at all. But if you hold overnight, then the charges for interest begin. This is one way brokerages and clearinghouses make money. Many people are under the mistaken impression that as long as they don't spend more than they have in cash they are not buying on margin. Every purchase in a margin account is "on margin" unless your clearinghouse has different rules or you specified "cash only" at time of purchase. In order to avoid using credit, you must tell your broker to purchase the securities outright with 100 percent cash. The better trading platforms even have a little box that you can check to specify 100 percent cash only. Of course, then, since you won't be using any lent money, your dollar amount of cash buying power will equal your dollar amount of cash.

Note: If you purchase a nonmarginable security in your margin account, you'll automatically pay 100 percent cash, since your brokerage house cannot or will not lend money toward its purchase. Remember, clearinghouses may be more restrictive than standard Reg T. For example, many brokerages require 100 percent cash to purchase some of the more volatile Internet stocks. Even though the Fed will allow clearinghouses to lend against these stocks, some believe they are simply too risky to make loans on, so their own house rules will not allow you to purchase them on margin.

Clearinghouses that do this are protecting the consumer and themselves. If they feel the stock is too risky, they may simply not allow for purchase of it using margin. There will be plenty of situations where one brokerage may offer the purchase of these stocks on margin, whereas others will not. Some brokerages even have standard policies requiring the trader to put up, say, 75 percent of the purchase cost on any volatile Internet stock. So let's say you've been trading with a brokerage that allows you to purchase these stocks with only 50 percent cash (standard Reg T), and you switch to an account where you must put up 75 percent cash but haven't bothered to check. And then you purchase the stock and are asked to send in cash to cover the purchase. This can happen and wind up causing your account to be liquidated and closed, if you don't send in the money within a short time. This is one of the "unpleasant surprises" I talked about. In short, if you are putting your assets on the line, every day, do your homework!

The reasons why you might want to buy on margin are obvious: You can double your returns. You can, of course, lose double when wrong. So is buying on margin more risky? Yes—you are increasing your exposure to profit *and* loss. But more on that later. See Chapter 9 for additional information. For now, let's discuss what happens when you actually make that $10,000 purchase in a standard Reg T margin account.

Okay, so you purchase $10,000 worth of a marginable stock in your margin account. You are subject to the "initial call"—the initial call for money. You must contribute 50 percent of the total initial cost of the position toward the purchase. In this case, the amount you must contribute is $5,000. The rest (the other $5,000) is lent to you. It is important to note that the value of the loan never changes, though the price of the securities likely will. So, let's say the stock appreciates in value to $20,000. You decide to sell. Well, $5,000 of that money is not yours, so it gets returned to the brokerage house, along with any interest charges if it was held overnight. Remember, the loan value never changes. The rest of the money goes back to you ($10,000 profit minus interest). Now let's suppose you held the stock for a year to achieve this appreciation; you will have to pay interest on the $5,000 you borrowed for each day you held the stock. While interest charges are usually relatively small, they are significant. They fluctuate with the prime rate, and the lending rate is called the "broker's call." Ask your broker what his rate is. Usually he will say something like "A quarter point above broker's call; currently $8\frac{1}{4}$ percent annually." Note that if you do hold the stock for a year, and you are paying $8\frac{1}{4}$ percent interest on the monies borrowed (and 50 percent of the money will be borrowed), you must have a total return of at least $4^1/_8$ percent on the position just to break even.

exceeding your equity: trading calls

Now let's say you made the same purchase, but this time you have only $4,000 cash (and no positions) to begin with in your account, not $10,000. Your "buying power" is going to be $8,000 on the day (excess equity × 2; or $4,000 × 2 = $8,000). Another way of putting it is that your $4,000 cash equals 50 percent (half) of your buying power. You have a good relationship with your broker, and so you go ahead and purchase $10,000 worth of stock.

How can you do this when you only have $8,000 in buying power? Well, by regulation, you have three days to bring in your payment for a purchase, and the broker knows you are responsible (because you read, initialed, and signed all the small print on your margin account agreement signifying that you have read *and understand it*) and knows that you intend to pay for any purchases you make. So how much will you need to bring in? Well, remember: The initial call for a purchase in a margin account is 50 percent, and in any case, the broker may never lend more than 50 percent toward a purchase. This means that for a $10,000 purchase of a marginable stock, in a standard Reg T account you will need to contribute $5,000 as the initial call. You have $4,000 already in the account, so you will need to send in an additional $1,000 to cover the initial call of $5,000.

But if you buy it on margin and then sell it before the end of the day, then you won't have to send any money in, right?

Wrong. You bought it, and you'll need to have money in your account to cover the initial call. Even if you made $1 million intraday trading it, you'll *still* need to send in that initial call. This is a stipulation of Regulation T. There's no getting around it. Keep in mind that, in the above case, you could pull the money right back out. But this situation is most serious, because if you fail to send the initial call in, the brokerage house will be required to liquidate your purchase and freeze your account for 90 days. If you fail to send in the initial call, many clearinghouses will simply consider you a risk and close your account altogether! This is not a form of penalty. (You can't expect them to pay for your positions, can you?) However, consider the following. Nowadays many brokerages utilize the services of the same few clearinghouses. Now, if the clearinghouse closes your account because it considers you a risk, it will not open another account for you. And, therefore, neither will any of the brokerages that clear through that clearinghouse! I hope this will never happen to you, but it is always good to know all possibilities in advance. Then you can plan your affairs with confidence.

The situation just described, in my experience, is a most common error and cause for major aggravation. Imagine if you grossly exceed your buying power, erroneously thinking that "Well, I'm selling all the positions before close, so I won't have to send in anything," then make a killing, and immediately go on vacation. Upon your return several days later, you find that you are suddenly required to send in $100,000 immediately or suffer your account being closed. You might not be able to. Even if you have the cash readily available, it might be past your bank's wire deadline. This happens all the time, believe me. And to highly intelligent, educated people too. If you have a good understanding of the way margin works, you'll never find yourself in this awful position.

Always keep in mind the initial call requirement. Calculate your intraday buying power at the start of every day, and *never exceed it*, and you will never have this nasty kind of surprise.

By the way, many software programs calculate your buying power for you. If yours does not, calculating your intraday buying power is fairly simple. Once you've done it for a couple or three days in a row it will become second nature. Please call your broker for details of the way to calculate your buying power. Of course, most top-end trading platforms do this for you or provide you with the information you need for the calculation. Saving that, you may always call your broker and ask "What's my buying power?" A full-service brokerage will always calculate it for you, as a part of the service. At many direct-access firms, the trader (*you*) will be responsible for keeping tabs on it. The better direct-access firms provide you with all the necessary information on your margin report.

maintaining a position overnight

Suppose you decide to hold your position ($10,000 worth of ABCD, a fictitious Nasdaq stock) overnight. You will be required to have 50 percent of the value of the position in equity to hold it overnight. If you have less, you will be required to send money in. So in this case, you will need to have at least $5,000 (50 percent of $10,000 = $5,000) in equity. The way you calculate equity is: the current market value of the stock ($10,000) minus the loan value ($5,000) equals your equity: $5,000.

Let's say, for sake of argument, that you decide to ignore all your best intentions to cut your losses and hold a terrible position overnight. News came out today, and ABCD said it is going to restate its earnings for the previous quarter (and they're going to be really, really bad), and ABCD Corp. has even fired its accountant. During the day the stock traded down so much that your total position is now worth only $7,000. Remember: The loan value never changes. So, to calculate your equity now, take the current market value (CMV) and subtract the loan value (which never changes!). You have the following result:

$7,000	CMV
− 5,000	LV—the loan value; never changes
= $2,000	your current equity

You can also figure it this way: your original equity plus or minus the change in the value of the position, like this:

$ 7,000	CMV
− 10,000	original cost
= ($ 3,000)	change in value of the position were you to close it now
	(Note: Parentheses indicate loss.)

Your original equity was $5,000, so

$5,000	original equity
− 3,000	change in value
= $2,000	current equity

If you keep less than 50 percent equity but more than 25 percent equity in a long position, you will not receive a maintenance call but your account will be frozen. If your equity dips below 25 percent, you will be required to send in money or liquidate enough stock to bring your equity up to 40 percent.

Okay, I lied. This stuff isn't so simple, and here's where it gets weird. Please believe me when I say the hard stuff is almost over. Just one more hurdle and you're halfway there. Just kidding: You're there! This little part concerns the dreaded "maintenance call." If you can get through this, you're well on your way to trading with complete confidence. Or at least you'll have fewer nasty surprises in a standard margin account. But keep in mind that special rules apply to pattern day trading accounts. You will need to know how these work too, if you plan to trade with confidence.

To hold overnight, you *must* maintain 50 percent of the value of the position(s) in equity. Getting back to the example, the position is now worth $7,000, and you have at this point $2,000 in equity. Clearly not a good situation. But you will not be *required* to send in money just yet—because at this point your equity is approximately 28.6 percent of the value of your position. If ABCD continues its downward descent, eventually you will be required to send in money or suffer your account being liquidated. The point of no return occurs when the equity in your account is equal to 25 percent (or less) of the total value of the position(s). If it ever gets to that point (and I sincerely hope you never ever let it get that bad; reread Chapter 9 and use common sense to keep yourself liquid and safe!), you will receive a maintenance call of an amount that would bring the equity in your account up to at least 40 percent of the value of the position. If you do not send it in, the brokerage will be required, per Regulation T, to liquidate stock in order to bring your equity up to at least 40 percent of the market value of the position. Until it gets that bad, however, you will not be required to send anything in. During this time, however, your account will be frozen. What this means is that you may sell anytime, but in order to buy, you will need to pay in advance. If you really like to be in control (can you guess I'm a fan of being in control?) and wish to calculate in advance at what point you would receive a maintenance call, please consult your broker. And keep in mind that all this becomes more complex as your number of positions increases. But the idea is the same: The total value of all your positions minus your total loan value equals your equity. And your equity minus your minimum maintenance requirement equals your overnight buying power. Minimum maintenance requirement refers to the minimum amount of equity you must maintain in your account in order to hold your current position(s). If holding overnight, it is 50 percent, as discussed above. There are several additional things to be aware of in pattern day trading accounts; I'll deal with those shortly. However, when holding short positions, even in a standard margin account, the requirements are different from the long position requirements. Let's deal with them first.

margin and short positions

When you sell stock short, you are borrowing the security and selling it, with the intention of closing the position (buying the security back and returning it to the lender) at some later date at some lower price, and keeping the difference. See Chapter 8 for more specifics concerning short selling. Keep in mind that when you sell short, you are borrowing securities; therefore, the transaction *must* take place in a margin account. Regulation T serves to govern extension of credit (loans, as in lending stock) toward the purchase or sale of securities.

There are several important differences with regard to margin when shorting stock. The first difference, of course, is that you are selling stock and therefore receiving cash in return for the sale. You will not have use of this cash; the brokerage house holds it, sort of like in escrow. And you will, weird as this sounds, pledge 50 percent of the value of the position in equity. This is similar to what happens when you buy stock, because, in effect, your selling power is double your equity. The clearing firm holds your initial call of 50 percent, sort of like in escrow. The brokerage house puts up the other 50 percent. However, it is not considered a debit, as when you purchase equities. It is a credit. The "credit" is also lent to you, so let's call the amount of the loan "loan value" for the sake of simplicity. The loan value (in this case a credit) never changes, though the price of the security likely will.

The rules regarding initial margin and maintenance that apply to purchases are similar in short positions, except for the fact that when you are calculating, you are calculating based on a *credit* loan balance rather than a debit loan balance, which is a significant difference.

The difference is that the maintenance threshold is higher. In a long position, when your equity drops below 25 percent, you will receive a margin call. In a short position, the maintenance threshold is higher: It is 30 percent.

In a short position, if your equity falls below 50 percent but not below 30 percent, you will not receive a call, but your account will be frozen. If your equity dips below 30 percent, you will be required to send in money or liquidate positions to bring your equity up to 40 percent of the value of the position(s).

Now let's look at an example. Let's say you have $4,000 cash in your account and no positions. You see ABCD stock—a fictitious Nasdaq security. Terrible news has just come out: ABCD is going to restate its earnings for the previous quarter, and the earnings are going to be really, really bad. Having access to real-time news and being a practiced observer of this stock, you short $10,000 worth of it immediately, expecting a harsh drop in price.

But if you have $4,000 in your account, that's only $8,000 "shorting power." You intend to cover the position later today, but you realize you will still need to send in $1,000 in initial margin anyway. (Remember: The initial margin requirement is 50 percent; total value of the position is $10,000, and the brokerage house is only able to lend you 50 percent of the value of the position; 50 percent of $10,000 is $5,000—the loan (credit) value. You must also contribute $5,000 as initial call, and only $4,000 is in your account, so you write a check immediately for $1,000 and send it overnight mail.) It is worth it to you, since you think this thing is gonna go to zero, and you'll make a killing.

So now you are short this ABCD stock and are pleased as it drops quickly as the news spreads and sellers emerge. At the end of the day, the position is worth only $7,000—and indeed, you have made your killing . . . on paper at least. Were you to cover the position now, you would have a profit of $3,000. A review of your equity is as follows:

$7,000	current market value
$10,000	initial sale proceeds
$5,000	equity you put up
$5,000	equity you put up (the loan value; credited by your brokerage)

Now the stock declines (which is what you want it to do since you are short), and presently the stock is marked to market at its current replacement value (CRV). I say "replacement" here, since you will have to "replace" the stock you borrowed and then sold.

$7,000   CRV

So you may calculate your account equity in the following way: the equity you started with, plus or minus the marked-to-market "paper" proceeds. The proceeds are:

$10,000	initial sales proceeds, credited to you
– 7,000	CRC (current replacement cost)
= $ 3,000	difference (paper profit)

So your equity is currently:

$5,000	initial sales proceeds, credited to you
+ 3,000	marked-to-market "paper" proceeds
= $8,000	

Another way to calculate it: Your equity also equals the value of the position if closed minus the amount lent to you:

$10,000	original sale proceeds
+ 3,000	"paper profit" achieved if you covered now
= $13,000	total value of position if closed now

So:

$13,000	total value of position if closed now calculated above
– 5,000	CV; "credit" (loan) value
= $ 8,000	equity

Now, here's the interesting part: This "paper" increase in equity (whether gained from a short sell as in the previous example or gained from the purchase of a security that has since appreciated in value) is only theoretical until you close the position, right? However, you may use the "paper profit" anyway: Your brokerage house will lend it to you by sending you a check for the amount (minus the maintenance withholding), or allowing you to use it toward the purchase or sale of additional securities, as long as use/removal of this money doesn't cause you to drop below your minimum maintenance requirement. The "paper" increase in equity is recorded in what is called "SMA" on your margin report. SMA stands for "special memorandum account." Whenever you have a "paper" increase in equity, it is recorded as a journal entry to your SMA.

So, following the example just given, you have this $3,000 increase in SMA, which the brokerage house can send to you or allow you to use subject to Regulation T. Remember, per Reg T, the brokerage house can lend up to 50 percent of the value of a position. This position has increased in value by $3,000, so the brokerage house can lend you $1,500 (50 percent of $3,000) right away. You can use this money however you see fit. Keep in mind that since the profit is for now "on paper," but not realized (by closing the position you will have real profit), any monies withdrawn are *loans*, backed by your position. And you will pay interest on loans held overnight.

But getting back to the example. Remember that when the stock goes against you—that is (if you are short), it appreciates in value—to the point where your equity is less than 50 percent of the value of the position, your account will be frozen in the same manner discussed concerning long positions. You will be able to cover your position at any time, but in order to initiate any new positions, you will be required to send in cash upfront.

And should the position keep increasing in value, if it ever reaches the point where your equity is 30 percent or less of the total value of the position, you will be required to send in money to maintain your position. If you don't, you will be subject to liquidation to bring your account back to at least 40 percent equity. The process and ramifications are the same as discussed for long positions, with one significant difference: the size of the threshold. With short positions, it is 30 percent, as opposed to 25 percent for long positions. The maintenance requirement is higher for short positions because short positions have added risk. Remember, in a long position, your loss is theoretically limited to 100 percent of the value of the position. If you are short, in theory, the stock may rise against you to a potentially unlimited loss. Can you imagine if you had shorted a ridiculous "online" bookseller (Amazon.com) that didn't even have a store or even inventory in the salad days of Internet commerce (three short years ago) when the "ridiculous" company, without even a hope of earnings anytime soon—was trading at $8? Can you say "bankrupt"?

To calculate in advance what price a short position would have to rise to to generate a maintenance call, please call your broker and get the facts on how to do this. Again, this is easy to do; a fifth grader could do it.

cash purchases (or purchases of nonmarginable securities) in a margin account

You may, of course, elect to purchase your stock with 100 percent cash. As mentioned, the better direct-access electronic brokerages have a button or box that you may select to designate your purchase as a 100 percent paid-for-in-cash purchase.

Obviously, if you purchase a nonmarginable security (one for which your clearinghouse won't lend money), you must do so in cash. So what happens if, say, you have $50,000 in cash (equity) and no open positions and you purchase $40,000 worth of a nonmarginable security? Your "buying power" on margin will then be $20,000. Calculate it this way:

$50,000	excess equity: equity free and clear of any open position
– 40,000	used to purchase a nonmarginable security, which "absorbs" 100 percent cash
= $10,000	$\frac{1}{2}$ or 50 percent of "buying power" in a margin account; then, $10,000 × 2 (because $10,000 is half of your buying power) = $20,000.

Or, of course, you may purchase $10,000 worth of securities in cash.

As a rule, new issues and securities that generally trade at prices under $5 will not be marginable and must be purchased with 100 percent cash. Generally speaking, securities that are well established and trade with good volume and at prices well above $5 will often be marginable and so may often be purchased on margin. However, even if a security has been designated as marginable, a brokerage house may elect *not* to allow purchase on margin, or may only be willing to lend a lesser amount toward its purchase. There is also the following situation: A security with a longstanding marginable history may fall on hard times and trade for less than $5. Such securities may in fact still be marginable because they haven't been reviewed again in light of their new status. Always check with your broker to determine the status of a desired stock *before* trading it. Safe is always better than sorry. And the "rules" are just general statements, not specific fact. Get the facts from your broker before trading.

pattern day trading accounts

A pattern day trading account is any account in which there is a "pattern" of day trading—that is, opening positions one day and closing them on the same day, therefore ending the day flat with no positions. In the "old days," "day trading" was largely limited to professional traders, who were given a special type of account, coded pattern day trading (PDT) account. Now, with the advent of new technologies allowing individual traders everywhere to participate and trade actively, these accounts are being utilized by many more people. Many of these traders previously had standard margin accounts, and so are not aware of the special effects the PDT coding has on their accounts. People who plan to trade actively for a living must be aware of these special effects.

PDT accounts, in addition to being subject to the calculations of Regulation T, are also subject to another calculation, the specifics of which will be discussed presently. This additional method of accounting provides some advantages for the active trader as well as some additional restrictions. However, because these accounts are subject to both Regulation T *and* special PDT calculations at the same time, the calculations are tremendously confusing to Joe Public. As mentioned earlier, the Fed is currently promulgating a new set of regulations that may clarify the situation. Until this is done, we must learn the current regulations, which are not user-friendly. Traders who fail to understand the special conditions of a PDT account often wind up with suddenly closed accounts.

If you have an account at a full-service brokerage or even at an on-line brokerage, chances are strong that the account is regulated only by Regulation T or more restrictive "house rules," even though you trade actively. Accounts at full-service brokerages are often designed for individual nonprofessional investors. Often they are actively traded (though for reasons enumerated earlier they may not be suitable or desirable for active intraday trading), but many times users still are subject only to Regulation T and/or any more restrictive house rules.

If you have an account with a "direct-access" firm, however, it will likely be coded pattern day trading and be subject to the special PDT methods of accounting in addition to Reg T.

the good news

There are advantages and disadvantages to pattern day trading accounts. One of the main differences between a standard margin account and a PDT is that in a PDT there are different requirements covering intraday and overnight buying power. One of the advantages of a PDT is that you will have a maintenance withhold on positions of only 25 percent intraday, as opposed to 50 percent, so you'll have greater money with which to play intraday.

In other words, for the purposes of day trading, in a PDT account you will be required to maintain only 25 percent (rather than 50 percent on positions held overnight) intraday. Therefore, your intraday buying power is greater in a PDT account than in one regulated by Regulation T alone.

However, there is a price to pay for this potentially greater intraday buying power. This price comes in the serious restrictions that exist regarding use of that money. If you trade in blissful ignorance of how Regulation T and the special PDT calculations interact in a PDT account, at some point you may have a brutal lesson that summarily finishes your trading career.

the bad news

The first restriction we'll look at is a killer. It is, in my personal opinion, the cause of more frustration and anguish than can be measured.

You *must* be aware of this particular situation if you have a PDT account. The way that the additional calculation works in a PDT is like this: At the end of the day, when calculating equity and margin calls and the like, the calculation looks *only* at all the trades made intraday. That is, it assumes you've held no positions overnight. It looks at buys and sells made during the day and matches them. It is hoped that you start the day flat and end the day flat. But if you held a stock overnight today, this fact goes unnoticed . . . for the PDT part of the calculation.

So, let's look at the effect of this. Let's say you have a full-service brokerage account or an online discount account. Let's say you maxed out your buying power and bought 1,000 YHOO yesterday, and held it overnight for the gap-up. It gaps, and today at market open, you sell all 1,000 shares. Then you buy 1,000 shares again and sell the 1,000 shares, at a profit, and then buy the 1,000 shares and sell them again, again for a profit.

In a standard account, you would end the day flat, having sold your overnight position and then traded YHOO intraday, finally going flat into the close. Provided you didn't exceed your buying power, you're fine: no calls.

Now let's look at the same scenario in a PDT account, which subjects you to both the Regulation T calculation and the PDT calculation. Remember, the PDT side of the calculation doesn't look at what you held overnight—only what you traded intraday. So let's see how the last example would work in a PDT. The first thing you did was sell the 1,000 shares that you held overnight. Well, in a PDT this is seen as a sell too, but with one big difference: Since the PDT calculation doesn't take into account your overnight position and only looks at trades made intraday, it sees the first thing you did as a sell short. Next you bought (the PDT calculation says you "covered the short") and then sold again (the PDT says "went short again") and then bought and sold again. So the PDT says you finished the day short.

This may sound nuts, but this is the way things work currently. Keep in mind that securities regulations have evolved over time and have been modified to take situations into account as they have arisen. Don't argue the logic—unless you've got way too much time on your hands. Just learn the way things work. And when they change, learn the new paradigms.

But now it gets *really* weird. Remember, you're still subject to Regulation T in a PDT, and the PDT calculation says you have a short position. So now you get a Reg T call on your short position! But the fun isn't over. What about the stock you held overnight (which the PDT calculation didn't notice)? You still "hold" that too—at least according to the calculations—so you'll have a maintenance requirement on it.

Now remember, for the purposes of this example, you held a substantial position in YHOO overnight. It is easy to see how the calls generated by this additional PDT calculation could run into the hundreds of thousands of dollars.

For this example, where for the purposes of calculating, you ended up with a position of 1,000 shares of YHOO—which is currently $320 a share—the 50 percent initial call would be $160,000! And you'll be required to send this in or have your account closed. This is seen as an initial call on the short position, and there is no way of getting around it—once the call is generated, it must be satisfied, or eventually the account will be closed.

This scenario is a typical one, generated by nothing other than arguably outdated rules. Of course, had you managed your risk properly, you would get no such call. But this example is predicated on the assumption that you maxed out your buying power with each purchase. Calculating where you stand on a moment-to-moment basis can be difficult in a PDT account, especially if you have made many trades intraday. And having this happen can mean the end of your account! So, please, please continue reading.

e-z rule on trading stock you've held overnight in a PDT account

The following rule of thumb will serve you well in a PDT account. This rule is designed for simplicity's sake, to keep you safe without having to make tedious calculations. You don't even have to understand the scenarios just discussed. And if you follow this rule, you'll have fewer surprises. Here it is: In a pattern day trading account, if you hold a stock overnight, *do not* day-trade it the next day.

In other words, if you hold a stock overnight, *do not* day-trade it the next day.

And furthermore, if you hold a stock overnight, *do not* day-trade it the next day.

So now you know that if you hold a stock overnight, *do not* day-trade it the next day.

Please repeat after me: If I hold a stock overnight, I *must not* day-trade it the next day. And again: If I hold a stock overnight, I *must not* day-trade it the next day. I recommend writing this sentence 100 times. I am absolutely serious. And I'm not being cute. As I said earlier, this "specific PDT regulation" has, in my opinion, been the cause of more frustration and anguish than can be measured.

Another example of what happens if you do trade a stock you just held overnight in a PDT follows. Again, you must understand that you are subject to all the conditions of Regulation T. So you will need to put up 50 percent of the purchase price of any stock bought. And in addition, you are subject to the additional calculation specific to a PDT.

Again, in a PDT, the additional calculation looks at every trade you have made intraday and matches them. It also allows you to use 25 percent of the Reg T hold, as discussed earlier. But again, here's where things get weird.

It looks at the trades you've made in a day. In other words, if I come in today with 200 AOL—that is, I bought it yesterday and held it overnight—and I sell it at market open, the calculation looks on the sell as my opening trade of the day. Again, the calculation doesn't take into account prior positions held overnight.

So now I've sold my AOL at a nice profit, and I'm flat AOL, right? In a Reg T account, yes. And in a PDT as well, provided I don't trade AOL again on that day. But let's say I do. Let's say I trade 100 shares of AOL five times today. Buy, sell; buy, sell; buy, sell; buy, sell; buy, sell. Well, I should still end the day flat, right? *Not in a PDT.*

Remember, the calculation looks at actual trades done today, irrespective of positions coming into the day. So now look at the first trade, a *sell*, which will be seen as a short, since the calculation doesn't look at the overnight hold; and then the first buy, which will be seen as a cover buy, and you run down the trades and guess what? The PDT calculation sees you as *short!* And if this isn't convoluted enough, you will then be required to send in Reg T 50 percent cash for the new "position" the calculation says you have. And what about your old position, the one you held overnight and sold first thing in the morning? PDT accounting doesn't see it . . . but Reg T does. It thinks you still own it, so you will be required to keep 50 percent in equity to hold the position overnight!

You can see how, if you were caught unawares, this could lead to an unmanageable call for cash, which on such short notice you might have no hope of meeting. And the rules cannot be bent or broken; you will be required to send in any funds necessary or suffer your account being closed!

KISS: Keep it simple, silly! And don't trade any position that you've held overnight!

More often than not, this error—almost always done unawares, in ignorance of the regulations governing the account, even though you said you read them and understand them and have agreed to abide and be bound by them—causes a hellacious margin call. It can mean game over, because the call generated by this event is often, by virtue of being unplanned and huge, insurmountable. Many otherwise good traders, who know how to pick a stock and how to buy and sell, and know risk management, fall short in this one fatal regard: not knowing this simple little killer.

Now you know. And the killer mad dog has just been reduced to a friendly puppy.

a final note on margin

This chapter is not a replacement for talking with your broker and finding out the specifics of margin and what "house rules" your account will be subject to. Additionally, these rules change! But it gives you some general principles so you will have a better idea of what questions you should be asking (e.g., you will want to determine *before* opening the account whether it will be a regular margin account or one coded pattern day trading). Once you have: (1) a grasp of the general rules and regulations in margin accounts; (2) done your due diligence to determine whether your account is standard Regulation T or a more restrictive one, and if so, in what way; and (3) determined any particular "house rules" of the brokerage, you will have the tools to always know where you stand. It will be up to you to monitor your account, to make sure you are always exactly where you ought to be, riskwise.

Make a practice of monitoring your account on a daily basis, just as if you were running any commodity-driven business. Always know where you stand, and accept the fact that the responsibility ultimately rests with you. If you don't do your due diligence, you have nobody to blame but yourself. I don't mean to be preachy or to belabor the subject, but I've seen totally avoidable situations create such aggravation and havoc that I feel it's warranted to spend real time considering these important issues.

So, always understand your overall position. Print out your margin report every day. Monitor your positions and make sure you are never, ever, overextended. Plan accordingly. Run your business as a business should be run. And suffer no surprises!

For the actual NASD explanation of Reg T and the calculation specific to a pattern day trading account, check the Web at investor.nasd.com/notices/98102ntm.txt.

chapter 12

philosophical perspective

"that's life . . . that's what all the people say . . ."

Direct individual access to the securities markets has unquestionably affected the markets, but the jury is still out on what it all means. Major institutions and individuals alike wanted the liquidity that individual access to the markets could supply, but now that it exists, many are arguing for some sort of restrictions due to the volatility and balance-of-power issues that have arisen. The media, encouraged by the powers-that-be, run shows on how greedy and awful traders are, but the reality is traders and speculators have been around since before the tulip days of seventeenth-century Holland. And now that transparent electronic access to the markets exists, one thing is for sure: Direct access to the markets is here to stay.

poor Willie Loman

With the advent of sophisticated electronic communications networks like Archipelago, the very job and definition of "market maker" has changed. Is it necessary to incur the legal responsibilities of making a market in a time when you can do virtually the same thing without the legal responsibilities? In fact, the very meaning of "market" has changed; the Nasdaq system was the first step in the electronic evolution of the markets, when it created a virtual floor. Market participants from anywhere in the world could suddenly participate directly in the over-the-counter market. But now *anyone* with access to an electronic communications network can enter orders through a computer with an Internet connection, 24 hours a day. What will this do to the market? What will the term "market hours" mean when humans are no longer required (or desired) to make markets?

I believe the securities markets are heading toward an ECN-dominated, 24-hour virtual floor, where anyone with a brokerage account will be able to buy and sell securities directly, without additional human intervention (in the form of broker or trader) anytime, from anywhere in the world.

Supporting my conjecture is the fact that companies like Goldman Sachs and J.P. Morgan have taken major stakes in major ECNs (I wouldn't bet against them) and that the Nasdaq is proposing major changes to its order execution systems as well as its quotations. Additionally, many trading desks are evolving, as more and more institutions utilize the services of ECNs themselves, further cutting out the traders and market makers.

And what happens to brokers when individuals can sell their stock directly and can research companies for free over the Internet? Research reports put together by financial analysts will always be needed, since individuals will not have the specific knowledge (or time) to evaluate companies in the detailed way analysts do. So analysts will always be around, and perhaps in greater numbers, as more and more individuals enter the markets. But again, what about brokers? It seems to me that things will be tougher and tougher for brokers. In the same way that the traveling salesman of the 1940s was edged out by major department stores where individuals could compare and make their own decisions, I think brokers will be largely evolved out of existence. Sure there will be a few left (there will probably always be a need to speak with an individual and get his thoughts before making a decision, but in this case, won't the job of broker be distilled down, as fewer and fewer are needed?).

I can't help but feel sorry for those many individuals who make a living by recommending and facilitating the purchase of securities recommended to them by their firms' analysts. I'm a licensed broker too, and if I listen real closely, I think I hear a bell somewhere. And I'm sure not asking what it's for.

sailing upstream into the wind

I've already explained what I think about scalping as a business. Sure there will be those quick eighths occasionally, but in my opinion trading by scalping as a play is, in most cases, accepting tremendous risk for little to no gain. It is like being satisfied with a sardine fished at great expense out of the mouth of a huge tuna. If you're in these markets, it seems to me that scalping should be an occasional thing, not the primary plan of action.

There will be people who say, "Yeah, but I can scalp 100 times a day, and make an eighth every time!" Well, this may be true in the short term, especially for the more experienced traders. But you'll be paying such a huge percentage on commissions that it may be an uneconomic activity. There are those who will argue that you're tripping over pennies on the way to dollars by worrying about transaction costs. Nonsense. If you're scalping 100 times a day, you know nothing about the stocks you're picking. What if you buy a stock and two minutes later the stock is halted? And when it opens (with terrible news), you're screwed! It happens. Frequently. That one lousy occurrence can set you back all of your gains. Several years ago, as I have mentioned, scalping was much easier. Starting with this as a plan in today's markets may be much more difficult.

And what about all the big fish you'd be missing? Dozens of stocks move five points or more in one day. Sure, these won't move in 30 seconds, but if you pick a few and watch them closely, you'll learn who the players are and how the stock tends to move. This information is very useful, in that you can plan your strategies and remove as much risk as possible. Buying the intraday low and selling the high or shorting the high and buying the low are strategies you can perfect. Holding overnight can be an excellent strategy, if you know the stock and circumstances surrounding it. For example, one person I know bought (in a transaction very typical for him) E*Trade (EGRP) one day during incredible buying pressure. Many people got in and out for an eighth, a quarter, during the day, because earnings had come out and they were great. But this person bought the stock and held it overnight, for a possible gap-up.

And gap-up it did—the next day it closed up $22! The man (who incidentally consistently has amazing profits over time) will not scalp and often holds overnight. If he is wrong (which he often is), he gets out quick, at a tiny loss; obviously he employs stellar money management techniques.

Consider the facts that, when scalping, you incur major commission costs, large losses when wrong (you need to trade size, maybe even inappropriate size to beat commissions when trading for such tiny gains), are subject to the vagaries of stocks you don't know, are subject to the difficulties of getting in and out of positions at a profit due to the new order-handling rules, and finally make only a small profit when you are right!

When your plan is scalping, you are fishing in an ocean of big fish and going for minnows. It may be a real niche, but the bottom line is: You incur greater risk and greater expense for a smaller profit. Someday, with scalping as a main strategy, you will probably blow up.

why market makers hate scalpers and day traders

As soon as market makers are pegged as buyers or sellers of size, scalpers try to get in front of them. Scalpers make it harder for them to transact their large institutional orders profitably. Additionally, the volatility created by individual participation in the market makes it harder for market makers to do their jobs; they can't slack off, even for a moment. And finally, if market makers mess up and enter an incorrect price, some scalper will profit off their error almost instantaneously.

Scalpers create larger costs for market makers too, since often they'll SOES them and transact so many tickets for small numbers of shares. As mentioned, market makers often must pay a ticket charge for each and every transaction, which greatly reduces their overall profitability. Additionally, market makers are human and may have difficulty keeping up with their current positions, given the vast number of executions in such little time. It will be interesting to see the effects of SuperSOES, which should make for many more transactions. The impact on costs to market makers may be huge.

But in the words of the great Frank Sinatra, "That's life!" You can talk about it all day, but in the end, market makers will just have to get over it and evolve, because the electronic revolution has only just begun.

a 24-hour, worldwide market

Well, maybe, at this point, we're a little far off. But given the electronic advances in back-office clearing operations, a worldwide market could be a real possibility. (The clearing operations are those mechanisms of the clearinghouses that establish, track, and transfer the identity of securities and their owners.) Currently it takes trade day plus three days for a purchased stock to hit your account; very soon the industry will move to trade day plus one—and after that it may evolve to real-time processing. Why not? The credit card companies can handle it. Stock exchanges all over the world are going or have already gone electronic. And there is a desire for convergence; if a trader in France can day-trade the U.S. stock markets as well as the markets of the European Union, it's only a matter of time until somebody comes up with the bright idea of creating a transparent order entry platform that will route orders to all the required exchanges. Of course, there are huge regulatory hurdles; every country has its own systems and rules. But eventually . . .

Eventually (and Moore's law suggests we're really not that far away), we may log in to our multiple-currency accounts over the wireless Internet from watch-size processor/modems and view the world through electronically linked quotes-colored glasses. Currently, with a laptop and a cell modem, you can trade from anywhere on the face of the planet (even if it is painfully slow). But high bandwidth is on the way, and high-bandwidth wireless is sure to follow. Companies are already marketing personal wireless computers that you view through eyeglass-size monitors. Who can imagine where this will evolve, in a year, in five years? With convergence of all these technologies, maybe we'll be able to trade any market in real time, at any time, from anywhere on earth. I'm getting my boat ready now.

index